Learn LLVM 12

A beginner's guide to learning LLVM compiler tools and core libraries with C++

Kai Nacke

BIRMINGHAM—MUMBAI

Learn LLVM 12

Copyright © 2021 Packt Publishing

Group Product Manager: Aaron Lazar
Publishing Product Manager: Shweta Bairoliya
Senior Editor: Ruvika Rao
Content Development Editor: Nithya Sadanandan
Technical Editor: Gaurav Gala
Copy Editor: Safis Editing
Project Coordinator: Deeksha Thakkar
Proofreader: Safis Editing
Indexer: Manju Arasan
Production Designer: Roshan Kawale

First published: April 2021
Production reference: 1290421

Published by Packt Publishing Ltd.
Livery Place
35 Livery Street
Birmingham
B3 2PB, UK.

978-1-83921-350-2

www.packt.com

Writing a book is a challenging task, especially when you are planning to move to Canada and suddenly a pandemic hits the world and changes everything. The team at Packt not only provided guidance on writing, but also showed understanding for my slow writing, and always motivated me to carry on. I owe them a great thank you.

Without the support of my family, this book would not have been possible. Thanks for putting all that faith in me!

Contributors

About the author

Kai Nacke is a professional IT architect currently living in Toronto, Canada. He holds a diploma in computer science from the Technical University of Dortmund, Germany. His diploma thesis about universal hash functions was recognized as the best of the semester.

He has been working in the IT industry for more than 20 years and has great experience in the development and architecture of business and enterprise applications. In his current role, he evolves an LLVM/Clang-based compiler.

For some years, he was the maintainer of LDC, the LLVM-based D compiler. He is the author of *D Web Development*, published by Packt. In the past, he was also a speaker in the LLVM developer room at the **Free and Open Source Software Developers' European Meeting** (**FOSDEM**).

About the reviewer

Suyog Sarda is a professional software engineer and an open source enthusiast. He focuses on compiler development and compiler tools. He is an active contributor to the LLVM open source community. Suyog was also involved in code performance improvements for the ARM and x86 architectures. He has been a part of the compiler team for the Tizen project. His interest in compiler development lies more in code optimization and vectorization. Previously, he has authored a book on LLVM, titled *LLVM Cookbook*, published by Packt. Apart from compilers, Suyog is also interested in Linux kernel development. He published a technical paper titled *Secure Co-resident Virtualization in Multicore Systems by VM Pinning and Page Coloring* at the IEEE Proceedings of the 2012 International Conference on Cloud Computing, Technologies, Applications, and Management at the Birla Institute of Technology, Dubai. He earned a bachelor's degree in computer technology from the College of Engineering, Pune, India.

Table of Contents

3
The Structure of a Compiler

Section 2 – From Source to Machine Code Generation

4
Turning the Source File into an Abstract Syntax Tree

5

Basics of IR Code Generation

6

IR Generation for High-Level Language Constructs

7

Advanced IR Generation

8
Optimizing IR

Section 3 – Taking LLVM to the Next Level

9
Instruction Selection

10
JIT Compilation

11
Debugging Using LLVM Tools

12
Create Your Own Backend

Other Books You May Enjoy

Index

Preface

Constructing a compiler is a complex and fascinating task. The LLVM project provides reusable components for your compiler. The LLVM core libraries implement a world-class optimizing code generator, which translates a source language-independent intermediate representation of machine code for all popular CPU architectures. The compilers for many programming languages already take advantage of LLVM technology.

This book teaches you how to implement your own compiler and how to use LLVM to achieve it. You will learn how the frontend of a compiler turns source code into an abstract syntax tree, and how to generate **intermediate representation** (**IR**) from it. Adding an optimization pipeline to your compiler, you can compile the IR to performant machine code.

The LLVM framework can be extended in several ways, and you will learn how to add new passes, new machine instructions, and even a completely new backend to LLVM. Advanced topics such as compiling for a different CPU architecture and extending clang and the clang static analyzer with your own plugins and checkers are also covered. This book follows a practical approach and is packed with example source code, which makes it easy to apply the knowledge gained in your own projects.

Who this book is for

This book is for compiler developers, enthusiasts, and engineers who are new to LLVM and are interested in learning about the LLVM framework. It is also useful for C++ software engineers looking to use compiler-based tools for code analysis and improvement, as well as casual users of LLVM libraries who want to gain more knowledge of LLVM essentials. Intermediate-level experience with C++ programming is mandatory to understand the concepts covered in this book more effectively.

What this book covers

Chapter 1, Installing LLVM, explains how to set up and use your development environment. At the end of the chapter, you will have compiled the LLVM libraries and learned how to customize the build process.

Chapter 2, Touring the LLVM Source, introduces you to the various LLVM projects and discusses the common directory layout shared by all projects. You will create your first project using the LLVM core libraries, and you will also compile it for a different CPU architecture.

Chapter 3, The Structure of a Compiler, gives you an overview of the components of a compiler. At the end of the chapter, you will have implemented your first compiler producing LLVM IR.

Chapter 4, Turning the Source File into an Abstract Syntax Tree, teaches you in detail how to implement the frontend of a compiler. You will create your own frontend for a small programming language, ending with the construction of an abstract syntax tree.

Chapter 5, Basics of IR Generation, shows you how to generate LLVM IR from an abstract syntax tree. At the end of the chapter, you will have implemented a compiler for the example language, emitting assembly text or object code files as a result.

Chapter 6, IR Generation for High-Level Language Constructs, illustrates how you translate source language features commonly found in high-level programming languages to LLVM IR. You will learn about the translation of aggregate data types, the various options to implement class inheritance and virtual functions, and how to comply with the application binary interface of your system.

Chapter 7, Advanced IR Generation, shows you how to generate LLVM IR for exception-handling statements in the source language. You will also learn how to add metadata for type-based alias analysis, and how to add debug information to the generated LLVM IR, and you will extend your compiler-generated metadata.

Chapter 8, Optimizing IR, explains the LLVM pass manager. You will implement your own pass, both as part of LLVM and as a plugin, and you will learn how to add your new pass to the optimizing pass pipeline.

Chapter 9, Instruction Selection, shows how LLVM lowers IR to machine instructions. You will learn how instructions are defined in LLVM, and you will add a new machine instruction to LLVM so that instruction selection takes the new instruction into account.

Chapter 10, JIT Compilation, discusses how you can use LLVM to implement a **just-in-time (JIT)** compiler. By the end of the chapter, you will have implemented your own JIT compiler for LLVM IR in two different ways.

Chapter 11, Debugging Using LLVM Tools, explores the details of various libraries and components of LLVM, which helps you to identify bugs in your application. You will use the sanitizers to identify buffer overflows and other bugs. With the libFuzzer library, you will test functions with random data as input, and XRay will help you to find performance bottlenecks. You will use the clang static analyzer to identify bugs at the source level, and you will learn that you can add your own checker to the analyzer. You will also learn how to extend clang with your own plugin.

Chapter 12, Creating Your Own Backend, explains how you can add a new backend to LLVM. You will implement all the necessary classes, and at the end of the chapter you will compile LLVM IR to yet another CPU architecture.

To get the most out of this book

You need a computer running Linux, Windows, macOS, or FreeBSD, with the development toolchain installed for the operating system. Please see the table for the required tools. All tools should be in the search path of your shell.

Software/hardware covered in the book	OS requirements
A C/C++ compiler: gcc 5.1.0 or later, clang 3.5 or later, Apple clang 6.0 or later, Visual Studio 2017 or later	Linux (any), Windows, macOS, or FreeBSD
CMake 3.13.4 or later	
Ninja 1.9.0	
Python 3.6 or later	
Git, 1.7.10 or later	

To view the DAG visualization in *Chapter 9, Instruction Selection*, you must have the Graphviz software from `https://graphviz.org/` installed. By default, the generated image is in PDF format, and you need a PDF viewer to show it.

To create the flame graph in *Chapter 11, Debugging Using LLVM Tools*, you need to install the scripts from `https://github.com/brendangregg/FlameGraph`. To run the script, you also need a recent version of Perl installed, and to view the graph you need a web browser capable of displaying SVG files, which all modern browsers do. To see the Chrome Trace Viewer visualization in the same chapter, you need to have the Chrome browser installed.

If you are using the digital version of this book, we advise you to type the code yourself or access the code via the GitHub repository (link available in the next section). Doing so will help you avoid any potential errors related to the copying and pasting of code.

Download the example code files

You can download the example code files for this book from GitHub at `https://github.com/PacktPublishing/Learn-LLVM-12`. In case there's an update to the code, it will be updated on the existing GitHub repository.

We also have other code bundles from our rich catalog of books and videos available at `https://github.com/PacktPublishing/`. Check them out!

Code in Action

Code in Action videos for this book can be viewed at `https://bit.ly/3nllhED`

Download the color images

We also provide a PDF file that has color images of the screenshots/diagrams used in this book. You can download it here: `https://static.packt-cdn.com/downloads/9781839213502_ColorImages.pdf`.

Conventions used

There are a number of text conventions used throughout this book.

`Code in text`: Indicates code words in text, database table names, folder names, filenames, file extensions, pathnames, dummy URLs, user input, and Twitter handles. Here is an example: "You can observe in the code that a quantum circuit operation is being defined and a variable called numOnes."

A block of code is set as follows:

```
#include "llvm/IR/IRPrintingPasses.h"
#include "llvm/IR/LegacyPassManager.h"
#include "llvm/Support/ToolOutputFile.h"
```

When we wish to draw your attention to a particular part of a code block, the relevant lines or items are set in bold:

```
    switch (Kind) {
// Many more cases
    case m88k:              return "m88k";
    }
```

Bold: Indicates a new term, an important word, or words that you see onscreen. For example, words in menus or dialog boxes appear in the text like this. Here is an example: "Select **System info** from the **Administration** panel."

> **Tips or important notes**
> Appear like this.

Get in touch

Feedback from our readers is always welcome.

General feedback: If you have questions about any aspect of this book, mention the book title in the subject of your message and email us at customercare@packtpub.com.

Errata: Although we have taken every care to ensure the accuracy of our content, mistakes do happen. If you have found a mistake in this book, we would be grateful if you would report this to us. Please visit www.packtpub.com/support/errata, selecting your book, clicking on the Errata Submission Form link, and entering the details.

Piracy: If you come across any illegal copies of our works in any form on the Internet, we would be grateful if you would provide us with the location address or website name. Please contact us at copyright@packt.com with a link to the material.

If you are interested in becoming an author: If there is a topic that you have expertise in and you are interested in either writing or contributing to a book, please visit authors.packtpub.com.

Reviews

Please leave a review. Once you have read and used this book, why not leave a review on the site that you purchased it from? Potential readers can then see and use your unbiased opinion to make purchase decisions, we at Packt can understand what you think about our products, and our authors can see your feedback on their book. Thank you!

For more information about Packt, please visit packt.com.

Section 1 – The Basics of Compiler Construction with LLVM

In this section, you will learn how to compile LLVM by yourself, and how you can tailor the build to your needs. You will understand how LLVM projects are organized, and you will create your first project utilizing LLVM. You will also learn how to compile LLVM and applications using LLVM for a different CPU architecture. Finally, you will explore the overall structure of a compiler, while creating a small compiler yourself.

This section comprises the following chapters:

- *Chapter 1, Installing LLVM*
- *Chapter 2, Touring the LLVM Source*
- *Chapter 3, The Structure of a Compiler*

1
Installing LLVM

To learn how to work with LLVM, it is best to begin by compiling LLVM from the source. LLVM is an umbrella project, and its GitHub repository contains the sources for all the projects that belong to LLVM. Each LLVM project is in a top-level directory of the repository. Besides cloning the repository, your system must also have all tools that are required by the build system installed.

In this chapter, you will learn about the following topics:

- Getting the prerequisites ready, which will show you how to set up your build system.

- Building with CMake, which will cover how to compile and install the LLVM core libraries and Clang with CMake and Ninja.

- Customizing the build process, which will talk about the various way we can influence the build process.

Getting the prerequisites ready

To work with LLVM, your development system must run a common operating system such as Linux, FreeBSD, macOS, or Windows. Building LLVM and Clang with debug symbols enabled easily need tens of gigabytes of disk space, so be sure that your system has plenty of disk space available – in this scenario, you should have 30 GB of free space.

The required disk space depends heavily on the chosen build options. For example, building only the LLVM core libraries in release mode, while targeting only one platform, requires about 2 GB of free disk space, which is the bare minimum needed. To reduce compile times, a fast CPU (such as a quadcore CPU with 2.5 GHz clock speed) and a fast SSD would also be helpful.

It is even possible to build LLVM on a small device such as a Raspberry Pi – it just takes a lot of time to do so. I developed the examples in this book on a laptop with an Intel quadcore CPU running at 2.7 GHz clock speed, with 40 GB RAM and 2.5 TB SSD disk space. This system is well-suited for the development task at hand.

Your development system must have some prerequisite software installed. Let's review the minimal required versions of these software packages.

> **Note**
>
> Linux distributions often contain more recent versions that can be used. The version numbers are suitable for LLVM 12. Later versions of LLVM may require more recent versions of the packages mentioned here.

To check out the source from **GitHub**, you need **git** (`https://git-scm.com/`). There is no requirement for a specific version. The GitHub help pages recommend using at least version 1.17.10.

The LLVM project uses **CMake** (`https://cmake.org/`) as the build file generator. At least version 3.13.4 is required. CMake can generate build files for various build systems. In this book, **Ninja** (`https://ninja-build.org/`) is being used because it is fast and available on all platforms. The latest version, 1.9.0, is recommended.

Obviously, you also need a **C/C++ compiler**. The LLVM projects are written in modern C++, based on the C++14 standard. A conforming compiler and standard library are required. The following compilers are known to work with LLVM 12:

- gcc 5.1.0 or later
- Clang 3.5 or later
- Apple Clang 6.0 or later
- Visual Studio 2017 or later

Please be aware that with further development of the LLVM project, the requirements for the compiler are most likely to change. At the time of writing, there are discussions to use C++17 and drop Visual Studio 2017 support. In general, you should use the latest compiler version available for your system.

Python (`https://python.org/`) is used to generate the build files and to run the test suite. It should be at least version 3.6.

Although not covered in this book, there may be reasons why you need to use Make instead of Ninja. In this case, you need to use **GNU Make** (`https://www.gnu.org/software/make/`) version 3.79 or later. The usage of both build tools is very similar. It is sufficient to replace `ninja` in each command with `make` for the scenarios described here.

To install the prerequisite software, the easiest thing to do is use the package manager from your operating system. In the following sections, the commands you must enter to install the software for the most popular operating systems are shown.

Ubuntu

Ubuntu 20.04 uses the APT package manager. Most of the basic utilities are already installed; only the development tools are missing. To install all the packages at once, type the following:

```
$ sudo apt install -y gcc g++ git cmake ninja-build
```

Fedora and RedHat

The package manager for Fedora 33 and RedHat Enterprise Linux 8.3 is called **DNF**. Like Ubuntu, most of the basic utilities are already installed. To install all the packages at once, type the following:

```
$ sudo dnf install -y gcc gcc-c++ git cmake ninja-build
```

FreeBSD

On FreeBSD 12 or later, you must use the PKG package manager. FreeBSD differs from Linux-based systems in that Clang is the preferred compiler. To install all the packages at once, type the following:

```
$ sudo pkg install -y clang git cmake ninja
```

OS X

For development on OS X, it is best to install **Xcode** from the Apple store. While the XCode IDE is not used in this book, it comes with the required C/C++ compilers and supporting utilities. To install the other tools, you can use the Homebrew package manager (https://brew.sh/). To install all the packages at once, type the following:

```
$ brew install git cmake ninja
```

Windows

Like OS X, Windows does not come with a package manager. The easiest way to install all the software is to use the **Chocolately** (https://chocolatey.org/) package manager. To install all the packages at once, type the following:

```
$ choco install visualstudio2019buildtools cmake ninja git\
   gzip bzip2 gnuwin32-coreutils.install
```

Please note that this only installs the build tools from **Visual Studio 2019**. If you would like to get the Community Edition (which includes the IDE), then you must install package visualstudio2019community instead of visualstudio2019buildtools. Part of the Visual Studio 2019 installation is the x64 Native Tools Command Prompt for VS 2019. Upon using this command prompt, the compiler is automatically added to the search path.

Configuring Git

The LLVM project uses Git for version control. If you have not used Git before, then you should do some basic configuration of Git first before continuing; that is, setting a username and email address. Both pieces of information are used if you commit changes. In the following commands, replace Jane with your name and jane@email.org with your email:

```
$ git config --global user.email "jane@email.org"
$ git config --global user.name "Jane"
```

By default, Git uses the **vi** editor for commit messages. If you would prefer using another editor, then you can change the configuration in a similar way. To use the **nano** editor, type the following:

```
$ git config --global core.editor nano
```

For more information about git, please see the *Git Version Control Cookbook - Second Edition* by Packt Publishing (`https://www.packtpub.com/product/git-version-control-cookbook/9781782168454`).

Building with CMake

With the build tools ready, you can now check out all the LLVM projects from GitHub. The command for doing this is essentially the same on all platforms. However, on Windows, it is recommended to turn off auto-translation for line endings.

Let's review this process in three parts: cloning the repository, creating a build directory, and generating the build system files.

Cloning the repository

On all non-Windows platforms, type in the following command to clone the repository:

```
$ git clone https://github.com/llvm/llvm-project.git
```

On Windows, you must add the option to disable line endings from being auto-translated. Here, type the following:

```
$ git clone --config core.autocrlf=false\  https://github.com/llvm/llvm-project.git
```

This `git` command clones the latest source code from GitHub into a local directory named `llvm-project`. Now, change the current directory to the new `llvm-project` directory with the following command:

```
$ cd llvm-project
```

Inside the directory is all the LLVM projects, each in its own directory. Most notably, the LLVM core libraries are in the `llvm` subdirectory. The LLVM project uses branches for subsequent release development ("release/12.x") and tags ("llvmorg-12.0.0") to mark a certain release. With the preceding `clone` command, you get the current development state. This book uses LLVM 12. To check out the first release of LLVM 12, type the following:

```
$ git checkout -b llvmorg-12.0.0
```

With this, you have cloned the whole repository and checked out a tag. This is the most flexible approach.

Git also allows you to clone only a branch or a tag (including history). With `git clone --branch llvmorg-12.0.0 https://github.com/llvm/llvm-project`, you check out the same label, as we did previously, but only the history for this tag is cloned. With the additional `--depth=1` option, you prevent the history from being cloned too. This saves time and space but obviously limits what you can do locally.

The next step is to create a build directory.

Creating a build directory

Unlike many other projects, LLVM does not support inline builds and requires a separate `build` directory. This can easily be created inside the `llvm-project` directory. Change into this directory with the following command:

```
$ cd llvm-project
```

Then, create a build directory called `build` for simplicity. Here, the commands for Unix and Windows systems differ. On Unix-likes system, you should use the following command:

```
$ mkdir build
```

On Windows, you should use the following command:

```
$ md build
```

Then, change into the `build` directory:

```
$ cd build
```

Now, you are ready to create the build system files with the CMake tool inside this directory.

Generating the build system files

To generate the build system files that will compile LLVM and Clang using Ninja, run the following command:

```
$ cmake -G Ninja -DLLVM_ENABLE_PROJECTS=clang ../llvm
```

> **Tip**
>
> On Windows, the backslash character, \, is the directory name separator.
> On Windows, CMake automatically translates the Unix separator, /, into the
> Windows one.

The -G option tells CMake which system to generate build files for. The most often used options are as follows:

- `Ninja`: For the Ninja build system

- `Unix Makefiles`: For GNU Make

- `Visual Studio 15 VS2017` and `Visual Studio 16 VS2019`: For Visual Studio and MS Build

- `Xcode`: For XCode projects

The generation process can be influenced by setting various variables with the –D option. Usually, they are prefixed with `CMAKE_` (if defined by CMake) or `LLVM_` (if defined by LLVM). With the `LLVM_ENABLE_PROJECTS=clang` variable setting, CMake generates build files for Clang in addition to LLVM. The last part of the command tells CMake where to find the LLVM core library source. More on that in the next section.

Once the build files have been generated, LLVM and Clang can be compiled with the following command:

```
$ ninja
```

Depending on the hardware resources, this command takes between 15 minutes (a server with lots of CPU cores and memory and fast storage) and several hours (dual-core Windows notebook with limited memory) to run. By default, Ninja utilizes all available CPU cores. This is good for compilation speed but may prevent other tasks from running. For example, on a Windows-based notebook, it is almost impossible to surf the internet while Ninja is running. Fortunately, you can limit resource usage with the –j option.

Let's assume you have four CPU cores available and that Ninja should only use two (because you have parallel tasks to run). Here, you should use the following command for compilation:

```
$ ninja -j2
```

Once compilation is finished, a best practice is to run the test suite to check if everything works as expected:

```
$ ninja check-all
```

Again, the runtime of this command varies widely due to the available hardware resources. The Ninja check-all target runs all test cases. Targets are generated for each directory containing test cases. Using check-llvm, instead of check-all runs the LLVM tests but not the Clang tests; check-llvm-codegen only runs the tests in the CodeGen directory from LLVM (that is, the llvm/test/CodeGen directory).

You can also do a quick manual check. One of the LLVM applications you will be using is **llc,** the LLVM compiler. If you run it with the -version option, it shows the LLVM version of it, its host CPU, and all its supported architectures:

```
$ bin/llc -version
```

If you have trouble getting LLVM compiled, then you should consult the *Common Problems* section of the *Getting Started with the LLVM System* documentation (https://llvm.org/docs/GettingStarted.html#common-problems) for solutions to typical problems.

Finally, install the binaries:

```
$ ninja install
```

On a Unix-like system, the install directory is /usr/local. On Windows, C:\Program Files\LLVM is used. This can be changed, of course. The next section explains how.

Customizing the build process

The CMake system uses a project description in the CMakeLists.txt file. The top-level file is in the llvm directory; that is, llvm/CMakeLists.txt. Other directories also contain CMakeLists.txt files, which are recursively included during the build-file generation.

Based on the information provided in the project description, CMake checks which compilers have been installed, detects libraries and symbols, and creates the build system files, such as build.ninja or Makefile (depending on the chosen generator). It is also possible to define reusable modules, such as a function to detect if LLVM is installed. These scripts are placed in the special cmake directory (llvm/cmake), which is searched automatically during the generation process.

The build process can be customized by defining CMake variables. The -D command-line option is used to set a variable to a value. These variables are used in CMake scripts. Variables defined by CMake itself are almost always prefixed with CMAKE_, and these variables can be used in all projects. Variables defined by LLVM are prefixed with LLVM_ but they can only be used if the project definition includes the use of LLVM.

Variables defined by CMake

Some variables are initialized with the values of environment variables. The most notable are CC and CXX, which define the C and C++ compilers to be used for building. CMake tries to locate a C and a C++ compiler automatically, using the current shell search path. It picks the first compiler that's found. If you have several compilers installed, such as gcc and Clang or different versions of Clang, then this might not be the compiler you want for building LLVM.

Suppose you like to use clang9 as a C compiler and clang++9 as a C++ compiler. Here, you can invoke CMake in a Unix shell in the following way:

```
$ CC=clang9 CXX=clang++9 cmake ../llvm
```

This sets the value of the environment variables for the invocation of cmake. If necessary, you can specify an absolute path for the compiler executables.

CC is the default value of the CMAKE_C_COMPILER CMake variable, while CXX is the default value of the CMAKE_CXX_COMPILER CMake variable. Instead of using the environment variables, you can set the CMake variables directly. This is equivalent to the preceding call:

```
$ cmake -DCMAKE_C_COMPILER=clang9\
  -DCMAKE_CXX_COMPILER=clang++9 ../llvm
```

Other useful variables defined by CMake are as follows:

- CMAKE_INSTALL_PREFIX: A path prefix that is prepended to every path during installation. The default is /usr/local on Unix and C:\Program Files\<Project> on Windows. To install LLVM in the /opt/llvm directory, you must specify -DCMAKE_INSTALL_PREFIX=/opt/llvm. The binaries are copied to /opt/llvm/bin, the library files are copied to /opt/llvm/lib, and so on.

- CMAKE_BUILD_TYPE: Different types of builds require different settings. For example, a debug build needs to specify options for generating debug symbols and are usually linking against debug versions of system libraries. In contrast, a release build uses optimization flags and links against production versions of libraries. This variable is only used for build systems that can only handle one build type, such as Ninja or Make. For IDE build systems, all variants are generated, and you must use the mechanism of the IDE to switch between build types. Some possible values are as follows:

  DEBUG: Build with debug symbols

  RELEASE: Build with optimization for speed

  RELWITHDEBINFO: Release build with debug symbols

  MINSIZEREL: Build with optimization for size

  The default build type is DEBUG. To generate build files for a release build, you must specify -DCMAKE_BUILD_TYPE=RELEASE.

- CMAKE_C_FLAGS and CMAKE_CXX_FLAGS: These are extra flags that are used when we're compiling C and C++ source files. The initial values are taken from the CFLAGS and CXXFLAGS environment variables, which can be used as alternatives.

- CMAKE_MODULE_PATH: Specifies additional directories that are searched for in CMake modules. The specified directories are searched before the default ones. The value is a semicolon-separated list of directories.

- PYTHON_EXECUTABLE: If the Python interpreter is not found or if the wrong one is picked if you have installed multiple versions of it, you can set this variable to the path of the Python binary. This variable only takes effect if the Python module of CMake is included (which is the case for LLVM).

CMake provides built-in help for variables. The --help-variable var option prints help for the var variable. For instance, you can type the following to get help for CMAKE_BUILD_TYPE:

```
$ cmake --help-variable CMAKE_BUILD_TYPE
```

You can also list all the variables with the following command:

```
$ cmake --help-variablelist
```

This list is very long. You may want to pipe the output to more or a similar program.

Variables defined by LLVM

The variables defined by LLVM work in the same way as those defined by CMake, except that there is no built-in help. The most useful variables are as follows:

- `LLVM_TARGETS_TO_BUILD`: LLVM supports code generation for different CPU architectures. By default, all these targets are built. Use this variable to specify the list of targets to build, separated by semicolons. The current targets are AArch64, AMDGPU, ARM, BPF, Hexagon, Lanai, Mips, MSP430, NVPTX, PowerPC, RISCV, Sparc, SystemZ, WebAssembly, X86, and XCore. all can be used as shorthand for all targets. The names are case-sensitive. To only enable PowerPC and the System Z target, you must specify -DLLVM_TARGETS_TO_BUILD="PowerPC;SystemZ".

- `LLVM_ENABLE_PROJECTS`: This is a list of the projects you want to build, separated by semicolons. The source for the projects must be at the same level as the llvm directory (side-by-side layout). The current list is clang, clang-tools-extra, compiler-rt, debuginfo-tests, lib, libclc, libcxx, libcxxabi, libunwind, lld, lldb, llgo, mlir, openmp, parallel-libs, polly, and pstl. all can be used as shorthand for all the projects in this list. To build Clang and llgo together with LLVM, you must specify -DLLVM_ENABLE_PROJECT="clang;llgo".

- `LLVM_ENABLE_ASSERTIONS`: If set to ON, then assertion checks are enabled. These checks help find errors and are very useful during development. The default value is ON for a DEBUG build and OFF otherwise. To turn assertion checks on (for example, for a RELEASE build), you must specify –DLLVM_ENABLE_ASSERTIONS=ON.

- `LLVM_ENABLE_EXPENSIVE_CHECKS`: This enables some expensive checks that can really slow down your compilation speed or consume large amounts of memory. The default value is OFF. To turn these checks on, you must specify -DLLVM_ENABLE_EXPENSIVE_CHECKS=ON.

- `LLVM_APPEND_VC_REV`: LLVM tools such as llc display the LLVM version they are based on, besides other information if the–version command-line option is provided. This version information is based on the LLVM_REVISION C macro. By default, not only the LLVM version but also the Git hash of the latest commit is part of the version information. This is handy in case you are following the development of the master branch because it makes it clear which Git commit the tool is based on. If this isn't required, then this can be turned off with –DLLVM_APPEND_VC_REV=OFF.

- `LLVM_ENABLE_THREADS`: LLVM automatically includes thread support if a threading library is detected (usually, the pthreads library). Furthermore, in this case, LLVM assumes that the compiler supports **thread-local storage** (TLS). If you don't want thread support or your compiler does not support TLS, then you can turn it off with `-DLLVM_ENABLE_THREADS=OFF`.

- `LLVM_ENABLE_EH`: The LLVM projects do not use C++ exception handling, so they turn exception support off by default. This setting can be incompatible with other libraries your project is linking with. If needed, you can enable exception support by specifying `-DLLVM_ENABLE_EH=ON`.

- `LLVM_ENABLE_RTTI`: LVM uses a lightweight, self-built system for runtime type information. Generating C++ RTTI is turned off by default. Like the exception handling support, this may be incompatible with other libraries. To turn generation for C++ RTTI on, you must specify `-DLLVM_ENABLE_RTTI=ON`.

- `LLVM_ENABLE_WARNINGS`: Compiling LLVM should generate no warning messages if possible. Due to this, the option to print warning messages is turned on by default. To turn it off, you must specify `-DLLVM_ENABLE_WARNINGS=OFF`.

- `LLVM_ENABLE_PEDANTIC`: The LLVM source should be C/C++ language standard-conforming; hence, pedantic checking of the source is enabled by default. If possible, compiler-specific extensions are also disabled. To reverse this setting, you must specify `-DLLVM_ENABLE_PEDANTIC=OFF`.

- `LLVM_ENABLE_WERROR`: If set to `ON`, then all the warnings are treated as errors – the compilation aborts as soon as warnings are found. It helps to find all the remaining warnings in the source. By default, it is turned off. To turn it on, you must specify `-DLLVM_ENABLE_WERROR=ON`.

- `LLVM_OPTIMIZED_TABLEGEN`: Usually, the tablegen tool is built with the same options as the other parts of LLVM. At the same time, tablegen is used to generate large parts of the code generator. As a result, tablegen is much slower in a debug build, thus increasing the compile time noticeably. If this option is set to `ON`, then tablegen is compiled with optimization turned on, even for a debug build, possibly reducing compile time. The default is `OFF`. To turn this on, you must specify `-DLLVM_OPTIMIZED_TABLEGEN=ON`.

- `LLVM_USE_SPLIT_DWARF`: If the build compiler is gcc or Clang, then turning on this option will instruct the compiler to generate the DWARF debug information in a separate file. The reduced size of the object files reduces the link time of debug builds significantly. The default is `OFF`. To turn this on, you must specify `-LLVM_USE_SPLIT_DWARF=ON`.

LLVM defines many more CMake variables. You can find the complete list in the LLVM documentation of CMake (`https://releases.llvm.org/12.0.0/docs/CMake.html#llvm-specific-variables`). The preceding list only contains the ones you are likely to need.

Summary

In this chapter, you prepared your development machine to compile LLVM. You cloned the LLVM GitHub repository and compiled your own versions of LLVM and Clang. The build process can be customized with CMake variables. You also learned about useful variables and how to change them. Equipped with this knowledge, you can tweak LLVM for your needs.

In the next chapter, we will take a closer look at the contents of the LLVM mono repository. You will learn which projects are in it and how the projects are structured. You will then use this information to create your own project using LLVM libraries. Finally, you will learn how to compile LLVM for a different CPU architecture.

2

Touring the
LLVM Source

The LLVM mono repository contains all the projects under the `llvm-project` root directory. All projects follow a common source layout. To use LLVM effectively, it is good to know what is available and where to find it. In this chapter, you will learn about the following:

- The contents of the LLVM mono repository, covering the most important top-level projects

- The layout of an LLVM project, showing the common source layout used by all projects

- How to create your own projects using LLVM libraries, covering all the ways you can use LLVM in your own projects

- How to target a different CPU architecture, showing the steps required to cross-compile to another system

Technical requirements

The code files for the chapter are available at `https://github.com/PacktPublishing/Learn-LLVM-12/tree/master/Chapter02/tinylang`

You can find the code in action videos at `https://bit.ly/3nllhED`

Contents of the LLVM mono repository

In *Chapter 1*, *Installing LLVM*, you cloned the LLVM mono repository. This repository contains all LLVM top-level projects. They can be grouped as follows:

- LLVM core libraries and additions

- Compilers and tools

- Runtime libraries

In the next sections, we will take a closer look at these groups.

LLVM core libraries and additions

The LLVM core libraries are in the `llvm` directory. This project provides a set of libraries with optimizers and code generation for well-known CPUs. It also provides tools based on these libraries. The LLVM static compiler `llc` takes a file written in LLVM **intermediate representation** (**IR**) as input and compiles it into either bitcode, assembler output, or a binary object file. Tools such as `llvm-objdump` and `llvm-dwarfdump` let you inspect object files, and those such as `llvm-ar` let you create an archive file from a set of object files. It also includes tools that help with the development of LLVM itself. For example, the `bugpoint` tool helps to find a minimal test case for a crash inside LLVM. `llvm-mc` is the machine code playground: this tool assembles and disassembles machine instructions and also outputs the encoding, which is a great help when adding new instructions.

The LLVM core libraries are written in C++. Additionally, a C interface and bindings for Go, Ocaml, and Python are provided.

The Polly project, located in the `polly` directory, adds another set of optimizations to LLVM. It is based on a mathematical representation called the **polyhedral model**. With this approach, complex optimizations such as loops optimized for cache locality are possible.

The **MLIR** project aims to provide a **multi-level intermediate representation** for LLVM. The LLVM IR is already at a low level, and certain information from the source language is lost during IR generation in the compiler. The idea of MLIR is to make the LLVM IR extensible and capture this information in a domain-specific representation. You will find the source in the `mlir` directory.

Compilers and tools

A complete C/C++/Objective-C/Object-C++ compiler named clang (http://clang.llvm.org/) is part of the LLVM project. The source is located in the clang directory. It provides a set of libraries for lexing, parsing, semantic analysis, and generation of LLVM IR from C, C++, Objective-C, and Objective-C++ source files. The small tool clang is the compiler driver, based on these libraries. Another useful tool is clang-format, which can format C/C++ source files and source fragments according to rules provided by the user.

Clang aims to be compatible with GCC, the GNU C/C++ compiler, and CL, the Microsoft C/C++ compiler.

Additional tools for C/C++ are provided by the clang-tools-extra project in the directory of the same name. Most notable here is clang-tidy which is a Lint style checker for C/C++. clang-tidy uses the clang libraries to parse the source code and checks the source with static analysis. The tool can catch more potential errors than the compiler, at the expense of more runtime.

Llgo is a compiler for the Go programming languages, located in the llgo directory. It is written in Go and uses the Go bindings from the LLVM core libraries to interface with LLVM. Llgo aims to be compatible with the reference compiler (https://golang.org/) but currently, the only supported target is 64-bit x86 Linux. The project seems unmaintained and may be removed in the future.

The object files created by a compiler must be linked together with runtime libraries to form an executable. This is the job of lld (http://lld.llvm.org/), the LLVM linker that is located in the lld directory. The linker supports the ELF, COFF, Mach-O, and WebAssembly formats.

No compiler toolset is complete without a debugger! The LLVM debugger is called lldb (http://lldb.llvm.org/) and is located in the directory of the same name. The interface is similar to GDB, the GNU debugger, and the tool supports C, C++, and Objective-C out of the box. The debugger is extensible so support for other programming languages can be added easily.

Runtime libraries

In addition to a compiler, runtime libraries are required for complete programming language support. All the listed projects are located in the top-level directory in a directory of the same name:

- The `compiler-rt` project provides programming language-independent support libraries. It includes generic functions, such as a 64-bit division for 32-bit i386, various sanitizers, the fuzzing library, and the profiling library.

- The `libunwind` library provides helper functions for stack unwinding based on the DWARF standard. This is usually used for implementing exception handling of languages such as C++. The library is written in C and the functions are not tied to a specific exception handling model.

- The `libcxxabi` library implements C++ exception handling on top of `libunwind` and provides the standard C++ functions for it.

- Finally, `libcxx` is an implementation of the C++ standard library, including iostreams and STL. In addition, the `pstl` project provides a parallel version of the STL algorithm.

- `libclc` is the runtime library for OpenCL. OpenCL is a standard for heterogeneous parallel computing and helps with moving computational tasks to graphics cards.

- `libc` aims to provide a complete C library. This project is still in its early stages.

- Support for the OpenMP API is provided by the `openmp` project. OpenMP helps with multithreaded programming and can, for instance, parallelize loops based on annotations in the source.

Even though this is a long list of projects, the good news is that all projects are structured similarly. We look at the general directory layout in the next section.

Layout of an LLVM project

All LLVM projects follow the same idea of directory layout. To understand the idea, let's compare LLVM with **GCC**, the **GNU Compiler Collection**. GCC has provided mature compilers for decades for almost every system you can imagine. But, except for the compilers, there are no tools that take advantage of the code. The reason is that it is not designed for reuse. This is different with LLVM.

Every functionality has a clearly defined API and is put in a library of its own. The clang project has (among others) a library to lex a C/C++ source file into a token stream. The parser library turns this token stream into an abstract syntax tree (also backed by a library). Semantic analysis, code generation, and even the compiler driver are provided as a library. The well-known `clang` tool is only a small application linked against these libraries.

The advantage is obvious: when you want to build a tool that requires the **abstract syntax tree (AST)** of a C++ file, then you can reuse the functionality from these libraries to construct the AST. Semantic analysis and code generation are not required and you do not link against these libraries. This principle is followed by all LLVM projects, including the core libraries!

Each project has a similar organization. Because CMake is used for build file generation, each project has a `CMakeLists.txt` file that describes the building of the projects. If additional CMake modules or support files are required, then they are stored in the `cmake` subdirectory, with modules placed in `cmake/modules`.

Libraries and tools are mostly written in C++. Source files are placed under the `lib` directory and header files under the `include` directory. Because a project typically consists of several libraries, there are directories for each library in the `lib` directory. If necessary, this repeats. For example, inside the `llvm/lib` directory is the `Target` directory, which holds the code for the target-specific lowering. Besides some source files, there are again subdirectories for each target that are again compiled into libraries. Each of these directories has a `CMakeLists.txt` file that describes how to build the library and which subdirectories also contain source.

The `include` directory has an additional level. To make the names of the include files unique, the path name includes the project name, which is the first subdirectory under `include`. Only in this folder is the structure from the `lib` directory repeated.

The source of applications is inside the `tools` and `utils` directories. In the `utils` directory are internal applications that are used during compilation or testing. They are usually not part of a user installation. The `tools` directory contains applications for the end user. In both directories, each application has its own subdirectory. As with the `lib` directory, each subdirectory that contains source has a `CMakeLists.txt` file.

Correct code generation is a *must* for a compiler. This can only be achieved with a good test suite. The `unittest` directory contains unit tests that use the *Google Test* framework. This is mainly used for single functions and isolated functionality that can't be tested otherwise. In the `test` directory are the LIT tests. These tests use the `llvm-lit` utility to execute tests. `llvm-lit` scans a file for shell commands and executes them. The file contains the source code used as input for the test, for example, LLVM IR. Embedded in the file are commands to compile it, executed by `llvm-lit`. The output of this step is then verified, often with the help of the `FileCheck` utility. This utility reads check statements from one file and matches them against another file. The LIT tests themselves are in subdirectories under the `test` directory, loosely following the structure of the `lib` directory.

Documentation (usually as **reStructuredText**) is placed in the `docs` directory. If a project provides examples, they are in the `examples` directory.

Depending on the needs of the project, there can be other directories too. Most notably, some projects that provide runtime libraries place the source code in a `src` directory and use the `lib` directory for library export definitions. The compiler-rt and libclc projects contain architecture-dependent code. This is always placed in a subdirectory named after the target architecture (for example, `i386` or `ptx`).

In summary, the general layout of a project that provides a sample library and has a driver tool looks like this:

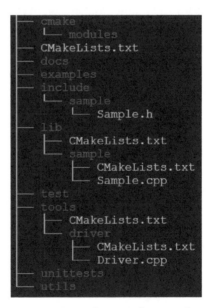

Figure 2.1 – General project directory layout

Our own project will follow this organization, too.

Creating your own project using LLVM libraries

Based on the information in the previous section, you can now create your own project using LLVM libraries. The following sections introduce a small language called **Tiny**. The project will be called tinylang. Here the structure for such a project is defined. Even though the tool in this section is only a **Hello, world** application, its structure has all the parts required for a real-world compiler.

Creating the directory structure

The first question is if the tinylang project should be built together with LLVM (like clang), or if it should be a standalone project that just uses the LLVM libraries. In the former case, it is also necessary to decide where to create the project.

Let's first assume that tinylang should be built together with LLVM. There are different options for where to place the project. The first solution is to create a subdirectory for the project inside the llvm-projects directory. All projects in this directory are picked up and built as part of building LLVM. Before the side-by-side project layout was created, this the standard way to build, for example, clang.

A second option is to place the tinylang project in the top-level directory. Because it is not an official LLVM project, the CMake script does not know about it. When running cmake, you need to specify –DLLVM_ENABLE_PROJECTS=tinylang to include the project in the build.

And the third option is to place the project directory somewhere else, outside the llvm-project directory. Of course, you need to tell CMake about this location. If the location is /src/tinylang, for example, then you need to specify –DLLVM_ENABLE_ PROJECTS=tinylang –DLLVM_EXTERNAL_TINYLANG_SOURCE_DIR=/src/ tinylang.

If you want to build the project as a standalone project, then it needs to find the LLVM libraries. This is done in the CMakeLists.txt file, which is discussed later in this section.

After learning about the possible options, which one is the best? Making your project part of the LLVM source tree is a bit inflexible because of the size. As long as you don't aim to add your project to the list of top-level projects, I recommend using a separate directory. You can maintain your project on GitHub or similar services without worrying about how to sync with the LLVM project. And as shown previously, you can still build it together with the other LLVM projects.

Let's create a project with a very simple library and application. The first step is to create the directory layout. Choose a location that's convenient for you. In the following steps, I assume it is in the same directory in which you cloned the llvm-project directory. Create the following directories with mkdir (Unix) or md (Windows):

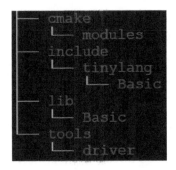

Figure 2.2 – Required directories for the project

Next, we will place the build description and source files in these directories.

Adding the CMake files

You should recognize the basic structure from the last section. Inside the tinylang directory, create a file called CMakeLists.txt with the following steps:

1. The file starts by calling cmake_minimum_required() to declare the minimal required version of CMake. It is the same version as in *Chapter 1, Installing LLVM*:

```
Cmake_minimum_required(VERSION 3.13.4)
```

2. The next statement is `if()`. If the condition is true, then the project is built standalone, and some additional setup is required. The condition uses two variables, `CMAKE_SOURCE_DIR` and `CMAKE_CURRENT_SOURCE_DIR`. The `CMAKE_SOURCE_DIR` variable is the top-level source directory that is given on the `cmake` command line. As we saw in the discussion about the directory layout, each directory with source files has a `CMakeLists.txt` file. The directory of the `CMakeLists.txt` file that CMake currently processes is recorded in the `CMAKE_CURRENT_SOURCE_DIR` variable. If both variables have the same string value, then the project is built standalone. Otherwise, `CMAKE_SOURCE_DIR` would be the `llvm` directory:

```
if(CMAKE_SOURCE_DIR STREQUAL CMAKE_CURRENT_SOURCE_DIR)
```

The standalone setup is straightforward. Each CMake project needs a name. Here, we set it to `Tinylang`:

```
project(Tinylang)
```

3. The LLVM package is searched and the found LLVM directory is added to the CMake module path:

```
find_package(LLVM REQUIRED HINTS
  "${LLVM_CMAKE_PATH}")
list(APPEND CMAKE_MODULE_PATH ${LLVM_DIR})
```

4. Then, three additional CMake modules provided by LLVM are included. The first is only needed when Visual Studio is used as the build compiler and sets the correct runtime library to link again. The other two modules add the macros used by LLVM and configure the build based on the provided options:

```
include(ChooseMSVCCRT)
include(AddLLVM)
include(HandleLLVMOptions)
```

5. Next, the path of the header files from LLVM is added to the include search path. Two directories are added. The `include` directory from the build directory is added because auto-generated files are saved here. The other `include` directory is the one inside the source directory:

```
include_directories("${LLVM_BINARY_DIR}/include"
                    "${LLVM_INCLUDE_DIR}")
```

6. With `link_directories()`, the path of the LLVM libraries is added for the linker:

```
link_directories("${LLVM_LIBRARY_DIR}")
```

7. As a last step, a flag is set to denote that the project is built standalone:

```
set(TINYLANG_BUILT_STANDALONE 1)
endif()
```

8. Now follows the common setup. The `cmake/modules` directory is added to the CMake modules search path. This allows us to later add our own CMake modules:

```
list(APPEND CMAKE_MODULE_PATH
  "${CMAKE_CURRENT_SOURCE_DIR}/cmake/modules")
```

9. Next, we check whether the user is performing an out-of-tree build. Like LLVM, we require that the user uses a separate directory for building the project:

```
if(CMAKE_SOURCE_DIR STREQUAL CMAKE_BINARY_DIR AND NOT
    MSVC_IDE)
  message(FATAL_ERROR "In-source builds are not
    allowed.")
endif()
```

10. The version number of `tinylang` is written to a generated file with the `configure_file()` command. The version number is taken from the `TINYLANG_VERSION_STRING` variable. The `configure_file()` command reads an input file, replaces CMake variables with their current value, and writes an output file. Please note that the input file is read from the source directory and is written to the build directory:

```
set(TINYLANG_VERSION_STRING "0.1")
configure_file(${CMAKE_CURRENT_SOURCE_DIR}/include/
tinylang/Basic/Version.inc.in
  ${CMAKE_CURRENT_BINARY_DIR}/include/tinylang/Basic/
Version.inc)
```

11. Next, another CMake module is included. The `AddTinylang` module has some helper functionality:

```
include(AddTinylang)
```

12. There follows another `include_directories()` statement. This adds our own `include` directories to the beginning of the search path. As in the standalone build, two directories are added:

```
include_directories(BEFORE
  ${CMAKE_CURRENT_BINARY_DIR}/include
  ${CMAKE_CURRENT_SOURCE_DIR}/include
  )
```

13. At the end of the file, the `lib` and the `tools` directories are declared as further directories in which CMake finds the `CMakeLists.txt` file. This is the basic mechanism to connect the directories. This sample application only has source files below the `lib` and the `tools` directories, so nothing else is needed. More complex projects will add more directories, for example, for the unit tests:

```
add_subdirectory(lib)
add_subdirectory(tools)
```

This is the main description for your project.

The `AddTinylang.cmake` helper module is placed in the `cmake/modules` directory. It has the following content:

```
macro(add_tinylang_subdirectory name)
  add_llvm_subdirectory(TINYLANG TOOL ${name})
endmacro()

macro(add_tinylang_library name)
  if(BUILD_SHARED_LIBS)
    set(LIBTYPE SHARED)
  else()
    set(LIBTYPE STATIC)
  endif()
  llvm_add_library(${name} ${LIBTYPE} ${ARGN})
  if(TARGET ${name})
    target_link_libraries(${name} INTERFACE
      ${LLVM_COMMON_LIBS})
    install(TARGETS ${name}
      COMPONENT ${name}
      LIBRARY DESTINATION lib${LLVM_LIBDIR_SUFFIX}
```

```
        ARCHIVE DESTINATION lib${LLVM_LIBDIR_SUFFIX}
        RUNTIME DESTINATION bin)
  else()
    add_custom_target(${name})
  endif()
endmacro()


macro(add_tinylang_executable name)
  add_llvm_executable(${name} ${ARGN} )
endmacro()


macro(add_tinylang_tool name)
  add_tinylang_executable(${name} ${ARGN})
  install(TARGETS ${name}
    RUNTIME DESTINATION bin
    COMPONENT ${name})
endmacro()
```

With inclusion of the module, the add_tinylang_subdirectory(), add_tinylang_library(), add_tinylang_executable(), and add_tinylang_tool() functions are available for use. Basically, these are wrappers around the equivalent functions provided by LLVM (in the AddLLVM module). add_tinylang_subdirectory() adds a new source directory for inclusion in the build. Additionally, a new CMake option is added. With this option, the user can control whether the content of the directory should be compiled or not. With add_tinylang_library(), a library is defined that is also installed. add_tinylang_executable() defines an executable and add_tinylang_tool() defines an executable that is also installed.

Inside the lib directory, a CMakeLists.txt file is needed even if there is no source. It must include the source directories of this project's libraries. Open your favorite text editor and save the following content in the file:

```
add_subdirectory(Basic)
```

A large project would create several libraries, and the source would be placed in subdirectories of lib. Each of these directories would have to be added in the CMakeLists.txt file. Our small project has only one library called Basic, so only one line is needed.

The `Basic` library has only one source file, `Version.cpp`. The `CMakeLists.txt` file in this directory is again simple:

```
add_tinylang_library(tinylangBasic
  Version.cpp
  )
```

A new library called `tinylangBasic` is defined, and the compiled `Version.cpp` is added to this library. An LLVM option controls whether this is a shared or static library. By default, a static library is created.

The same steps repeat in the `tools` directory. The `CMakeLists.txt` file in this folder is almost as simple as in the `lib` directory:

```
create_subdirectory_options(TINYLANG TOOL)
add_tinylang_subdirectory(driver)
```

First, a CMake option is defined that controls whether the content of this directory is compiled. Then the only subdirectory, `driver`, is added, this time with a function from our own module. Again, this allows us to control if this directory is included in compilation or not.

The `driver` directory contains the source of the application, `Driver.cpp`. The `CMakeLists.txt` file in this directory has all the steps to compile and link this application:

```
set(LLVM_LINK_COMPONENTS
  Support
  )

add_tinylang_tool(tinylang
  Driver.cpp
  )

target_link_libraries(tinylang
  PRIVATE
  tinylangBasic
  )
```

First, the LLVM_LINK_COMPONENTS variable is set to the list of LLVM components that we need to link our tool against. An LLVM component is a set of one or more libraries. Obviously, this depends on the implemented functionality of the tools. Here, we need only the Support component.

With add_tinylang_tool() a new installable application is defined. The name is tinylang and the only source file is Driver.cpp. To link against our own libraries, we have to specify them with target_link_libraries(). Here, only tinylangBasic is needed.

Now the files required for the CMake system are in place. Next, we will add the source files.

Adding the C++ source files

Let's start in the include/tinylang/Basic directory. First, create the Version.inc.in template file, which holds the configured version number:

```
#define TINYLANG_VERSION_STRING "@TINYLANG_VERSION_STRING@"
```

The @ symbols around TINYLANG_VERSION_STRING denote that this is a CMake variable that should be replaced with their content.

The Version.h header file only declares a function to retrieve the version string:

```
#ifndef TINYLANG_BASIC_VERSION_H
#define TINYLANG_BASIC_VERSION_H

#include "tinylang/Basic/Version.inc"
#include <string>

namespace tinylang {
std::string getTinylangVersion();
}
#endif
```

The implementation for this function is in the lib/Basic/Version.cpp file. It's similarly simple:

```
#include "tinylang/Basic/Version.h"

std::string tinylang::getTinylangVersion() {
  return TINYLANG_VERSION_STRING;
}
```

And finally, in the `tools/driver/Driver.cpp` file there is the application source:

```
#include "llvm/Support/InitLLVM.h"
#include "llvm/Support/raw_ostream.h"
#include "tinylang/Basic/Version.h"

int main(int argc_, const char **argv_) {
  llvm::InitLLVM X(argc_, argv_);
  llvm::outs() << "Hello, I am Tinylang "
               << tinylang::getTinylangVersion()
               << "\n";
}
```

Despite being only a friendly tool, the source uses typical LLVM functionality. The `llvm::InitLLVM()` call does some basic initialization. On Windows, the arguments are converted to Unicode for the uniform treatment of command-line parsing. And in the (hopefully unlikely) case that the application crashes, a pretty print stack trace handler is installed. It outputs the call hierarchy, beginning with the function inside which the crash happened. To see the real function names instead of hex addresses, the debug symbols must be present.

LLVM does not use the `iostream` classes of the C++ standard library. It comes with its own implementation. `llvm::outs()` is the output stream and is used here to send a friendly message to the user.

Compiling the tinylang application

Now all files for the first application are in place, the application can be compiled. To recap, you should have the following directories and files:

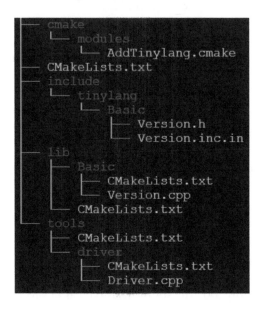

Figure 2.3 – All directories and files of the tinylang project

As discussed previously, there are several ways to build tinylang. Here is how to build tinylang as a part of LLVM:

1. Change into the build directory with this:

   ```
   $ cd build
   ```

2. Then, run CMake as follows:

   ```
   $ cmake -G Ninja -DCMAKE_BUILD_TYPE=Release \
     -DLLVM_EXTERNAL_PROJECTS=tinylang \
     -DLLVM_EXTERNAL_TINYLANG_SOURCE_DIR=../tinylang \
     -DCMAKE_INSTALL_PREFIX=../llvm-12 \
     ../llvm-project/llvm
   ```

With this command, CMake generates build files for **Ninja** (`-G Ninja`). The build type is set to `Release`, thus producing optimized binaries (`-DCMAKE_BUILD_TYPE=Release`). Tinylang is built as an external project alongside LLVM (`-DLLVM_EXTERNAL_PROJECTS=tinylang`) and the source is found in a directory parallel to the build directory (`-DLLVM_EXTERNAL_TINYLANG_SOURCE_DIR=../tinylang`). A target directory for the build binaries is also given (`-DCMAKE_INSTALL_PREFIX=../llvm-12`). As the last parameter, the path of the LLVM project directory is specified (`../llvm-project/llvm`).

3. Now, build and install everything:

```
$ ninja
$ ninja install
```

4. After building and installing, the `../llvm-12` directory contains the LLVM and the `tinylang` binaries. Please check that you can run the application:

```
$ ../llvm-12/bin/tinylang
```

5. You should see the friendly message. Please also check that the Basic library was installed:

```
$ ls ../llvm-12/lib/libtinylang*
```

This will show that there is a `libtinylangBasic.a` file.

Building together with LLVM is useful when you closely follow LLVM development, and you want to be aware of API changes as soon as possible. In *Chapter 1, Installing LLVM*, we checked out a specific version of LLVM. Therefore, we see no changes to LLVM sources.

In this scenario, it makes sense to build LLVM once and compile `tinylang` as a standalone project using the compiled version of LLVM. Here is how to do it:

1. Start again with entering the `build` directory:

```
$ cd build
```

This time, CMake is used only to build LLVM:

```
$ cmake -G Ninja -DCMAKE_BUILD_TYPE=Release \
    -DCMAKE_INSTALL_PREFIX=../llvm-12 \
    ../llvm-project/llvm
```

2. Compare this with the preceding CMake command: the parameters referring to `tinylang` are missing; everything else is identical.

3. Build and install LLVM with Ninja:

```
$ ninja
$ ninja install
```

4. Now you have an LLVM installation in the `llvm-12` directory. Next, the `tinylang` project will be built. As it is a standalone build, a new `build` directory is required. Leave the LLVM build directory like so:

```
$ cd ..
```

5. Now create a new `build-tinylang` directory. On Unix, you use the following command:

```
$ mkdir build-tinylang
```

And on Windows, you would use this command:

```
$ md build-tinylang
```

6. Enter the new directory with the following command on either operating system:

```
$ cd build-tinylang
```

7. Now run CMake to create the build files for `tinylang`. The only peculiarity is how LLVM is discovered, because CMake does not know the location where we installed LLVM. The olution is to specify the path to the `LLVMConfig.cmake` file from LLVM with the `LLVM_DIR` variable. The command is as follows:

```
$ cmake -G Ninja -DCMAKE_BUILD_TYPE=Release \
  -DLLVM_DIR=../llvm-12/lib/cmake/llvm \
  -DCMAKE_INSTALL_PREFIX=../tinylang ../tinylang/
```

8. The installation directory is now separate, too. As usual, build and install with the following:

```
$ ninja
$ ninja install
```

9. After the commands are finished, you should run the `../tinylang/bin/`
    `tinylang` application to check that the application works.

An alternate way to include LLVM

If you do not want to use CMake for your project, then you need to find out where the
include files and libraries are, which libraries to link against, which build mode was used,
and much more. This information is provided by the `llvm-config` tool, which is in the
`bin` directory of an LLVM installation. Assuming that this directory is included in your
shell search path, you run `$ llvm-config` to see all options.

For example, to get the LLVM libraries to link against the `support` component (which is
used in the preceding example), you run this:

```
$ llvm-config –libs support
```

The output is a line with the library names including the link option for the compiler,
for example, `-lLLVMSupport -lLLVMDemangle`. Obviously, this tool can be easily
integrated with your build system of choice.

With the project layout shown in this section, you have a structure that scales for large
projects such as compilers. The next section lays another foundation: how to cross-
compile for a different target architecture.

Targeting a different CPU architecture

Today, many small computers such as the Raspberry Pi are in use and have only limited
resources. Running a compiler on such a computer is often not possible or takes too much
runtime. Hence, a common requirement for a compiler is to generate code for a different
CPU architecture. The whole process of creating an executable is called cross-compiling.
In the previous section, you created a small example application based on the LLVM
libraries. Now we will take this application and compile it for a different target.

With cross-compiling, there are two systems involved: the compiler runs on the host system and produces code for the target system. To denote the systems, the so-called **triple** is used. This is a configuration string that usually consists of the CPU architecture, the vendor, and the operating system. More information about the environment is often added. For example, the triple x86_64-pc-win32 is used for a Windows system running on a 64-bit X86 CPU. The CPU architecture is x86_64, pc is a generic vendor, and win32 is the operating system. The parts are connected by a hyphen. A Linux system running on an ARMv8 CPU uses aarch64-unknown-linux-gnu as the triple. aarch64 is the CPU architecture. The operating system is linux, running a gnu environment. There is no real vendor for a Linux-based system, so this part is unknown. Parts that are not known or unimportant for a specific purpose are often omitted: the triple aarch64-linux-gnu describes the same Linux system.

Let's assume your development machine runs Linux on an X86 64-bit CPU and you want to cross-compile to an ARMv8 CPU system running Linux. The host triple is x86_64-linux-gnu and the target triple is aarch64-linux-gnu. Different systems have different characteristics. Your application must be written in a portable fashion, otherwise you will be surprised by failures. Common pitfalls are as follows:

- **Endianness**: The order in which multi-byte values are stored in memory can be different.

- **Pointer size**: The size of a pointer varies with the CPU architecture (usually 16, 32, or 64 bit). The C type int may not be large enough to hold a pointer.

- **Type differences**: Data types are often closely related to the hardware. The type long double can use 64 bit (ARM), 80 bit (X86), or 128 bit (ARMv8). PowerPC systems may use double-double arithmetic for long double, which gives more precision by using a combination of two 64-bit double values.

If you do not pay attention to these points, then your application can act surprisingly or crash on the target platform even if it runs perfectly on your host system. The LLVM libraries are tested on different platforms and also contain portable solutions to the mentioned issues.

For cross-compiling, you need the following tools:

- A compiler that generates code for the target

- A linker capable of generating binaries for the target

- Header files and libraries for the target

Ubuntu and Debian distributions have packages that support cross-compiling. In the following setup, we take advantage of this. The gcc and g++ compilers, the ld linker, and the libraries are available as precompiled binaries producing ARMv8 code and executables. To install all these packages, type the following:

```
$ sudo apt install gcc-8-aarch64-linux-gnu \
  g++-8-aarch64-linux-gnu binutils-aarch64-linux-gnu \
  libstdc++-8-dev-arm64-cross
```

The new files are installed under the /usr/aarch64-linux-gnu. directory This directory is the (logical) root directory of the target system. It contains the usual bin, lib, and include directories. The cross-compilers (aarch64-linux-gnu-gcc-8 and aarch64-linux-gnu-g++-8) know about this directory.

> **Cross-compiling on other systems**
>
> If your distribution does not come with the required toolchain, then you can build it from source. The gcc and g++ compilers must be configured to produce code for the target system and the binutils tools need to handle files for the target system. Moreover, the C and the C++ library need to be compiled with this toolchain. The steps vary with the used operating systems and host and target architecture. On the web, you can find instructions if you search for gcc cross-compile <architecture>.

With this preparation, you are almost ready to cross-compile the sample application (including the LLVM libraries) except for one little detail. LLVM uses the **tablegen tool** during the build. During cross-compilation, everything is compiled for the target architecture, including this tool. You can use llvm-tblgen from the build of *Chapter 1, Installing LLVM,* or you can compile only this tool. Assuming you are in the directory that contains the clone of the GitHub repository, type this:

```
$ mkdir build-host
$ cd build-host
$ cmake -G Ninja \
  -DLLVM_TARGETS_TO_BUILD="X86" \
  -DLLVM_ENABLE_ASSERTIONS=ON \
  -DCMAKE_BUILD_TYPE=Release \
  ../llvm-project/llvm
$ ninja llvm-tblgen
$ cd ..
```

These steps should be familiar by now. A build directory is created and entered. The CMake command creates LLVM build files for the X86 target only. To save space and time, a release build is done but assertions are enabled to catch possible errors. Only the `llvm-tblgen` tool is compiled with Ninja.

With the `llvm-tblgen` tool at hand, you can now start the cross-compilation. The CMake command line is very long so you may want to store the command in a script file. The difference from previous builds is that more information must be provided:

```
$ mkdir build-target
$ cd build-target
$ cmake -G Ninja \
  -DCMAKE_CROSSCOMPILING=True \
  -DLLVM_TABLEGEN=../build-host/bin/llvm-tblgen \
  -DLLVM_DEFAULT_TARGET_TRIPLE=aarch64-linux-gnu \
  -DLLVM_TARGET_ARCH=AArch64 \
  -DLLVM_TARGETS_TO_BUILD=AArch64 \
  -DLLVM_ENABLE_ASSERTIONS=ON \
  -DLLVM_EXTERNAL_PROJECTS=tinylang \
  -DLLVM_EXTERNAL_TINYLANG_SOURCE_DIR=../tinylang \
  -DCMAKE_INSTALL_PREFIX=../target-tinylang \
  -DCMAKE_BUILD_TYPE=Release \
  -DCMAKE_C_COMPILER=aarch64-linux-gnu-gcc-8 \
  -DCMAKE_CXX_COMPILER=aarch64-linux-gnu-g++-8 \
  ../llvm-project/llvm
$ ninja
```

Again, you create a build directory and enter it. Some of the CMake parameters have not been used before and need some explanation:

- `CMAKE_CROSSCOMPILING` set to `ON` tells CMake that we are cross-compiling.

- `LLVM_TABLEGEN` specifies the path to the `llvm-tblgen` tool to use. This is the one from the previous build.

- `LLVM_DEFAULT_TARGET_TRIPLE` is the triple of the target architecture.

- `LLVM_TARGET_ARCH` is used for **just-in-time (JIT)** code generation. It defaults to the architecture of the host. For cross-compiling, this must be set to the target architecture.

- `LLVM_TARGETS_TO_BUILD` is the list of target(s) for which LLVM should include code generators. The list should at least include the target architecture.

- `CMAKE_C_COMPILER` and `CMAKE_CXX_COMPILER` specify the C and C++ compilers used for the build. The binaries of the cross-compilers are prefixed with the target triple and are not found automatically by CMake.

With the other parameters, a release build with assertions enabled is requested and our tinylang application is built as part of LLVM (as shown in the previous section). After the compilation process is finished, you can check with the `file` command that you have really created a binary for ARMv8. Run `$ file bin/tinylang` and check that the output says that it is an ELF 64-bit object for the ARM aarch64 architecture.

Cross-compiling with clang

As LLVM generates code for different architectures, it seems obvious to use clang to cross-compile. The obstacle here is that LLVM does not provide all required parts; for example, the C library is missing. Because of this, you have to use a mix of LLVM and GNU tools, and as a result you need to tell CMake even more about the environment you are using. As a minimum, you need to specify the following options for clang and clang++: `--target=<target-triple>` (enables code generation for a different target), `--sysroot=<path>` (path to the root directory for the target; see previous), `I` (search path for header files), and `-L` (search path for libraries). During the CMake run, a small application is compiled and CMake complains if something is wrong with your setup. This step is sufficient to check if you have a working environment. Common problems include picking the wrong header files, link failures due to different library names, and the wrong search path.

Cross-compiling is surprisingly complex. With the instructions from this section, you will be able to cross-compile your application for a target architecture of your choice.

Summary

In this chapter, you learned about the projects that are part of the LLVM repository and the common layout used. You replicated this structure for your own small application, laying the foundation for more complex applications. As the supreme discipline of compiler construction, you also learned how to cross-compile your application for another target architecture.

In the next chapter, the sample language `tinylang` will be outlined. You will learn about the tasks a compiler has to do and where LLVM library support is available.

3
The Structure of a Compiler

Compiler technology is a well-studied field of computer science. Its high-level task is to translate a source language into machine code. Typically, this task is divided into two parts: the frontend and the backend. The frontend mainly deals with the source language, while the backend is responsible for generating machine code.

In this chapter, we will cover the following topics:

- The building blocks of a compiler, in which you will learn about the components typically found in a compiler.

- An arithmetic expression language, which will introduce you to an example language. You will learn how grammar is used to define a language.

- Lexical analysis, which will discuss how you implement lexers for the language.

- Syntactical analysis, which covers how to construct a parser from grammar.

- Semantic analysis, in which you will learn how a sematic check can be implemented.

- Code generation with the LLVM backend, which will discuss how to interface with the LLVM backend and how you can glue all the phases together to create a complete compiler.

Technical requirements

The code files for the chapter are available at `https://github.com/PacktPublishing/Learn-LLVM-12/tree/master/Chapter03/calc`

You can find the code in action videos at `https://bit.ly/3nllhED`

Building blocks of a compiler

After computers became available in the middle of the last century, it quickly became apparent that a more abstract language than assembler would be useful for programming. As early as 1957, Fortran was the first available higher programming language. Since then, thousands of programming languages have been developed. It turns out that all compilers must solve the same tasks and that the implementation of a compiler is best structured according to these tasks.

At the highest level, a compiler consists of two parts: the frontend and the backend. The frontend is responsible for language-specific tasks. It reads a source file and computes a semantic analyzed representation of it, usually an annotated **abstract syntax tree** (**AST**). The backend creates optimized machine code from the frontend's result. The motivation behind there being a distinction between the frontend and the backend is reusability. Let's assume that the interface between the frontend and the backend is well defined. Here, you can connect a C and a Modula-2 frontend to the same backend. Alternatively, if you have one backend for X86 and one for Sparc, then you can connect your C++ frontend to both.

The frontend and backend have specific structures. The frontend usually performs the following tasks:

1. The lexer reads the source file and produces a token stream.
2. The parser creates an AST from the token stream.
3. The semantic analyzer adds semantic information to the AST.
4. The code generator produces an **intermediate representation** (**IR**) from the AST.

The intermediate representation is the interface of the backend. The backend does the following tasks:

1. The backend performs target-independent optimization on the IR.
2. It then selects instructions for the IR code.
3. After, it performs target-dependent optimizations on the instructions.
4. Finally, it emits assembler code or an object file.

Of course, these instructions are only at a conceptual level. The implementations vary a lot. The LLVM core libraries define an intermediate representation as a standard interface to the backend. Other tools could use the annotated AST. The C preprocessor is a language of its own. It can be implemented as a standalone application that outputs preprocessed C source or as an additional component between the lexer and the parser. In some cases, the AST must not be constructed explicitly. If the language to be implemented is not too complex, then combining the parser and the semantic analyzer, and then emitting code while parsing, is a common approach. Even if a given implementation of a programing language does not explicitly name these components, it is good to remember that the tasks must still be done.

In the following sections, we will construct a compiler for an expression language that produces LLVM IR from its input. The LLVM static compiler, `llc`, which represents the backend, can then be used to compile the IR into object code. It all begins with defining the language.

An arithmetic expression language

Arithmetic expressions are part of every programming language. Here is an example of an arithmetic expression calculation language called **calc**. calc expressions are compiled into an application that evaluates the following expression:

```
with a, b: a * (4 + b)
```

The variables that are used in the expression must be declared with the `with` keyword. This program is compiled into an application, which asks the user for the values of the a and b variables and prints the result.

Examples are always welcome but as a compiler writer, you need a more thorough specification than this for implementation and testing. The vehicle for the syntax of the programming language is its grammar.

Formalism for specifying the syntax of a programming language

The elements of a language, such as its keywords, identifiers, strings, numbers, and operators, are called **tokens**. In this sense, a program is a sequence of tokens, and the grammar specifies which sequences are valid.

Usually, grammar is written in the **extended Backus-Naur form (EBNF)**. One of the rules of grammar is that it has a left-hand side and a right-hand side. The left-hand side is just a single symbol called a **non-terminal**. The right-hand side of a rule consists of non-terminals, tokens, and meta-symbols for alternatives and repetitions. Let's have a look at the grammar for the calc language:

```
calc : ("with" ident ("," ident)* ":")? expr ;
expr : term (( "+" | "-" ) term)* ;
term : factor (( "*" | "/") factor)* ;
factor : ident | number | "(" expr ")" ;
ident : ([a-zAZ])+ ;
number : ([0-9])+ ;
```

In the first line, `calc` is a non-terminal. If not otherwise stated, then the first non-terminal of grammar is the start symbol. The colon, `:`, is the separator between the left-hand side and the right-hand side of the rule. `"with"`, `","`, and `":"` are tokens that represent this string. Parentheses are used for grouping. A group can be optional or repeated. A question mark, `?`, after the closing parenthesis denotes an optional group. A star, `*`, denotes zero or more repetitions, while a plus, `+`, denotes one or more repetitions. `ident` and `expr` are non-terminals. For each, another rule exists. The semicolon, `;`, marks the end of a rule. The pipe, `|`, in the second line, denotes an alternative. Finally, the brackets, `[ ]`, in the last two lines denote a character class. The valid characters are written inside the brackets. For example, the `[a-zA-Z]` character classes matches an uppercase or lowercase letter and `([a-zA-Z])+` matches one or more of these letters. This corresponds to a regular expression.

How grammar helps the compiler writer

Such grammar may look like a theoretical toy, but it is of value to the compiler writer. First, all the tokens are defined, which is needed to create the lexical analyzer. The rules of the grammar can be translated into the parser. And of course, if questions arise regarding whether the parser works correctly, then the grammar serves as a good specification.

However, grammar does not define all the aspects of a programming language. The meaning – the semantics – of the syntax must also be defined. Formalisms for this purpose were developed too, but often, it is specified in plain text, similar to when the language was first introduced.

Equipped with this knowledge, the next two sections will show you how lexical analysis turns the input into a sequence of tokens and how grammar is coded in C++ for syntactical analysis.

Lexical analysis

As we saw in the example in the previous section, a programming language consists of many elements, such as keywords, identifiers, numbers, operators, and so on. The task of lexical analysis is to take the textual input and create a sequence of tokens from it. The calc language consists of the with, :, +, -, *, /, (, and) tokens and the ([a-zA-Z]) + (an identifier) and ([0-9]) + (a number) regular expressions. We assign a unique number to each token to make handling them easier.

A handwritten lexer

The implementation of a lexical analyzer is often called a Lexer. Let's create a header file called Lexer.h and start defining Token. It begins with the usual header guard and the required headers:

```
#ifndef LEXER_H
#define LEXER_H

#include "llvm/ADT/StringRef.h"
#include "llvm/Support/MemoryBuffer.h"
```

The llvm::MemoryBuffer class provides read-only access to a block of memory, filled with the content of a file. On request, a trailing zero character ('\x00') is added to the end of the buffer. We use this feature to read through the buffer without checking the length of the buffer at each access. The llvm::StringRef class encapsulates a pointer to a C string and its length. Because the length is stored, the string doesn't need to be terminated with a zero character ('\x00') like normal C strings. This allows an instance of StringRef to point to the memory managed by MemoryBuffer. Let's take a look at this in more detail:

1. First, the Token class contains the definition of the enumeration for the unique token numbers mentioned previously:

```
class Lexer;

class Token {
  friend class Lexer;

public:
  enum TokenKind : unsigned short {
    eoi, unknown, ident, number, comma, colon, plus,
```

```
      minus, star, slash, l_paren, r_paren, KW_with
   };
```

Besides defining a member for each token, we added two additional values: `eoi` and `unknown`. `eoi` stands for **end of input** and is returned if all the characters of the input are processed. `unknown` is used in case of an error at the lexical level; for example, # is not a token of the language, so it would be mapped to `unknown`.

2. In addition to the enumeration, the class has a member, `Text`, which points to the start of the text of the token. It uses the `StringRef` class mentioned previously:

```
private:
   TokenKind Kind;
   llvm::StringRef Text;


public:
   TokenKind getKind() const { return Kind; }
   llvm::StringRef getText() const { return Text; }
```

This is useful for semantic processing, in that it is useful to know the identifier's name.

3. The `is()` and `isOneOf()` methods are used to test if the token is of a certain kind. The `isOneOf()` method uses a variadic template, which allows a variable number of arguments:

```
   bool is(TokenKind K) const { return Kind == K; }
   bool isOneOf(TokenKind K1, TokenKind K2) const {
     return is(K1) || is(K2);
   }
   template <typename... Ts>
   bool isOneOf(TokenKind K1, TokenKind K2, Ts... Ks)
 const {
     return is(K1) || isOneOf(K2, Ks...);
   }
};
```

4. The `Lexer` class itself has a similar simple interface and comes next in the header file:

```
class Lexer {
   const char *BufferStart;
```

```
      const char *BufferPtr;


public:
    Lexer(const llvm::StringRef &Buffer) {
      BufferStart = Buffer.begin();
      BufferPtr = BufferStart;
    }


    void next(Token &token);


private:
    void formToken(Token &Result, const char *TokEnd,
                   Token::TokenKind Kind);
};
#endif
```

Except for the constructor, the public interface only contains the next() method, which returns the next token. The method acts like an iterator, always advancing to the next available token. The only members of the class are pointers to the beginning of the input and to the next unprocessed character. It is assumed that the buffer ends with a terminating 0 (like a C string).

5. Let's implement the Lexer class in the Lexer.cpp file. It begins with some helper functions to help classify characters:

```
#include "Lexer.h"


namespace charinfo {
LLVM_READNONE inline bool isWhitespace(char c) {
    return c == ' ' || c == '\t' || c == '\f' ||
           c == '\v' ||
           c == '\r' || c == '\n';
}


LLVM_READNONE inline bool isDigit(char c) {
    return c >= '0' && c <= '9';
}
```

```
LLVM_READNONE inline bool isLetter(char c) {
  return (c >= 'a' && c <= 'z') ||
         (c >= 'A' && c <= 'Z');
}
}
```

These functions are used to make conditions more readable.

> **Note**
>
> We are not using the functions provided by the <cctype> standard library
> header for two reasons. First, these functions change behavior based on the
> locale defined in the environment. For example, if the locale is a German-
> language local, then German umlauts can be classified as letters. This is usually
> not wanted in a compiler. Second, since the functions have int as a parameter
> type, we must convert from the char type. The result of this conversion
> depends on whether char is treated as a signed or unsigned type, which
> causes portability problems.

6. From the grammar in the previous section, we know all the tokens of the language.
    But the grammar does not define the characters that should be ignored. For
    example, a space or a new line only adds whitespace and is often ignored. The
    next() method begins by ignoring these characters:

```
void Lexer::next(Token &token) {
  while (*BufferPtr &&
         charinfo::isWhitespace(*BufferPtr)) {
    ++BufferPtr;
  }
```

7. Next, make sure that there are still characters left to process:

```
if (!*BufferPtr) {
  token.Kind = Token::eoi;
  return;
}
```

There is at least one character to process.

8. So, we first check whether the character is lowercase or uppercase. In this case, the token is either an identifier or the `with` keyword, because the regular expression for the identifier also matches the keyword. The common solution is to collect the characters that are matched by the regular expression and check if the string happens to be the keyword:

```
if (charinfo::isLetter(*BufferPtr)) {
  const char *end = BufferPtr + 1;
  while (charinfo::isLetter(*end))
    ++end;
  llvm::StringRef Name(BufferPtr, end - BufferPtr);
  Token::TokenKind kind =
      Name == "with" ? Token::KW_with : Token::ident;
  formToken(token, end, kind);
  return;
}
```

The private `formToken()` method is used to populate the token.

9. Next, we check for a number. The following code is very similar to the code shown previously:

```
else if (charinfo::isDigit(*BufferPtr)) {
  const char *end = BufferPtr + 1;
  while (charinfo::isDigit(*end))
    ++end;
  formToken(token, end, Token::number);
  return;
}
```

10. Now, only the tokens defined by fixed strings are left. This is done easily with a `switch`. Since all these tokens have only one character, the `CASE` preprocessor macro is used to reduce typing:

```
else {
    switch (*BufferPtr) {
#define CASE(ch, tok) \
case ch: formToken(token, BufferPtr + 1, tok); break
CASE('+', Token::plus);
CASE('-', Token::minus);
```

```
CASE('*', Token::star);
CASE('/', Token::slash);
CASE('(', Token::Token::l_paren);
CASE(')', Token::Token::r_paren);
CASE(':', Token::Token::colon);
CASE(',', Token::Token::comma);
#undef CASE
```

11. Finally, we need to check for unexpected characters:

```
        default:
            formToken(token, BufferPtr + 1, Token::unknown);
        }
        return;
    }
}
```

Only the private helper method, formToken(), is still missing.

12. This private helper method populates the members of the Token instance and updates the pointer to the next unprocessed character:

```
void Lexer::formToken(Token &Tok, const char *TokEnd,
                      Token::TokenKind Kind) {
    Tok.Kind = Kind;
    Tok.Text = llvm::StringRef(BufferPtr, TokEnd -
                               BufferPtr);
    BufferPtr = TokEnd;
}
```

In the next section, we'll have a look at how to construct a parser for syntactical analysis.

Syntactical analysis

Syntactical analysis is done by the parser, which we will implement next. Its base is the grammar and the lexer from the previous sections. The result of the parsing process is a dynamic data structure called an **abstract syntax tree** (**AST**). The AST is a very condensed representation of the input and is well-suited for semantic analysis. First, we will implement the parser. After that, we will have a look at the AST.

A handwritten parser

The interface of the parser is defined in the `Parser.h` header file. It begins with some `include` statements:

```
#ifndef PARSER_H
#define PARSER_H

#include "AST.h"
#include "Lexer.h"
#include "llvm/Support/raw_ostream.h"
```

The `AST.h` header file declares the interface for the AST and will be shown later. The coding guidelines from LLVM forbid the use of the `<iostream>` library, so the header of the equivalent LLVM functionality must be included. It is required to emit an error message. Let's take a look at this in more detail:

1. First, the `Parser` class declares some private members:

```
class Parser {
  Lexer &Lex;
  Token Tok;
  bool HasError;
```

   Lex and Tok are instances of the classes from the previous section. Tok stores the next token (the look-ahead), while Lex is used to retrieve the next token from the input. The `HasError` flag indicates if an error was detected.

2. A couple of methods deal with the token:

```
  void error() {
    llvm::errs() << "Unexpected: " << Tok.getText()
                 << "\n";
    HasError = true;
  }

  void advance() { Lex.next(Tok); }

  bool expect(Token::TokenKind Kind) {
    if (Tok.getKind() != Kind) {
      error();
```

```
      return true;
    }
  return false;
}


bool consume(Token::TokenKind Kind) {
  if (expect(Kind))
    return true;
  advance();
  return false;
}
```

advance() retrieves the next token from the lexer. expect() tests whether the look-ahead is of the expected kind and emits an error message if not. Finally, consume() retrieves the next token if the look-ahead is of the expected kind. If an error message is emitted, the HasError flag is set to true.

3. For each non-terminal in the grammar, a method to parse the rule is declared:

```
AST *parseCalc();
Expr *parseExpr();
Expr *parseTerm();
Expr *parseFactor();
```

> **Note**
>
> There are no methods for ident and number. Those rules only return the token and are replaced by the corresponding token.

4. The public interface follows. The constructor initializes all the members and retrieves the first token from the lexer:

```
public:
  Parser(Lexer &Lex) : Lex(Lex), HasError(false) {
    advance();
  }
```

5. A function is required to get the value of the error flag:

```
bool hasError() { return HasError; }
```

6. Finally, the `parse()` method is the main entry point into parsing:

```
    AST *parse();
};

#endif
```

In the next section, we will learn to implement the parser.

Parser implementation

Let's dive into the implementation of the parser:

1. The implementation of the parser can be found in the `Parser.cpp` file and begins with the `parse()` method:

```
#include "Parser.h"

AST *Parser::parse() {
  AST *Res = parseCalc();
  expect(Token::eoi);
  return Res;
}
```

The main point of the `parse()` method is that the whole input has been consumed. Do you remember that the parsing example in the first section added a special symbol to denote the end of the input? We'll check this here.

2. The `parseCalc()` method implements the corresponding rule. It's worth having a closer look at this method as the other parsing methods follow the same patterns. Let's recall the rule from the first section:

```
calc : ("with" ident ("," ident)* ":")? expr ;
```

3. The method begins by declaring some local variables:

```
AST *Parser::parseCalc() {
  Expr *E;
  llvm::SmallVector<llvm::StringRef, 8> Vars;
```

4. The first decision to be made is whether the optional group must be parsed or not. The group begins with the `with` token, so we compare the token to this value:

    ```
    if (Tok.is(Token::KW_with)) {
        advance();
    ```

5. Next, we expect an identifier:

    ```
    if (expect(Token::ident))
        goto _error;
    Vars.push_back(Tok.getText());
    advance();
    ```

    If there is an identifier, then we save it in the `Vars` vector. Otherwise, it is a syntax error, which is handled separately.

6. In the grammar now follows a repeating group, which parses more identifiers, it's separated by a comma:

    ```
    while (Tok.is(Token::comma)) {
        advance();
        if (expect(Token::ident))
            goto _error;
        Vars.push_back(Tok.getText());
        advance();
    }
    ```

    At this point, this should not be surprising to you. The repetition group begins with the, token. The test for the token becomes the condition of the `while` loop, implementing zero or more repetition. The identifier inside the loop is treated as it was previously.

7. Finally, the optional group requires a colon at the end:

    ```
    if (consume(Token::colon))
        goto _error;
    }
    ```

8. Now, the rule for `expr` must be parsed:

    ```
    E = parseExpr();
    ```

9. With this call, the rule has been parsed successfully. The information that we've collected is now used to create the AST node for this rule:

```
if (Vars.empty()) return E;
else return new WithDecl(Vars, E);
```

Now, only the error handling code is missing. Detecting a syntax error is easy but recovering from it is surprisingly complicated. Here, a simple approach called **panic mode** must be used.

In panic mode, tokens are deleted from the token stream until one is found that the parser can use to continue its work. Most programming languages have symbols that denote an end; for example, in C++, we can use ; (end of a statement) or } (end of a block). Such tokens are good candidates to look for.

On the other hand, the error can be that the symbol we are looking for is missing. In this case, a lot of tokens are probably deleted before the parser can continue. This is not as bad as it sounds. Today, it is more important that a compiler is fast. In case of an error, the developer looks at the first error message, fixes it, and restarts the compiler. This is quite different from using punch cards, where it was important to get as many error messages as possible, since the next run of the compiler would only be possible on the next day.

Error handling

Instead of using some arbitrary tokens, another set of tokens is used. For each non-terminal, there is a set of tokens that can follow this non-terminal in a rule. Let's take a look:

1. In the case of calc, only the end of the input follows this non-terminal. Its implementation is trivial:

```
_error:
    while (!Tok.is(Token::eoi))
        advance();
    return nullptr;
}
```

2. The other parsing methods are constructed in a similar fashion. parseExpr() is the translation of the rule for expr:

```
Expr *Parser::parseExpr() {
    Expr *Left = parseTerm();
    while (Tok.isOneOf(Token::plus, Token::minus)) {
```

```
        BinaryOp::Operator Op =
            Tok.is(Token::plus) ? BinaryOp::Plus :
                                    BinaryOp::Minus;
        advance();
        Expr *Right = parseTerm();
        Left = new BinaryOp(Op, Left, Right);
    }
    return Left;
}
```

The repeated group inside the rule is translated into a `while` loop. Note how the use of the `isOneOf()` method simplifies the check for several tokens.

3. The coding of the `term` rule looks the same:

```
Expr *Parser::parseTerm() {
    Expr *Left = parseFactor();
    while (Tok.isOneOf(Token::star, Token::slash)) {
        BinaryOp::Operator Op =
            Tok.is(Token::star) ? BinaryOp::Mul :
                                    BinaryOp::Div;
        advance();
        Expr *Right = parseFactor();
        Left = new BinaryOp(Op, Left, Right);
    }
    return Left;
}
```

This method is strikingly similar to `parseExpr()`, and you may be tempted to combine them into one. In grammar, it is possible to have one rule that deals with multiplicative and additive operators. The advantage of using two rules instead of one is that the precedence of the operators fits well with the mathematical order of evaluation. If you combine both rules, then you need to figure out the evaluation order somewhere else.

4. Finally, you need to implement the rule for `factor`:

```
Expr *Parser::parseFactor() {
    Expr *Res = nullptr;
    switch (Tok.getKind()) {
```

```
case Token::number:
  Res = new Factor(Factor::Number, Tok.getText());
  advance(); break;
```

Instead of using a chain of `if` and `else if` statements, a `switch` statement seems more suitable here, because each alternative begins with just one token. In general, you should think about which translation patterns you like to use. If you need to change the parsing methods later, then it is an advantage if not every method has a different way of implementing a grammar rule.

5. If you use a `switch` statement, then error handling happens in the `default` case:

```
case Token::ident:
  Res = new Factor(Factor::Ident, Tok.getText());
  advance(); break;
case Token::l_paren:
  advance();
  Res = parseExpr();
  if (!consume(Token::r_paren)) break;
default:
  if (!Res) error();
```

We guard emitting the error message here because of the fall-through.

6. If there was a syntax error in the parenthesis expression, then an error message would have been emitted. The guard prevents a second error message from being emitted:

```
  while (!Tok.isOneOf(Token::r_paren, Token::star,
                      Token::plus, Token::minus,
                      Token::slash, Token::eoi))
    advance();
  }
  return Res;
}
```

That was easy, wasn't it? As soon as you have memorized the used patterns, it is almost tedious to code the parser based on the grammar rules. This type of parser is called a **recursive descent parser**.

> **A recursive descent parser can't be constructed from all grammar**
>
> Grammar must satisfy certain conditions to be suitable for constructing a recursive descent parser. This class of grammar is called LL(1). In fact, most grammar that you can find on the internet does not belong to this class of grammar. Most books about the theory of compiler construction explain the reason for this. The classic book on this topic is the so-called "dragon book", *Compilers: Principles, Techniques, and Tools* by Aho, Lam, Sethi, and Ullman.

The abstract syntax tree

The result of the parsing process is an **AST**. The AST is another compact representation of the input program. It captures essential information. Many programming languages have symbols that are needed as separators and that do not carry further meaning. For example, in C++, a semicolon, ;, denotes the end of a single statement. Of course, this information is important for the parser. As soon as we turn the statement into an in-memory representation, the semicolon is not important anymore and can be dropped.

If you look at the first rule of the example expression language, then it is clear that the with keyword, the comma, ,, and the colon, :, are not really important for the meaning of a program. What is important is the list of declared variables that could be used in the expression. The result is that only a couple of classes are required to record the information: Factor holds a number or an identifier, BinaryOp holds the arithmetic operator and the left-hand and right-hand sides of an expression, and WithDecl stores the list of declared variables and the expression. AST and Expr are only used to create a common class hierarchy.

In addition to the information from the parsed input, tree traversal while using the **visitor pattern** is also supported. It's all in the AST.h header file. Let's take a look:

1. It begins with the visitor interface:

```
#ifndef AST_H
#define AST_H

#include "llvm/ADT/SmallVector.h"
#include "llvm/ADT/StringRef.h"

class AST;
class Expr;
class Factor;
class BinaryOp;
```

```
class WithDecl;
```

```
class ASTVisitor {
public:
  virtual void visit(AST &){};
  virtual void visit(Expr &){};
  virtual void visit(Factor &) = 0;
  virtual void visit(BinaryOp &) = 0;
  virtual void visit(WithDecl &) = 0;
};
```

The visitor pattern needs to know each class it must visit. Because each class also refers to the visitor, we declare all the classes at the top of the file. Please note that the `visit()` methods for `AST` and `Expr` have a default implementation, which does nothing.

2. The `AST` class is the root of the hierarchy:

```
class AST {
public:
  virtual ~AST() {}
  virtual void accept(ASTVisitor &V) = 0;
};
```

3. Similarly, `Expr` is the root for the `AST` classes related to expressions:

```
class Expr : public AST {
public:
  Expr() {}
};
```

4. The `Factor` class stores a number or the name of a variable:

```
class Factor : public Expr {
public:
  enum ValueKind { Ident, Number };

private:
  ValueKind Kind;
  llvm::StringRef Val;
```

```
public:
  Factor(ValueKind Kind, llvm::StringRef Val)
      : Kind(Kind), Val(Val) {}
  ValueKind getKind() { return Kind; }
  llvm::StringRef getVal() { return Val; }
  virtual void accept(ASTVisitor &V) override {
    V.visit(*this);
  }
};
```

In this example, numbers and variables are treated almost identically, so we decided to create only one AST node class to represent them. The `Kind` member tells us which of both cases the instances represent. In more complex languages, you usually want to have different AST classes, such as a `NumberLiteral` class for numbers and a `VariableAccess` class for a reference to a variable.

5. The `BinaryOp` class holds the data that's needed to evaluate an expression:

```
class BinaryOp : public Expr {
public:
  enum Operator { Plus, Minus, Mul, Div };

private:
  Expr *Left;
  Expr *Right;
  Operator Op;

public:
  BinaryOp(Operator Op, Expr *L, Expr *R)
      : Op(Op), Left(L), Right(R) {}
  Expr *getLeft() { return Left; }
  Expr *getRight() { return Right; }
  Operator getOperator() { return Op; }
  virtual void accept(ASTVisitor &V) override {
    V.visit(*this);
  }
};
```

In contrast to the parser, the `BinaryOp` class makes no distinction between multiplicative and additive operators. The precedence of the operators is implicitly available in the tree structure.

6. Finally, `WithDecl` stores the declared variables and the expression:

```
class WithDecl : public AST {
  using VarVector =
                llvm::SmallVector<llvm::StringRef, 8>;
  VarVector Vars;
  Expr *E;

public:
  WithDecl(llvm::SmallVector<llvm::StringRef, 8> Vars,
           Expr *E)
      : Vars(Vars), E(E) {}
  VarVector::const_iterator begin()
                            { return Vars.begin(); }
  VarVector::const_iterator end() { return Vars.end(); }
  Expr *getExpr() { return E; }
  virtual void accept(ASTVisitor &V) override {
    V.visit(*this);
  }
};
#endif
```

The AST is constructed during parsing. The semantic analysis checks that the tree adheres to the meaning of the language (for example, that used variables are declared) and possibly augments the tree. After that, the tree is used for code generation.

Semantic analysis

The semantic analyzer walks the AST and checks for various semantic rules of the language; for example, a variable must be declared before use or types of variables must be compatible in an expression. The semantic analyzer can also print out warnings if it finds a situation that can be improved. For the example expression language, the sematic analyzer must check that each used variable is declared, because that is what the language requires. A possible extension (which will not be implemented here) is to print a warning message if a declared variable is not used.

The semantic analyzer is implemented in the `Sema` class, and semantic analysis is performed by the `semantic()` method. Here is the complete `Sema.h` header file:

```
#ifndef SEMA_H
#define SEMA_H

#include "AST.h"
#include "Lexer.h"

class Sema {
public:
  bool semantic(AST *Tree);
};

#endif
```

The implementation is in the `Sema.cpp` file. The interesting part is the semantic analysis, which is implemented using a visitor. The basic idea is that the name of each declared variable is stored in a set. While the set it being created, we can check that each name is unique and then check that the name is in the set later:

```
#include "Sema.h"
#include "llvm/ADT/StringSet.h"

namespace {
class DeclCheck : public ASTVisitor {
  llvm::StringSet<> Scope;
  bool HasError;

  enum ErrorType { Twice, Not };

  void error(ErrorType ET, llvm::StringRef V) {
    llvm::errs() << "Variable " << V << " "
                 << (ET == Twice ? "already" : "not")
                 << " declared\n";
    HasError = true;
  }
```

```
public:
  DeclCheck() : HasError(false) {}

  bool hasError() { return HasError; }
```

Like in the `Parser` class, a flag is used to indicate that an error occurred. The names are stored in a set called `Scope`. In a `Factor` node that holds a variable name, we check that the variable name is in the set:

```
virtual void visit(Factor &Node) override {
  if (Node.getKind() == Factor::Ident) {
    if (Scope.find(Node.getVal()) == Scope.end())
      error(Not, Node.getVal());
  }
};
```

For a `BinaryOp` node, we only need to check that both sides exist and have been visited:

```
virtual void visit(BinaryOp &Node) override {
  if (Node.getLeft())
    Node.getLeft()->accept(*this);
  else
    HasError = true;
  if (Node.getRight())
    Node.getRight()->accept(*this);
  else
    HasError = true;
};
```

In a `WithDecl` node, the set is populated and the walk over the expression is started:

```
virtual void visit(WithDecl &Node) override {
  for (auto I = Node.begin(), E = Node.end(); I != E;
       ++I) {
    if (!Scope.insert(*I).second)
      error(Twice, *I);
  }
  if (Node.getExpr())
    Node.getExpr()->accept(*this);
```

```
        else
          HasError = true;
    };
  };
}
```

The `semantic()` method only starts the tree walk and returns an error flag:

```
bool Sema::semantic(AST *Tree) {
  if (!Tree)
    return false;
  DeclCheck Check;
  Tree->accept(Check);
  return Check.hasError();
}
```

If required, much more could be done here. It would also be possible to print a warning message if a declared variable is not used. We leave it to you to implement this. If the semantic analysis finishes without error, then we can generate the LLVM IR from the AST. We will do this in the next section.

Generating code with the LLVM backend

The backend's task is to create optimized machine code from an **IR** of a module. The IR is the interface to the backend and can be created using a C++ interface or in textual form. Again, the IR is generated from the AST.

Textual representation of the LLVM IR

Before trying to generate the LLVM IR, we need to understand what we want to generate. For the example expression language, the high-level plan is as follows:

1. Ask the user for the value of each variable.

2. Calculate the value of the expression.

3. Print the result.

To ask the user to provide a value for a variable and to print the result, two library functions, `calc_read()` and `calc_write()`, are used. For the `with a: 3*a` expression, the generated IR is as follows:

1. The library functions must be declared, like in C. The syntax also resembles C. The type before the function name is the return type. The type names surrounded by parenthesis are the argument types. The declaration can appear anywhere in the file:

    ```
    declare i32 @calc_read(i8*)
    declare void @calc_write(i32)
    ```

2. The `calc_read()` function takes the variable name as a parameter. The following construct defines a constant, holding a and the null byte that's used as a string terminator in C:

    ```
    @a.str = private constant [2 x i8] c"a\00"
    ```

3. It follows the `main()` function. The parameter's names are omitted because they are not used. Like in C, the body of the function is enclosed in braces:

    ```
    define i32 @main(i32, i8**) {
    ```

4. Each basic block must have a label. Because this is the first basic block of the function, we name it `entry`:

    ```
    entry:
    ```

5. The `calc_read()` function is called to read the value for the a variable. The nested `getelemenptr` instruction performs an index calculation to compute the pointer to the first element of the string constant. The function's result is assigned to the unnamed `%2` variable:

    ```
    %2 = call i32 @calc_read(i8* getelementptr inbounds
                    ([2 x i8], [2 x i8]* @a.str, i32 0, i32
    0))
    ```

6. Next, the variable is multiplied by 3:

    ```
    %3 = mul nsw i32 3, %2
    ```

7. The result is printed to the console via a call to the `calc_write()` function:

    ```
    call void @calc_write(i32 %3)
    ```

8. Finally, the `main()` function returns 0 to indicate successful execution:

    ```
    ret i32 0
    }
    ```

Each value in LLVM IR is typed, with `i32` denoting the 32-bit bit integer type and `i8*` denoting a pointer to a byte. IR code is very readable (maybe except for the `getelementptr` operation, which will be explained in detail in *Chapter 5, Basics of IR Generation*). Since it is now clear what the IR looks like, let's generate it from the AST.

Generating the IR from the AST

The interface, which is provided in the `CodeGen.h` header file, is very small:

```
#ifndef CODEGEN_H
#define CODEGEN_H

#include "AST.h"

class CodeGen
{
public:
  void compile(AST *Tree);
};
#endif
```

Because the AST contains the information from semantic analysis phase, the basic idea is to use a visitor to walk the AST. The `CodeGen.cpp` file is implemented as follows:

1. The required includes are at the top of the file:

    ```
    #include "CodeGen.h"
    #include "llvm/ADT/StringMap.h"
    #include "llvm/IR/IRBuilder.h"
    #include "llvm/IR/LLVMContext.h"
    #include "llvm/Support/raw_ostream.h"
    ```

2. The namespace of the LLVM libraries is used for name lookups:

    ```
    using namespace llvm;
    ```

3. First, some private members are declared in the visitor. Each compilation unit is represented in LLVM by the `Module` class and the visitor has a pointer to the module call, `M`. For easy IR generation, the `Builder` (of the `IRBuilder<>` type) is used. LLVM has a class hierarchy to represent types in IR. You can look up the instances for basic types such as `i32` in the LLVM context. These basic types are used often. To avoid repeated lookup, we cache the needed type instance, which can be either `VoidTy`, `Int32Ty`, `Int8PtrTy`, `Int8PtrPtrTy`, or `Int32Zero`. `V` is the current calculated value, which is updated through tree traversal. Finally, `nameMap` maps a variable name to the value that's returned by the `calc_read()` function:

    ```
    namespace {
    class ToIRVisitor : public ASTVisitor {
      Module *M;
      IRBuilder<> Builder;
      Type *VoidTy;
      Type *Int32Ty;
      Type *Int8PtrTy;
      Type *Int8PtrPtrTy;
      Constant *Int32Zero;
      Value *V;
      StringMap<Value *> nameMap;
    ```

4. The constructor initializes all the members:

    ```
    public:
      ToIRVisitor(Module *M) : M(M), Builder(M->getContext())
      {
        VoidTy = Type::getVoidTy(M->getContext());
        Int32Ty = Type::getInt32Ty(M->getContext());
        Int8PtrTy = Type::getInt8PtrTy(M->getContext());
        Int8PtrPtrTy = Int8PtrTy->getPointerTo();
        Int32Zero = ConstantInt::get(Int32Ty, 0, true);
      }
    ```

5. For each function, a `FunctionType` instance must be created. In C++
    terminology, this is a function prototype. A function itself is defined with a
    `Function` instance. First, the `run()` method defines the `main()` function in
    LLVM IR:

    ```
    void run(AST *Tree) {
      FunctionType *MainFty = FunctionType::get(
          Int32Ty, {Int32Ty, Int8PtrPtrTy}, false);
      Function *MainFn = Function::Create(
          MainFty, GlobalValue::ExternalLinkage,
          "main", M);
    ```

6. Then, we create the `BB` basic block with the `entry` label and attach it to the
    IR builder:

    ```
    BasicBlock *BB = BasicBlock::Create(M->getContext(),
                                        "entry", MainFn);
    Builder.SetInsertPoint(BB);
    ```

7. With this preparation done, tree traversal can begin:

    ```
    Tree->accept(*this);
    ```

8. After tree traversal, the computed value is printed via a call to the `calc_write()`
    function. Again, a function prototype (an instance of `FunctionType`) must be
    created. The only parameter is the current value, V:

    ```
    FunctionType *CalcWriteFnTy =
        FunctionType::get(VoidTy, {Int32Ty}, false);
    Function *CalcWriteFn = Function::Create(
        CalcWriteFnTy, GlobalValue::ExternalLinkage,
        "calc_write", M);
    Builder.CreateCall(CalcWriteFnTy, CalcWriteFn, {V});
    ```

9. The generation finishes by returning a 0 from the `main()` function:

    ```
    Builder.CreateRet(Int32Zero);
    }
    ```

10. A `WithDecl` node holds the names of the declared variables. First, we must create a function prototype for the `calc_read()` function:

```
virtual void visit(WithDecl &Node) override {
  FunctionType *ReadFty =
      FunctionType::get(Int32Ty, {Int8PtrTy}, false);
  Function *ReadFn = Function::Create(
      ReadFty, GlobalValue::ExternalLinkage,
      "calc_read", M);
```

11. The method loops through the variable names:

```
for (auto I = Node.begin(), E = Node.end(); I != E;
     ++I) {
```

12. For each variable, a string with a variable name is created:

```
StringRef Var = *I;
Constant *StrText = ConstantDataArray::getString(
    M->getContext(), Var);
GlobalVariable *Str = new GlobalVariable(
    *M, StrText->getType(),
    /*isConstant=*/true,
    GlobalValue::PrivateLinkage,
    StrText, Twine(Var).concat(".str"));
```

13. Then, the IR code to call the `calc_read()` function is created. The string that we created in the previous step is passed as a parameter:

```
Value *Ptr = Builder.CreateInBoundsGEP(
    Str, {Int32Zero, Int32Zero}, "ptr");
CallInst *Call =
    Builder.CreateCall(ReadFty, ReadFn, {Ptr});
```

14. The returned value is stored in the `mapNames` map for later use:

```
nameMap[Var] = Call;
}
```

15. Tree traversal continues with the expression:

```
        Node.getExpr()->accept(*this);
    };
```

16. A `Factor` node is either a variable name or a number. For a variable name, the value is looked up in the `mapNames` map. For a number, the value is converted into an integer and turned into a constant value:

```
    virtual void visit(Factor &Node) override {
        if (Node.getKind() == Factor::Ident) {
          V = nameMap[Node.getVal()];
        } else {
          int intval;
          Node.getVal().getAsInteger(10, intval);
          V = ConstantInt::get(Int32Ty, intval, true);
        }
    };
```

17. Finally, for a `BinaryOp` node, the right calculation operation must be used:

```
    virtual void visit(BinaryOp &Node) override {
      Node.getLeft()->accept(*this);
      Value *Left = V;
      Node.getRight()->accept(*this);
      Value *Right = V;
      switch (Node.getOperator()) {
      case BinaryOp::Plus:
        V = Builder.CreateNSWAdd(Left, Right); break;
      case BinaryOp::Minus:
        V = Builder.CreateNSWSub(Left, Right); break;
      case BinaryOp::Mul:
        V = Builder.CreateNSWMul(Left, Right); break;
      case BinaryOp::Div:
        V = Builder.CreateSDiv(Left, Right); break;
      }
    };
  };
  }
```

18. With this, the visitor class is complete. The `compile()` method creates the global context and the module, runs the tree traversal, and dumps the generated IR to the console:

```
void CodeGen::compile(AST *Tree) {
  LLVMContext Ctx;
  Module *M = new Module("calc.expr", Ctx);
  ToIRVisitor ToIR(M);
  ToIR.run(Tree);
  M->print(outs(), nullptr);
}
```

With that, we have implemented the frontend of the compiler, from reading the source to generating the IR. Of course, all these components must work together on user input, which is the task of the compiler driver. We also need to implement the functions that are required at runtime. We will cover both of these in the next section.

The missing pieces – the driver and the runtime library

All the phases from the previous sections are glued together by the `Calc.cpp` driver, which we will implement here. At this point, a parameter for the input expression is declared, the LLVM is initialized, and all the phases from the previous sections are called. Let's take a look:

1. First, we must include the required header files:

```
#include "CodeGen.h"
#include "Parser.h"
#include "Sema.h"
#include "llvm/Support/CommandLine.h"
#include "llvm/Support/InitLLVM.h"
#include "llvm/Support/raw_ostream.h"
```

2. LLVM comes with its own system for declaring command-line options. You only need to declare a static variable for each option you need. In doing so, the option is registered with a global command-line parser. The advantage of this approach is that each component can add command-line options when needed. We must declare an option for the input expression:

```
static llvm::cl::opt<std::string>
    Input(llvm::cl::Positional,
```

```
        llvm::cl::desc("<input expression>"),
        llvm::cl::init(""));
```

3. Inside the `main()` function, the LLVM libraries are initialized. You need to call `ParseCommandLineOptions` to handle the options on the command line. This also handles printing help information. In the case of an error, this method exits the application:

```
int main(int argc, const char **argv) {
  llvm::InitLLVM X(argc, argv);
  llvm::cl::ParseCommandLineOptions(
      argc, argv, "calc - the expression compiler\n");
```

4. Next, we call the lexer and the parser. After syntactical analysis, we check if errors occurred. If this is the case, then we exit the compiler with a return code, indicating a failure:

```
Lexer Lex(Input);
Parser Parser(Lex);
AST *Tree = Parser.parse();
if (!Tree || Parser.hasError()) {
  llvm::errs() << "Syntax errors occured\n";
  return 1;
}
```

5. And we do the same if there was a semantic error:

```
Sema Semantic;
if (Semantic.semantic(Tree)) {
  llvm::errs() << "Semantic errors occured\n";
  return 1;
}
```

6. Finally, in the driver, the code generator is called:

```
CodeGen CodeGenerator;
CodeGenerator.compile(Tree);
return 0;
}
```

With that, we have successfully created IR code for the user input. We delegated the object code generation to the LLVM static compiler, `llc`, so this finishes the implementation of our compiler. We must link all the components together to create the `calc` application.

The runtime library consists of a single file called `rtcalc.c`. It contains the implementation of the `calc_read()` and `calc_write()` functions, written in C:

```
#include <stdio.h>
#include <stdlib.h>

void calc_write(int v)
{
  printf("The result is: %d\n", v);
}
```

`calc_write()` only writes the resulting value to the terminal:

```
int calc_read(char *s)
{
  char buf[64];
  int val;
  printf("Enter a value for %s: ", s);
  fgets(buf, sizeof(buf), stdin);
  if (EOF == sscanf(buf, "%d", &val))
  {
    printf("Value %s is invalid\n", buf);
    exit(1);
  }
  return val;
}
```

`calc_read()` reads an integer number from the terminal. Nothing prevents the user from entering letters or other characters, so we must carefully check the input. If the input is not a number, we exit the application. A more complex approach would be to make the user aware of the problem and ask for a number again.

Now, we can try out our compiler. The `calc` application creates IR from an expression. The LLVM static compiler, `llc`, compiles the IR as an object file. Then, you can use your favorite C compiler to link against the small runtime library. On Unix, you can type the following:

```
$ calc "with a: a*3" | llc -filetype=obj -o=expr.o
$ clang -o expr expr.o rtcalc.c
$ expr
Enter a value for a: 4
The result is: 12
```

On Windows, you will most likely use the `cl` compiler:

```
$ calc "with a: a*3" | llc -filetype=obj -o=expr.obj
$ cl expr.obj rtcalc.c
$ expr
Enter a value for a: 4
The result is: 12
```

With that, you have created your first LLVM-based compiler! Please take some time to play around with the various expressions. Also check that multiplicative operators are evaluated before additive operators and that using parentheses changes the evaluation order, as we expect from a basic calculator.

Summary

In this chapter, you learned about the typical components of a compiler. An arithmetic expression language was used to introduce you to grammar for programming languages. You then learned how to develop the typical components of a frontend for this language: a lexer, a parser, a semantic analyzer, and a code generator. The code generator only produced LLVM IR, and the LLVM static compiler, `llc`, was used to create object files from it. Finally, you developed your first LLVM-based compiler!

In the next chapter, you will deepen this knowledge to construct the frontend for a programming language.

Section 2 – From Source to Machine Code Generation

In this section, you will learn how to develop your own compiler. You will begin by constructing the frontend, which reads the source file and creates an abstract syntax tree of it. Then, you will learn how to generate LLVM IR from the source file. Using the optimization capabilities of LLVM, you will then create optimized machine code. You will also learn about a number of advanced topics, including generating LLVM IR for object-oriented language constructs, and how to add debug metadata.

This section comprises the following chapters:

- *Chapter 4, Turning the Source File into an Abstract Syntax Tree*
- *Chapter 5, Basics of IR Generation*
- *Chapter 6, IR Generation for High-Level Language Constructs*
- *Chapter 7, Advanced IR Generation*
- *Chapter 8, Optimizing IR*

4
Turning the Source File into an Abstract Syntax Tree

A compiler is typically divided into two parts: the frontend and the backend. In this chapter, we will implement the frontend of a programming language; that is, the part that deals with the source language. We will learn about the techniques real-world compilers use and apply them to our own programming languages.

We'll begin our journey by defining our programming language's grammar and end it with an **abstract syntax tree (AST)**, which will become the basis for code generation. You can use this approach for every programming language that you would like to implement a compiler for.

In this chapter, you will learn about the following topics:

- Defining a real programming language introduces you to the `tinylang` language, which is a subset of a real programming language, and for which you must implement a compiler frontend.

- Creating the project layout, in which you will create the project layout for the compiler.

- Managing source files and user messages, which gives you knowledge of how to handle several input files and how to inform the user about problems in a pleasant way.

- Structuring the lexer, which discusses how the lexer is broken down into modular pieces.

- Constructing a recursive descent parser, which will talk about the rules you can use to derive a parser from grammar to perform syntax analysis.

- Generating a parser and lexer with bison and flex, in which you will use tools to comfortably generate parsers and lexers from a specification.

- Performing semantic analysis, in which you will create the AST and evaluate its attributes, which will be intertwined with the parser.

With the skills you will acquire in this chapter, you will be able to build a compiler frontend for any programming language.

Technical requirements

The code files for the chapter are available at `https://github.com/PacktPublishing/Learn-LLVM-12/tree/master/Chapter04`

You can find the code in action videos at `https://bit.ly/3nllhED`

Defining a real programming language

A real programming language brings up more challenges than the simple **calc language** from the previous chapter. To look at this in more detail, I will be using a tiny subset of *Modula-2* in this and the following chapters. Modula-2 is well-designed and optionally supports **generics** and **object-oriented programming** (**OOP**). I don't claim to create a complete Modula-2 compiler in this book. Therefore, I will call my subset `tinylang`.

Let's take a quick tour of subset of the `tinylang` grammar that will be used in this chapter. In the upcoming sections, we will derive the lexer and the parser from this grammar:

```
compilationUnit
  : "MODULE" identifier ";" ( import )* block identifier "." ;
Import : ( "FROM" identifier )? "IMPORT" identList ";" ;
Block
  : ( declaration )* ( "BEGIN" statementSequence )? "END" ;
```

A compilation unit in Modula-2 begins with the MODULE keyword, followed by the name of the module. The content of a module can be a list of imported modules, declarations, and a block containing statements that run at initialization time:

```
declaration
    : "CONST" ( constantDeclaration ";" )*
    | "VAR" ( variableDeclaration ";" )*
    | procedureDeclaration ";" ;
```

A declaration introduces constants, variables, and procedures. Constants that have been declared are prefixed with the CONST keyword. Similarly, variable declarations begin with the VAR keyword. Declaring a constant is very simple:

```
constantDeclaration : identifier "=" expression ;
```

The identifier is the name of the constant. The value is derived from an expression, which must be computable at compile time. Declaring variables is a bit more complex:

```
variableDeclaration : identList ":" qualident ;
qualident : identifier ( "." identifier )* ;
identList : identifier ( "," identifier)* ;
```

To be able to declare more than one variable in one go, a list of identifiers must be used. The type's name can potentially come from another module and is prefixed with the module name in this case. This is called a qualified identifier. A procedure requires the most details:

```
procedureDeclaration
    : "PROCEDURE" identifier ( formalParameters )? ";"
      block identifier ;
formalParameters
    : "(" ( formalParameterList )? ")" ( ":" qualident )? ;
formalParameterList
    : formalParameter (";" formalParameter )* ;
formalParameter : ( "VAR" )? identList ":" qualident ;
```

In the preceding code, you can see how constants, variables, and procedures are declared. Procedures can have parameters and a return type. Normal parameters are passed as values, while VAR parameters are passed by reference. The other part missing from the preceding block rule is statementSequence, which is only a list of single statements:

```
statementSequence
  : statement ( ";" statement )* ;
```

A statement is delimited by a semicolon if it is followed by another statement. Again, only a subset of the *Modula-2* statements is supported:

```
statement
  : qualident ( ":=" expression | ( "(" ( expList )? ")" )? )
  | ifStatement | whileStatement | "RETURN" ( expression )? ;
```

The first part of this rule describes an assignment or procedure call. A qualified identifier followed by : = is an assignment. On the other hand, if it is followed by (, then it is a procedure call. The other statements are the usual control statements:

```
ifStatement
  : "IF" expression "THEN" statementSequence
    ( "ELSE" statementSequence )? "END" ;
```

The IF statement has a simplified syntax too, since it can only have a single ELSE block. With that statement, we can conditionally guard a statement:

```
whileStatement
  : "WHILE" expression "DO" statementSequence "END" ;
```

The WHILE statement describes a loop, guarded by a condition. Together with the IF statement, this enables us to write simple algorithms in tinylang. Finally, the definition of an expression is missing:

```
expList
  : expression ( "," expression )* ;
expression
  : simpleExpression ( relation simpleExpression )? ;
relation
  : "=" | "#" | "<" | "<=" | ">" | ">=" ;
simpleExpression
  : ( "+" | "-" )? term ( addOperator term )* ;
```

```
addOperator
  : "+" | "-" | "OR" ;
term
  : factor ( mulOperator factor )* ;
mulOperator
  : "*" | "/" | "DIV" | "MOD" | "AND" ;
factor
  : integer_literal | "(" expression ")" | "NOT" factor
  | qualident ( "(" ( expList )? ")" )? ;
```

The expression syntax is very similar to that of calc in the previous chapter. Only the INTEGER and BOOLEAN data types are supported.

Additionally, the `identifier` and `integer_literal` tokens are used. An **identifier** is a name that begins with a letter or an underscore, followed by letters, digits, and underscores. An **integer literal** is either a sequence of decimal digits or a sequence of hexadecimal digits, followed by the letter H.

That's already a lot of rules, and we're only covering a part of Modula-2 here! Nevertheless, it is possible to write small applications in this subset. Let's implement a compiler for `tinylang`!

Creating the project layout

The project layout for `tinylang` follows the approach we laid out in *Chapter 2, Touring the LLVM Source*. The source code for each component is in a subdirectory of the `lib` directory, while the header files are in a subdirectory of `include/tinylang`. The subdirectory is named after the component. In *Chapter 2, Touring the LLVM Source*, we only created the `Basic` component.

From the previous chapter, we know that we need to implement a lexer, a parser, an AST, and a semantic analyzer. Each is a component of its own, called `Lexer`, `Parser`, `AST`, and `Sema`. The directory layout that was used in the previous chapter looks like this:

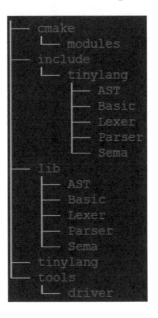

Figure 4.1 – The directory layout of the tinylang project

The components have clearly defined dependencies. Here, `Lexer` only depends on `Basic`. `Parser` depends on `Basic`, `Lexer`, `AST`, and `Sema`. Finally, `Sema` only depends on `Basic` and `AST`. These well-defined dependencies help with reusing components.

Let's have a closer look at their implementation!

Managing source files and user messages

A real compiler must deal with many files. Usually, the developer calls the compiler with the name of the main compilation unit. This compilation unit can refer to other files, for example, via `#include` directives in C or `import` statements in Python or Modula-2. An imported module can import other modules and so on. All these files must be loaded into memory and run through the analysis stages of the compiler. During development, a developer may make syntactical or semantical errors. When detected, an error message, including the source line and a marker, should be printed. At this point, it should be obvious that this essential component is not trivial.

Luckily, LLVM comes with a solution: the `llvm::SourceMgr` class. A new source file is added to `SourceMgr` with a call to the `AddNewSourceBuffer()` method. Alternatively, a file can be loaded with a call to the `AddIncludeFile()` method. Both methods return an ID to identify the buffer. You use this ID to retrieve a pointer to the memory buffer of the associated file. To define a location in the file, the `llvm::SMLoc` class must be used. This class encapsulates a pointer into the buffer. Various `PrintMessage()` methods allow us to emit errors and other informational messages to the user.

Only a way to centrally define messages is missing. In a large piece of software (such as a compiler), you do not want to sprinkle message strings all over the place. If there is a request to change messages or translate them into another language, then you'd better have them in a central place!

A simple approach is that each message has an ID (an `enum` member), a severity level, and a string containing the messages. In your code, you only refer to the message ID. The severity level and message string are only used when the message is printed. These three items (the ID, the security level, and the message) must be managed consistently. The LLVM libraries use a preprocessor to solve this. The data is stored in a file with a `.def` suffix and is wrapped in a macro name. That file is usually included several times, with different definitions for the macro. The definition of this is in the `include/tinylang/Basic/Diagnostic.def` file path and looks as follows:

```
#ifndef DIAG
#define DIAG(ID, Level, Msg)
#endif

DIAG(err_sym_declared, Error, "symbol {0} already declared")
#undef DIAG
```

The first macro parameter, `ID`, is the enumeration label, the second parameter, `Level`, is the severity, and the third parameter, `Msg`, is the message text. With this definition at hand, we can define a `DiagnosticsEngine` class to emit error messages. The interface is in the `include/tinylang/Basic/Diagnostic.h` file:

```
#ifndef TINYLANG_BASIC_DIAGNOSTIC_H
#define TINYLANG_BASIC_DIAGNOSTIC_H

#include "tinylang/Basic/LLVM.h"
#include "llvm/ADT/StringRef.h"
#include "llvm/Support/FormatVariadic.h"
```

```
#include "llvm/Support/SMLoc.h"
#include "llvm/Support/SourceMgr.h"
#include "llvm/Support/raw_ostream.h"
#include <utility>


namespace tinylang {
```

After including the necessary header files, `Diagnostic.def` is now used to define the enumeration. To not pollute the global namespace, a nested namespace, `diag`, must be used:

```
namespace diag {
enum {
#define DIAG(ID, Level, Msg) ID,
#include "tinylang/Basic/Diagnostic.def"
};
} // namespace diag
```

The `DiagnosticsEngine` class uses a `SourceMgr` instance to emit the messages via the `report()` method. Messages can have parameters. To implement this facility, the variadic-format support from LLVM must be used. The message text and the severity level are retrieved with the help of the `static` method. As a bonus, the number of emitted error messages is also counted:

```
class DiagnosticsEngine {
   static const char *getDiagnosticText(unsigned DiagID);
   static SourceMgr::DiagKind
   getDiagnosticKind(unsigned DiagID);
```

The message string is returned by `getDiagnosticText()`, while the level is returned by `getDiagnosticKind()`. Both methods will be implemented in the `.cpp` file later:

```
   SourceMgr &SrcMgr;
   unsigned NumErrors;


public:
   DiagnosticsEngine(SourceMgr &SrcMgr)
      : SrcMgr(SrcMgr), NumErrors(0) {}


   unsigned nunErrors() { return NumErrors; }
```

Since messages can have a variable number of parameters, the solution in C++ is to use a variadic template. Of course, this is also used by the formatv() function provided by LLVM. To get the formatted message, we need only to forward the template parameters:

```
template <typename... Args>
void report(SMLoc Loc, unsigned DiagID,
            Args &&... Arguments) {
  std::string Msg =
      llvm::formatv(getDiagnosticText(DiagID),
                    std::forward<Args>(Arguments)...)
          .str();
  SourceMgr::DiagKind Kind = getDiagnosticKind(DiagID);
  SrcMgr.PrintMessage(Loc, Kind, Msg);
  NumErrors += (Kind == SourceMgr::DK_Error);
  }
};


} // namespace tinylang


#endif
```

With that, we have implemented most of the class. Only getDiagnosticText() and getDiagnosticKind() are missing. They are defined in the lib/Basic/Diagnostic.cpp file and also make use of the Diagnostic.def file:

```
#include "tinylang/Basic/Diagnostic.h"


using namespace tinylang;


namespace {
const char *DiagnosticText[] = {
#define DIAG(ID, Level, Msg) Msg,
#include "tinylang/Basic/Diagnostic.def"
};
```

As in the header file, the `DIAG` macro is defined to retrieve the desired part. Here, we will define an array that will hold the text messages. Therefore, the `DIAG` macro only returns the `Msg` part. We will use the same approach for the level:

```
SourceMgr::DiagKind DiagnosticKind[] = {
#define DIAG(ID, Level, Msg) SourceMgr::DK_##Level,
#include "tinylang/Basic/Diagnostic.def"
};
} // namespace
```

Not surprisingly, both functions simply index the array to return the desired data:

```
const char *
DiagnosticsEngine::getDiagnosticText(unsigned DiagID) {
   return DiagnosticText[DiagID];
}
```

```
SourceMgr::DiagKind
DiagnosticsEngine::getDiagnosticKind(unsigned DiagID) {
   return DiagnosticKind[DiagID];
}
```

This combination of the `SourceMgr` and `DiagnosticsEngine` classes provides a good basis for the other components. Let's use them in the lexer first!

Structuring the lexer

As we know from the previous chapter, we need a `Token` class and a `Lexer` class. Additionally, a `TokenKind` enumeration is required to give each token class a unique number. Having an all-in-one header and an implementation file does not scale, so let's restructure things. The `TokenKind` enumeration can be used universally and is placed in the `Basic` component. The `Token` and `Lexer` classes belong to the `Lexer` component but are placed in different header and implementation files.

There are three different classes of tokens: **keywords, punctuators**, and the **tokens** representing sets of many values. Examples include the `CONST` keyword, the `;` delimiter, and the `ident` token, which represent the identifiers in the source. Each token needs a member name for the enumeration. Keywords and punctuators have natural display names that can be used for messages.

Like in many programming languages, the keywords are a subset of the identifiers. To classify a token as a keyword, we need a keyword filter, which checks if the identifier that's been found is indeed a keyword. This is the same behavior as in C or C++, where keywords are also a subset of identifiers. Programming languages evolve over time and new keywords may be introduced. As an example, the original K&R C language had no enumerations defined with the `enum` keyword. Due to this, a flag indicating the language level of a keyword should be present.

We've collected several pieces of information, all of which belong to a member of the `TokenKind` enumeration: the label for the enumeration member, the spelling of the punctuators, and a flag for the keywords. As for the diagnostic messages, we centrally store the information in a `.def` file called `include/tinylang/Basic/TokenKinds.def`, which looks as follows. One thing to note is that keywords are prefixed with `kw_`:

```
#ifndef TOK
#define TOK(ID)
#endif
#ifndef PUNCTUATOR
#define PUNCTUATOR(ID, SP) TOK(ID)
#endif
#ifndef KEYWORD
#define KEYWORD(ID, FLAG) TOK(kw_ ## ID)
#endif

TOK(unknown)
TOK(eof)
TOK(identifier)
TOK(integer_literal)

PUNCTUATOR(plus,                  "+")
PUNCTUATOR(minus,                 "-")
// ...

KEYWORD(BEGIN                   , KEYALL)
KEYWORD(CONST                   , KEYALL)
// ...
```

```
#undef KEYWORD
#undef PUNCTUATOR
#undef TOK
```

With these centralized definitions, it's easy to create the `TokenKind` enumeration in the `include/tinylang/Basic/TokenKinds.h` file. Again, the enumeration is put into its own namespace, called `tok`:

```
#ifndef TINYLANG_BASIC_TOKENKINDS_H
#define TINYLANG_BASIC_TOKENKINDS_H

namespace tinylang {

namespace tok {
enum TokenKind : unsigned short {
#define TOK(ID) ID,
#include "TokenKinds.def"
  NUM_TOKENS
};
```

The pattern you must use to fill the array should be familiar by now. The `TOK` macro is defined to only return the enumeration label's `ID`. As a useful addition, we also define `NUM_TOKENS` as the last member of the enumeration, denoting the number of defined tokens:

```
    const char *getTokenName(TokenKind Kind);
    const char *getPunctuatorSpelling(TokenKind Kind);
    const char *getKeywordSpelling(TokenKind Kind);
  }
}

#endif
```

The implementation file, `lib/Basic/TokenKinds.cpp`, also uses the `.def` file to retrieve the names:

```
#include "tinylang/Basic/TokenKinds.h"
#include "llvm/Support/ErrorHandling.h"

using namespace tinylang;

static const char * const TokNames[] = {
#define TOK(ID) #ID,
#define KEYWORD(ID, FLAG) #ID,
#include "tinylang/Basic/TokenKinds.def"
  nullptr
};
```

The textual name of a token is derived from its enumeration label's `ID`. There are two particularities. First, we need two define the `TOK` and `KEYWORD` macros because the default definition of `KEYWORD` does not use the `TOK` macro. Second, a `nullptr` value is added at the end of the array, accounting for the added NUM_TOKENS enumeration member:

```
const char *tok::getTokenName(TokenKind Kind) {
  return TokNames[Kind];
}
```

We take a slightly different approach for the `getPunctuatorSpelling()` and `getKeywordSpelling()` functions. These functions only return meaningful values for a subset of the enumeration. This can be realized with a `switch` statement, which returns a `nullptr` value by default:

```
const char *tok::getPunctuatorSpelling(TokenKind Kind) {
  switch (Kind) {
#define PUNCTUATOR(ID, SP) case ID: return SP;
#include "tinylang/Basic/TokenKinds.def"
    default: break;
  }
  return nullptr;
}
```

```
const char *tok::getKeywordSpelling(TokenKind Kind) {
  switch (Kind) {
#define KEYWORD(ID, FLAG) case kw_ ## ID: return #ID;
#include "tinylang/Basic/TokenKinds.def"
    default: break;
  }
  return nullptr;
}
```

> **Tip**
> Note how the macros are defined to retrieve the piece of information that's required from the file.

In the previous chapter, the Token class was declared in the same header file as the Lexer class. To make this more modular, we will put the Token class into its own header file in include/Lexer/Token.h. As in the previous case, Token stores a pointer to the start of the token, the length, and the token's kind, as defined previously:

```
class Token {
  friend class Lexer;

  const char *Ptr;
  size_t Length;
  tok::TokenKind Kind;

public:
  tok::TokenKind getKind() const { return Kind; }
  size_t getLength() const { return Length; }
```

The SMLoc instance, which denotes the source's position in the messages, is created from the pointer to the token:

```
  SMLoc getLocation() const {
    return SMLoc::getFromPointer(Ptr);
  }
```

The `getIdentifier()` and `getLiteralData()` methods allow us to access the text of the token for identifiers and literal data. It is not necessary to access the text for any other token type, as this is implied by the token's type:

```
StringRef getIdentifier() {
  assert(is(tok::identifier) &&
        "Cannot get identfier of non-identifier");
  return StringRef(Ptr, Length);
}
StringRef getLiteralData() {
  assert(isOneOf(tok::integer_literal,
                 tok::string_literal) &&
        "Cannot get literal data of non-literal");
  return StringRef(Ptr, Length);
}
};
```

We declare the Lexer class in the `include/Lexer/Lexer.h` header file and put the implementation in the `lib/Lexer/lexer.cpp` file. The structure is the same as for the calc language from the previous chapter. Here, we must take a closer look at two details:

- First, there are operators that share the same prefix; for example, `<` and `<=`. When the current character we're looking at is a `<`, we must check the next character first, before deciding which token we found. Remember that we required that the input ends with a null byte. Therefore, the next character can always be used if the current character is valid:

```
case '<':
  if (*(CurPtr + 1) == '=')
    formTokenWithChars(token, CurPtr + 2, tok::lessequal);
  else
    formTokenWithChars(token, CurPtr + 1, tok::less);
  break;
```

- The other detail is that at this point, there are far more keywords. How can
  we handle this? A simple and fast solution is to populate a hash table with the
  keywords, which are all stored in the TokenKinds.def file. This can be done
  while we instantiate the Lexer class. In this approach, it is also possible to support
  different levels of the language, as the keywords can be filtered with the attached
  flag. Here, this flexibility is not needed yet. In the header file, the keyword filter is
  defined as follows, using an instance of llvm::StringMap for the hash table:

```
class KeywordFilter {
  llvm::StringMap<tok::TokenKind> HashTable;
  void addKeyword(StringRef Keyword,
                  tok::TokenKind TokenCode);

public:
  void addKeywords();
```

The getKeyword() method returns the token kind of the given string, or a default
value if the string does not represent a keyword:

```
tok::TokenKind getKeyword(
    StringRef Name,
    tok::TokenKind DefaultTokenCode = tok::unknown) {
  auto Result = HashTable.find(Name);
  if (Result != HashTable.end())
    return Result->second;
  return DefaultTokenCode;
  }
};
```

In the implementation file, the keyword table is filled in:

```
void KeywordFilter::addKeyword(StringRef Keyword,
                               tok::TokenKind TokenCode)
{
  HashTable.insert(std::make_pair(Keyword, TokenCode));
}

void KeywordFilter::addKeywords() {
#define KEYWORD(NAME, FLAGS)
  addKeyword(StringRef(#NAME), tok::kw_##NAME);
```

```
#include "tinylang/Basic/TokenKinds.def"
}
```

With these techniques, it's not difficult to write an efficient lexer class. Since compilation speed matters, many compilers use a handwritten lexer, an example of which is Clang.

Constructing a recursive descent parser

As shown in the previous chapter, the parser is derived from its grammar. Let's recall all the *construction rules*. For each rule of grammar, you create a method that's named after the non-terminal on the left-hand side of the rule in order to parse the right-hand side of the rule. Following the definition of the right-hand side, you must do the following:

- For each non-terminal, the corresponding method is called.

- Each token is consumed.

- For alternatives and optional or repeating groups, the look-ahead token (the next unconsumed token) is examined to decide where we can continue from.

Let's apply these construction rules to the following rule of the grammar:

```
ifStatement
  : "IF" expression "THEN" statementSequence
    ( "ELSE" statementSequence )? "END" ;
```

We can easily translate this into the following C++ method:

```
void Parser::parseIfStatement() {
  consume(tok::kw_IF);
  parseExpression();
  consume(tok::kw_THEN);
  parseStatementSequence();
  if (Tok.is(tok::kw_ELSE)) {
    advance();
    parseStatementSequence();
  }
  consume(tok::kw_END);
}
```

The whole grammar of `tinylang` can be turned into C++ in this way. In general, you must be careful and avoid some pitfalls.

One issue to look out for is left-recursive rules. A rule is **left-recursive** if the right-hand side begins with the same terminal that's on the left-hand side. A typical example can be found in the grammar for expressions:

```
expression : expression "+" term ;
```

If it's not already clear from the grammar, then the following translation into C++ should make it obvious that this results in infinite recursion:

```
Void Parser::parseExpression() {
  parseExpression();
  consume(tok::plus);
  parseTerm();
}
```

Left recursion can also indirectly occur and involve more rules, which is much more difficult to spot. That's why an algorithm exists that can detect and eliminate left recursion.

At each step, the parser decides how to continue just by using the look-ahead token. The grammar is said to have conflicts if this decision cannot be made deterministically. To illustrate this, let's have a look at the `using` statement in C#. Like in C++, the `using` statement can be used to make a symbol visible in a namespace, such as in `using Math;`. It is also possible to define an alias name for the imported symbol; that is, `using M = Math;`. In grammar, this can be expressed as follows:

```
usingStmt : "using" (ident "=")? ident ";"
```

Obviously, there's is a problem here. After the parser consumed the `using` keyword, the look-ahead token is `ident`. But this information is not enough for us to decide if the optional group must be skipped or parsed. This situation always arises if the set of tokens that the optional group can begin with overlap with the set of tokens that follow the optional group.

Let's rewrite the rule with an alternative instead of an optional group:

```
usingStmt : "using" ( ident "=" ident | ident ) ";" ;
```

Now, there is a different conflict: both alternatives begin with the same token. Looking only at the look-ahead token, the parser can't decide which of the alternatives is the right one.

These conflicts are very common. Therefore, it's good to know how to handle them. One approach is to rewrite the grammar in such a way that the conflict disappears. In the previous example, both alternatives begin with the same token. This can be factored out, resulting in the following rule:

```
usingStmt : "using" ident ("=" ident)? ";" ;
```

This formulation has no conflict. However, it should also be noted that it is less expressive. In the other two formulations, it is obvious which `ident` is the alias name and which `ident` is the namespace name. In this conflict-free rule, the left-most `ident` changes its role. First, it is the namespace name, but if an equals sign (=) follows it, then it turns into the alias name.

The second approach is to add an additional predicate to distinguish between both cases. This predicate, often called a **resolver**, could use context information for the decision (such as a name lookup in a symbol table), though it could have a look at more than one token. Let's assume that the lexer has a `Token &peek(int n)` method, which returns the nth token after the current look-ahead token. Here, the existence of an equals sign can be used as an additional predicate in the decision:

```
if (Tok.is(tok::ident) && Lex.peek(0).is(tok::equal)) {
    advance();
    consume(tok::equal);
}
consume(tok::ident);
```

Now, let's incorporate error recovery. In the previous chapter, I introduced the so-called *panic mode* as a technique for error recovery. The basic idea is to skip tokens until one is found that is suitable for continuing parsing. For example, in `tinylang`, a statement is followed by a semicolon (`:`).

If there is a syntax problem in an `IF` statement, then you skip all the tokens until you find a semicolon. Then, you continue with the next statement. Instead of using an ad hoc definition for the token set, it's better to use a systematic approach.

For each non-terminal, you compute the set of tokens that can follow the non-terminal anywhere (called the **FOLLOW set**). For the non-terminal statement, the `;`, `ELSE`, and `END` tokens can follow. So, you use this set in the error recovery part of `parseStatement()`. This method assumes that a syntax error can be handled locally. In general, this is not possible. Because the parser skips tokens, it could happen that so many are skipped that the end of the input is reached. At this point, local recovery is not possible.

To prevent meaningless error messages, the calling method needs to be informed that error recovery has still not finished. This can be done with the `bool` return value: `true` means that error recovery hasn't finished yet, while `false` means that parsing (including possible error recovery) was successful.

There are numerous ways to extend this error recovery scheme. One popular way is to also use the FOLLOW sets of the active callers. As a simple example, let's assume that `parseStatement()` was called by `parseStatementSequence()`, which was itself called by `parseBlock()` and that that was called from `parseModule()`.

Here, each of the corresponding non-terminals has a FOLLOW set. If the parser detects a syntax error in `parseStatement()`, then tokens are skipped until the token is in at least one of the FOLLOW sets of the active callers. If the token is in the FOLLOW set of a statement, then the error was recovered locally, and a `false` value is returned to the caller. Otherwise, a `true` value is returned, meaning that error recovery must continue. A possible implementation strategy for this extension is passing a `std::bitset` or `std::tuple` to represent the union of the current FOLLOW sets to the callee.

One last question is still open: how can we call error recovery? In the previous chapter, a `goto` was used to jump to the error recovery block. This works but is not a pleasing solution. Given the discussion earlier, we can skip tokens in a separate method. Clang has a method called `skipUntil()` for this purpose, and we can also use this for `tinylang`.

Because the next step is to add semantic actions to the parser, it would be nice to have a central place to put cleanup code if necessary. A nested function would be ideal for this. C++ does not have a nested function. Instead, a lambda function can serve a similar purpose. The `parseIfStatement()` method with complete error recovery looks as follows:

```
bool Parser::parseIfStatement() {
  auto _errorhandler = [this] {
    return SkipUntil(tok::semi, tok::kw_ELSE, tok::kw_END);
  };

  if (consume(tok::kw_IF))
    return _errorhandler();
  if (parseExpression(E))
    return _errorhandler();
  if (consume(tok::kw_THEN))
    return _errorhandler();
  if (parseStatementSequence(IfStmts))
```

```
      return _errorhandler();
   if (Tok.is(tok::kw_ELSE)) {
      advance();
      if (parseStatementSequence(ElseStmts))
         return _errorhandler();
   }
   if (expect(tok::kw_END))
      return _errorhandler();
   return false;
}
```

Generating a parser and lexer with bison and flex

Manually constructing a lexer and a parser is not difficult and usually results in fast components. The disadvantage is that it is not easy to introduce changes, especially in the parser. This can be important if you are prototyping a new programming language. Using specialized tools can mitigate this issue.

There are many tools available that generate either a lexer or a parser from a specification file. In the Linux world, **flex** (https://github.com/westes/flex) and **bison** (https://www.gnu.org/software/bison/) are the most commonly used tools. Flex generates a lexer from a set of regular expressions, while bison generates a parser from a grammar description. Usually, both tools are used together.

Bison produces an **LALR(1) parser** from a grammar description. An LALR(1) parser is a bottom-up parser and is implemented using an automaton. The input for bison is a grammar file very similar to the one presented at beginning of this chapter. The main difference is that regular expressions are not supported on the right-hand side. Optional groups and repetitions must be rewritten as rules. A bison specification for tinylang, stored in a tinylang.yy file, begins with the following prologue:

```
%require "3.2"
%language "c++"
%defines "Parser.h"
%define api.namespace {tinylang}
%define api.parser.class {Parser}
%define api.token.prefix {T_}
%token
```

```
identifier integer_literal string_literal
PLUS MINUS STAR SLASH
```

We instruct bison to generate C++ code with the %language directive. Using the %define directive, we override some default values for the code generation: the generated class should be named Parser and be inside the tinylang namespace Additionally, the members of the enumeration representing the token kind should be prefixed with T_. We require version 3.2 or later, because some of these variables were introduced with this version. To be able to interact with flex, we tell bison to write a Parser.h header file with the %defines directive. Finally, we must declare all used tokens with the %token directive. The grammar rules come after %%:

```
%%
compilationUnit
    : MODULE identifier SEMI imports block identifier PERIOD ;
imports : %empty | import imports ;
import
    : FROM identifier IMPORT identList SEMI
    | IMPORT identList SEMI ;
```

Please compare these rules with the grammar specification shown in the first section of this chapter. Bison does not know repeating groups, so we need to add a new rule called imports to model this repetition. In the import rule, we must introduce an alternative to model the optional group.

We also need to rewrite other rules of the tinylang grammar in this style. For example, the rule for the IF statement becomes the following:

```
ifStatement
    : IF expression THEN statementSequence
      elseStatement END ;
elseStatement : %empty | ELSE statementSequence ;
```

Again, we must introduce a new rule to model the optional ELSE statement. The %empty directive could be omitted, but the use of it makes it clear that this is an empty branch of the alternative.

Once we've rewritten all the grammar rules in the bison style, we can generate the parser with the following command:

```
$ bison tinylang.yy
```

That's all it takes to create a parser that's similar to the handwritten one in the previous section!

Similarly, flex is easy to use. The specification for flex is a list of regular expressions and the associated action, which is executed if the regular expression matches. The `tinylang.l` file specifies the lexer for `tinylang`. Like the bison specification, it begins with a prologue:

```
%{
#include "Parser.h"
%}
%option noyywrap nounput noinput batch
id        [a-zA-Z_][a-zA-Z_0-9]*
digit     [0-9]
hexdigit  [0-9A-F]
space     [ \t\r]
```

The text inside `%{ }%` is copied into the file generated by flex. We use this mechanism to include the header file generated by bison. With the `%option` directive, we control which features the generated lexer should have. We only read one file and do not want to continue to read another file once we've reached the end of it, so we specify `noyywrap` to disable this feature. We also do not need access to the underlying file stream and disable it with `nounput` and `noinout`. Finally, because we do not need an interactive lexer, we request that a `batch` scanner is generated.

Inside the prologue, we can also define character patterns for later use. After `%%` follows the definition section:

```
%%
{space}+
{digit}+        return
                tinylang::Parser::token::T_integer_literal;
```

In the definition section, you specify a regular expression pattern and an action to execute if the pattern matches the input. The action can also be empty.

The `{space}+` pattern uses the `space` character pattern defined in the prologue. It matches one or more white space characters. We defined no action, so all white space will be ignored.

To match a number, we use the {digit}+ pattern. As an action, we only return the associated token kind. The same is done for all the tokens. For example, we do the following for the arithmetic operators:

```
"+"                return tinylang::Parser::token::T_PLUS;
"-"                return tinylang::Parser::token::T_MINUS;
"*"                return tinylang::Parser::token::T_STAR;
"/"                return tinylang::Parser::token::T_SLASH;
```

If several patterns match the input, then the pattern with the longest match is selected. If there is still more than one pattern that matches the input, then the pattern that comes first lexicographically in the specification file is chosen. That's why it is important to define the patterns for the keywords first and the pattern for identifiers only after all the keywords:

```
"VAR"              return tinylang::Parser::token::T_VAR;
"WHILE"            return tinylang::Parser::token::T_WHILE;
{id}               return tinylang::Parser::token::T_identifier;
```

The actions are not limited to just a return statement. If your code needs more than one line, then you must surround your code with curly braces { }.

The scanner is generated with the following command:

```
$ flex -c++ tinylang.l
```

Which approach should you use for your language project? Parser generators usually generate LALR(1) parsers. The LALR(1) class is larger than the LL(1) class, which recursive descent parsers can be constructed for. If you can't tweak your grammar so that it fits in the LL(1) class, then you should consider using a parser generator. It's not feasible to construct such a bottom-up parser by hand. Even if your grammar is LL(1), a parser generator provides more comfort while producing similar code to what you could write by hand. Often, this is a choice that's influenced by many factors. Clang uses a handwritten parser, while GCC uses a bison-generated parser.

Performing semantic analysis

The parser that we constructed in the previous section only checks the syntax of the input. The next step is to add the ability to perform semantic analysis. In the calc example in the previous chapter, the parser constructed an AST. In a separate phase, the semantic analyzer worked on this tree. This approach can always be used. In this section, we will use a slightly different approach and intertwine the parser and the semantic analyzer more.

These are some of the tasks a semantic analyzer must perform:

- For each declaration, the semantic analyzer must check if the used name has not been declared elsewhere already.

- For each occurrence of a name in an expression or statement, the semantic analyzer must check that the name is declared and that the desired use fits the declaration.

- For each expression, the semantic analyzer must compute the resulting type. It is also necessary to compute if the expression is constant and if so, which value it has.

- For assignment and parameter passing, the semantic analyzer must check that the types are compatible. Furthermore, we must check that the conditions in the IF and WHILE statements are of the BOOLEAN type.

That's already a lot to check for such a small subset of a programming language!

Handling the scope of names

Let's have a look at the scope of names first. The scope of a name is the range where the name is visible. Like C, tinylang uses a declare-before-use model. For example, the B and X variables are declared at the module level so that they're of the INTEGER type:

```
VAR B, X: INTEGER;
```

Before the declaration, the variables are not known and cannot be used. This is only possible after the declaration. Inside a procedure, more variables can be declared:

```
PROCEDURE Proc;
VAR B: BOOLEAN;
BEGIN
   (* Statements *)
END Proc;
```

Inside this procedure, at the point where the comment is, using B refers to the local variable B, while using X refers to the global variable X. The scope of the local variable, B, is the Proc procedure. If a name cannot be found in the current scope, then the search continues in the enclosing scope. Therefore, the X variable can be used inside the procedure. In tinylang, only modules and procedures open a new scope. Other language constructs such as struct and class usually also open a scope. Predefined entities such as the INTEGER type or the TRUE literal are declared in a global scope, enclosing the scope of the module.

In tinylang, only the name is crucial. Therefore, a scope can be implemented as a mapping from a name to its declaration. A new name can only be inserted if it is not already present. For the lookup, the enclosing or parent scope must also be known. The interface (in the include/tinylang/Sema/Scope.h file) is as follows:

```
#ifndef TINYLANG_SEMA_SCOPE_H
#define TINYLANG_SEMA_SCOPE_H

#include "tinylang/Basic/LLVM.h"
#include "llvm/ADT/StringMap.h"
#include "llvm/ADT/StringRef.h"

namespace tinylang {

class Decl;

class Scope {
  Scope *Parent;
  StringMap<Decl *> Symbols;

public:
  Scope(Scope *Parent = nullptr) : Parent(Parent) {}

  bool insert(Decl *Declaration);
  Decl *lookup(StringRef Name);

  Scope *getParent() { return Parent; }
};
```

```
} // namespace tinylang
#endif
```

The implementation in the lib/Sema/Scope.cpp file looks as follows:

```
#include "tinylang/Sema/Scope.h"
#include "tinylang/AST/AST.h"


using namespace tinylang;


bool Scope::insert(Decl *Declaration) {
  return Symbols
      .insert(std::pair<StringRef, Decl *>(
          Declaration->getName(), Declaration))
      .second;
}
```

Please note that the StringMap::insert() method does not override an existing entry. The second member of the resulting std::pair indicates whether the table was updated. This information is returned to the caller.

To implement the search for the declaration of a symbol, the lookup() method searches the current scope; if nothing is found, it searches the scopes that have been linked by the parent member:

```
Decl *Scope::lookup(StringRef Name) {
  Scope *S = this;
  while (S) {
    StringMap<Decl *>::const_iterator I =
        S->Symbols.find(Name);
    if (I != S->Symbols.end())
      return I->second;
    S = S->getParent();
  }
  return nullptr;
}
```

The variable declaration is then processed as follows:

- The current scope is the module scope.

- The INTEGER type declaration is looked up. It's an error if no declaration is found or if it is not a type declaration.

- A new AST node, VariableDeclaration, is instantiated, with the important attributes being the name, B, and the type.

- The name, B, is inserted into the current scope, mapped to the declaration instance. If the name is already present in the scope, then this is an error. The content of the current scope is not changed in this case.

- The same is done for the X variable.

Two tasks are performed here. Like in the calc example, AST nodes are constructed. At the same time, the attributes of the node, such as its type, are computed. Why is this possible?

The semantic analyzer can fall back on two different sets of attributes. The scope is inherited from the caller. The type declaration can be computed (or synthesized) by evaluating the name of the type declaration. The language is designed in such a way that these two sets of attributes are sufficient to compute all the attributes of the AST node.

An important aspect of this is the *declare-before-use* model. If a language allows the use of names before declaration, such as the members inside a class in C++, then it is not possible to compute all the attributes of an AST node at once. In such a case, the AST node must be constructed with only partially computed attributes or just with plain information (such as in the calc example).

The AST must be visited one or more times to determine the missing information. In the case of tinylang (and Modula-2), it would also be possible to dispense with the AST construction – the AST is indirectly represented through the call hierarchy of the parseXXX() methods. Code generation from an AST is much more common, so we construct an AST here, too.

Before we put all the pieces together, we need to understand the LLVM style of using **runtime type information (RTTI)**.

Using LLVM-style RTTI for the AST

Naturally, the AST nodes are a part of a class hierarchy. A declaration always has a name. Other attributes depend on what is being declared. If a variable is declared, then a type is required. A constant declaration needs a type and a value, and so on. Of course, at runtime, you need to find out which kind of declaration you are working with. The `dynamic_cast<>` C++ operator could be used for this. The problem is that the required RTTI is only available if the C++ class has a virtual table attached to it; that is, it uses virtual functions. Another disadvantage is that C++ RTTI is bloated. To avoid these disadvantages, the LLVM developers introduced a self-made RTTI style that is used throughout the LLVM libraries.

The (abstract) base class of our hierarchy is `Decl`. To implement the LLVM-style RTTI, a public enumeration containing a label for each subclass is added. Also, a private member of this type and a public getter is required. The private member is usually called `Kind`. In our case, this looks like this:

```
class Decl {
public:
  enum DeclKind { DK_Module, DK_Const, DK_Type,
                  DK_Var, DK_Param, DK_Proc };
private:
  const DeclKind Kind;
public:
  DeclKind getKind() const { return Kind; }
};
```

Each subclass now needs a special function member called `classof`. The purpose of this function is to determine if a given instance is of the requested type. For a `VariableDeclaration`, it is implemented as follows:

```
static bool classof(const Decl *D) {
  return D->getKind() == DK_Var;
}
```

Now, you can use the `llvm::isa<>` special templates to check if an object is of the requested type and `llvm::dyn_cast<>` to dynamically cast the object. There are more templates that exist, but these two are the most commonly used ones. For the other templates, see `https://llvm.org/docs/ProgrammersManual.html#the-isa-cast-and-dyn-cast-templates` and for more information about the LLVM style, including more advanced uses, see `https://llvm.org/docs/HowToSetUpLLVMStyleRTTI.html`.

Creating the semantic analyzer

Equipped with this knowledge, we can now implement the semantic analyzer, operating on AST nodes created by the parser. First, we will implement the definition of the AST node for a variable, which is stored in the `include/llvm/tinylang/AST/AST.h` file. Besides support for the LLVM-style RTTI, the base class stores the name of the declaration, the location of its name, and a pointer to the enclosing declaration. The latter is required to code-generate nested procedures. The `Decl` base class is declared as follows:

```
class Decl {
public:
  enum DeclKind { DK_Module, DK_Const, DK_Type,
                  DK_Var, DK_Param, DK_Proc };

private:
  const DeclKind Kind;

protected:
  Decl *EnclosingDecL;
  SMLoc Loc;
  StringRef Name;

public:
  Decl(DeclKind Kind, Decl *EnclosingDecL, SMLoc Loc,
       StringRef Name)
      : Kind(Kind), EnclosingDecL(EnclosingDecL), Loc(Loc),
        Name(Name) {}

  DeclKind getKind() const { return Kind; }
  SMLoc getLocation() { return Loc; }
```

```
  StringRef getName() { return Name; }
  Decl *getEnclosingDecl() { return EnclosingDecL; }
};
```

The declaration for a variable only adds a pointer to the type declaration:

```
class TypeDeclaration;

class VariableDeclaration : public Decl {
  TypeDeclaration *Ty;

public:
  VariableDeclaration(Decl *EnclosingDecL, SMLoc Loc,
                       StringRef Name, TypeDeclaration *Ty)
      : Decl(DK_Var, EnclosingDecL, Loc, Name), Ty(Ty) {}

  TypeDeclaration *getType() { return Ty; }

  static bool classof(const Decl *D) {
    return D->getKind() == DK_Var;
  }
};
```

The method in the parser needs to be extended with a semantic action and variables for the information that's been collected:

```
bool Parser::parseVariableDeclaration(DeclList &Decls) {
  auto _errorhandler = [this] {
    while (!Tok.is(tok::semi)) {
      advance();
      if (Tok.is(tok::eof)) return true;
    }
    return false;
  };

  Decl *D = nullptr; IdentList Ids;
  if (parseIdentList(Ids)) return _errorhandler();
  if (consume(tok::colon)) return _errorhandler();
```

```
  if (parseQualident(D)) return _errorhandler();
  Actions.actOnVariableDeclaration(Decls, Ids, D);
  return false;
}
```

A `DeclList` is a list of declarations called `std::vector<Decl*>`, while `IdentList` is a list of locations and identifiers called `std::vector<std::pair<SMLoc, StringRef>>`.

The `parseQualident()` method returns a declaration, which in this case is expected to be a type declaration.

The parser class knows an instance of the semantic analyzer class, `Sema`, which is stored in the `Actions` member. A call to `actOnVariableDeclaration()` runs the semantic analyzer and the AST construction. The implementation is in the `lib/Sema/Sema.cpp` file:

```
void Sema::actOnVariableDeclaration(DeclList &Decls,
                                    IdentList &Ids,
                                    Decl *D) {
  if (TypeDeclaration *Ty = dyn_cast<TypeDeclaration>(D)) {
    for (auto I = Ids.begin(), E = Ids.end(); I != E; ++I) {
      SMLoc Loc = I->first;
      StringRef Name = I->second;
      VariableDeclaration *Decl = new VariableDeclaration(
          CurrentDecl, Loc, Name, Ty);
      if (CurrentScope->insert(Decl))
        Decls.push_back(Decl);
      else
        Diags.report(Loc, diag::err_symbold_declared, Name);
    }
  } else if (!Ids.empty()) {
    SMLoc Loc = Ids.front().first;
    Diags.report(Loc, diag::err_vardecl_requires_type);
  }
}
```

First, the type declaration is check with `llvm::dyn_cast<TypeDeclaration>`. If it is not a type declaration, then an error message is printed. Otherwise, for each name in the `Ids` list, a `VariableDeclaration` is instantiated and added to the list of declarations. If adding the variable to the current scope fails because the name has already been declared, then an error message is printed.

Most of the other entities are constructed in the same way, with the complexity of their semantic analysis being the only difference. More work is required for modules and procedures because they open a new scope. Opening a new scope is easy: only a new `Scope` object must be instantiated. As soon as the module or procedure has been parsed, the scope must be removed.

This must be done in a reliable fashion because we do not want to add names to the wrong scope in case of a syntax error. This is a classic use of the **Resource Acquisition Is Initialization (RAII)** idiom in C++. Another complication comes from the fact that a procedure can recursively call itself. Due to this, the name of the procedure must be added to the current scope before it can be used. The semantic analyzer has two methods to enter and leave a scope. The scope is associated with a declaration:

```
void Sema::enterScope(Decl *D) {
  CurrentScope = new Scope(CurrentScope);
  CurrentDecl = D;
}
```

```
void Sema::leaveScope() {
  Scope *Parent = CurrentScope->getParent();
  delete CurrentScope;
  CurrentScope = Parent;
  CurrentDecl = CurrentDecl->getEnclosingDecl();
}
```

A simple helper class is used to implement the RAII idiom:

```
class EnterDeclScope {
  Sema &Semantics;

public:
  EnterDeclScope(Sema &Semantics, Decl *D)
      : Semantics(Semantics) {
    Semantics.enterScope(D);
```

```
    }
    ~EnterDeclScope() { Semantics.leaveScope(); }
};
```

While parsing a module or procedure, there are now two interactions with the semantic analyzer. The first is after the name is parsed. Here, the (almost empty) AST node is constructed, and a new scope is established:

```
bool Parser::parseProcedureDeclaration(/* … */) {
    /* … */
    if (consume(tok::kw_PROCEDURE)) return _errorhandler();
    if (expect(tok::identifier)) return _errorhandler();
    ProcedureDeclaration *D =
        Actions.actOnProcedureDeclaration(
            Tok.getLocation(), Tok.getIdentifier());
    EnterDeclScope S(Actions, D);
    /* … */
}
```

The semantic analyzer does more than check the name in the current scope and return the AST node:

```
ProcedureDeclaration *
Sema::actOnProcedureDeclaration(SMLoc Loc, StringRef Name) {
    ProcedureDeclaration *P =
        new ProcedureDeclaration(CurrentDecl, Loc, Name);
    if (!CurrentScope->insert(P))
        Diags.report(Loc, diag::err_symbold_declared, Name);
    return P;
}
```

The real work is done once all the declarations and the procedure's body have been parsed. Basically, the semantic analyzer must only check if the name at the end of the procedure declaration is equal to the name of the procedure, and also if the declaration that's used for the return type is really a type declaration:

```
void Sema::actOnProcedureDeclaration(
        ProcedureDeclaration *ProcDecl, SMLoc Loc,
        StringRef Name, FormalParamList &Params, Decl *RetType,
```

```
          DeclList &Decls, StmtList &Stmts) {

  if (Name != ProcDecl->getName()) {
    Diags.report(Loc, diag::err_proc_identifier_not_equal);
    Diags.report(ProcDecl->getLocation(),
                 diag::note_proc_identifier_declaration);
  }
  ProcDecl->setDecls(Decls);
  ProcDecl->setStmts(Stmts);

  auto RetTypeDecl =
      dyn_cast_or_null<TypeDeclaration>(RetType);
  if (!RetTypeDecl && RetType)
    Diags.report(Loc, diag::err_returntype_must_be_type,
                 Name);
  else
    ProcDecl->setRetType(RetTypeDecl);
}
```

Some declarations are inherently present and cannot be defined by the developer. This includes the BOOLEAN and INTEGER types and the TRUE and FALSE literals. These declarations exist in the global scope and must be added programmatically. Modula-2 also predefines some procedures, such as INC or DEC, which should also be added to the global scope. Given our classes, the initialization of the global scope is simple:

```
void Sema::initialize() {
  CurrentScope = new Scope();
  CurrentDecl = nullptr;
  IntegerType =
      new TypeDeclaration(CurrentDecl, SMLoc(), "INTEGER");
  BooleanType =
      new TypeDeclaration(CurrentDecl, SMLoc(), "BOOLEAN");
  TrueLiteral = new BooleanLiteral(true, BooleanType);
  FalseLiteral = new BooleanLiteral(false, BooleanType);
  TrueConst = new ConstantDeclaration(CurrentDecl, SMLoc(),
                                      "TRUE", TrueLiteral);
  FalseConst = new ConstantDeclaration(
```

```
        CurrentDecl, SMLoc(), "FALSE", FalseLiteral);
  CurrentScope->insert(IntegerType);
  CurrentScope->insert(BooleanType);
  CurrentScope->insert(TrueConst);
  CurrentScope->insert(FalseConst);
}
```

With this scheme, all the required calculations for tinylang can be done. For example, to compute if an expression results in a constant value, you must ensure the following occurs:

- A literal or a reference to a constant declaration is constant.
- If both sides of an expression are constant, then applying the operator also yields a constant.

These rules are easily embedded into the semantic analyzer while creating the AST nodes for an expression. Likewise, the type and the constant value can be computed.

It should be noted that not all kinds of computations can be done in this way. For example, to detect the use of uninitialized variables, a method called symbolic interpretation can be used. In its general form, the method requires a special walk order through the AST, which is not possible during construction time. The good news is that the presented approach creates a fully decorated AST, which is ready for code generation. This AST can, of course, be used for further analysis, given the fact that costly analysis can be turned on or off on demand.

To play around with the frontend, you also need to update the driver. Since the code generation is missing, a correct tinylang program produces no output. Still, it can be used to explore error recovery and to provoke semantic errors:

```
#include "tinylang/Basic/Diagnostic.h"
#include "tinylang/Basic/Version.h"
#include "tinylang/Parser/Parser.h"
#include "llvm/Support/InitLLVM.h"
#include "llvm/Support/raw_ostream.h"

using namespace tinylang;

int main(int argc_, const char **argv_) {
  llvm::InitLLVM X(argc_, argv_);
```

```cpp
  llvm::SmallVector<const char *, 256> argv(argv_ + 1,
                                            argv_ + argc_);

  llvm::outs() << "Tinylang "
               << tinylang::getTinylangVersion() << "\n";

  for (const char *F : argv) {
    llvm::ErrorOr<std::unique_ptr<llvm::MemoryBuffer>>
        FileOrErr = llvm::MemoryBuffer::getFile(F);
    if (std::error_code BufferError =
            FileOrErr.getError()) {
      llvm::errs() << "Error reading " << F << ": "
                   << BufferError.message() << "\n";
      continue;
    }

    llvm::SourceMgr SrcMgr;
    DiagnosticsEngine Diags(SrcMgr);
    SrcMgr.AddNewSourceBuffer(std::move(*FileOrErr),
                              llvm::SMLoc());
    auto lexer = Lexer(SrcMgr, Diags);
    auto sema = Sema(Diags);
    auto parser = Parser(lexer, sema);
    parser.parse();
  }
}
```

Congratulations! You've finished implementing the frontend for tinylang!

Now, let's try out what we have learned so far. Save the following source, which is an implementation of Euclid's greatest common divisor algorithm, as a Gcd.mod file:

```
MODULE Gcd;

PROCEDURE GCD(a, b: INTEGER):INTEGER;
VAR t: INTEGER;
BEGIN
  IF b = 0 THEN RETURN a; END;
```

```
    WHILE b # 0 DO
        t := a MOD b;
        a := b;
        b := t;
    END;
    RETURN a;
END GCD;


END Gcd.
```

Let's run the compiler on this file with the following command:

```
$ tinylang Gcm.mod
Tinylang 0.1
```

There is no output except the version number being printed. This is because only the frontend part has been implemented. However, if you change the source so that it contains syntax errors, then error messages will be printed.

We'll continue this fun by adding code generation, which is the topic of the next chapter.

Summary

In this chapter, you learned about the techniques a real-world compiler uses in the frontend. Starting with the project's layout, you created separate libraries for the lexer, the parser, and the semantic analyzer. To output messages to the user, you extended an existing LLVM class, which allowed the messages to be stored centrally. The lexer has now been separated into several interfaces.

You then learned how to construct a recursive descent parser from a grammar description, which pitfalls to avoid, and how to use generators to do the job. The semantic analyzer you constructed performs all the semantic checks that are required by the language while being intertwined with the parser and AST construction.

The result of your coding effort was a fully decorated AST, which will be used in the next chapter to generate IR code and object code.

5

Basics of IR Code Generation

Having created a decorated **Abstract Syntax Tree (AST)** for your programming language, the next task is to generate the LLVM IR code from it. LLVM IR code resembles three-address code, with a human-readable representation. Therefore, we need a systematic approach to translate language concepts such as control structures into the lower level of LLVM IR.

In this chapter, you will learn about the basics of LLVM IR, and how to generate IR for control flow structures from the AST. You will also learn how to generate LLVM IR for expressions in **Static Single Assignment (SSA) form**, using a modern algorithm. Finally, you will learn how to emit assembler text and object code.

This chapter will cover the following topics:

- Generating IR from the AST
- Using AST numbering to generate IR code in SSA form
- Setting up the module and the driver

By the end of the chapter, you will have acquired the knowledge to create a code generator for your own programming language, and how to integrate it into your own compiler.

Technical requirements

The code files for the chapter are available at https://github.com/
PacktPublishing/Learn-LLVM-12/tree/master/Chapter05/tinylang

You can find the code in action videos at https://bit.ly/3nllhED

Generating IR from the AST

The LLVM code generator takes a module as described in IR as input and turns it into
object code or assembly text. We need to transform the AST representation into IR. To
implement an IR code generator, we will look at a simple example first and then develop
the classes required for the code generator. The complete implementation will be divided
into three classes: the CodeGenerator, the CGModule, and the CGProcedure classes.
The CodeGenerator class is the general interface used by the compiler driver. The
CGModule and the CGProcedure classes hold the state required for generating the IR
code for a compilation unit and a single function.

We begin with a look at the clang-generated IR in the next section.

Understanding the IR code

Before generating the IR code, it's good to know the main elements of the IR language.
In *Chapter 3, The Structure of a Compiler*, we already had a brief look at IR. An easy way
to get more knowledge of IR is to study the output from clang. For example, save this
C source code, which implements the Euclidean algorithm for calculating the greatest
common divisor of two numbers, as gcd.c:

```
unsigned gcd(unsigned a, unsigned b) {
  if (b == 0)
    return a;
  while (b != 0) {
    unsigned t = a % b;
    a = b;
    b = t;
  }
  return a;
}
```

You can then create the IR file, gcd.ll, with the following command:

```
$ clang --target=aarch64-linux-gnu -O1 -S -emit-llvm gcd.c
```

The IR code is not target-independent, even if it often looks like it. The preceding command compiles the source file for an ARM 64-bit CPU on Linux. The -S option instructs clang to output an assembly file, and with the additional specification of -emit-llvm, an IR file is created. The optimization level, -O1, is used to get an easy readable IR code. Let's have a look at the generated file and understand how the C source maps to IR. At the top of the file, some basic properties are established:

```
; ModuleID = 'gcd.c'
source_filename = "gcd.c"
target datalayout = "e-m:e-i8:8:32-i16:16:32-i64:64-
                     i128:128-n32:64-S128"
target triple = "aarch64-unknown-linux-gnu"
```

The first line is a comment, informing you about which module identifier was used. On the following line, the filename of the source file is named. With clang, both are the same.

The target datalayout string establishes some basic properties. Its parts are separated by -. The following information is included:

- A small e means that bytes in memory are stored using the little endian schema. To specify a big endian, you use a big E.

- m: specifies the name mangling applied to symbols. Here, m:e means that ELF name mangling is used.

- The entries on the iN:A:P form, for example, i8:8:32, specify the alignment of data, given in bits. The first number is the alignment required by the ABI, and the second number is the preferred alignment. For bytes (i8), the ABI alignment is 1 byte (8) and the preferred alignment is 4 bytes (32).

- n specifies which native register sizes are available. n32:64 means that 32-bit and 64-bit wide integers are natively supported.

- S specifies the alignment of the stack, again in bits. S128 means that the stack maintains a 16-byte alignment.

> **Note**
>
> A lot more information can be provided with the target data layout. You can find the full information in the reference manual at `https://llvm.org/docs/LangRef.html#data-layout`.

Last, the `target triple` string specifies the architecture we are compiling for. This is essential for the information we gave on the command line. You will find a more in-depth discussion of the triple in *Chapter 2, Touring the LLVM Source*.

Next, the `gcd` function is defined in the IR file:

```
define i32 @gcd(i32 %a, i32 %b) {
```

This resembles the function signature in the C file. The `unsigned` data type is translated to the 32-bit integer type, `i32`. The function name is prefixed with `@`, and the parameter names are prefixed with `%`. The body of the function is enclosed in curly braces. The code of the body follows:

```
entry:
  %cmp = icmp eq i32 %b, 0
  br i1 %cmp, label %return, label %while.body
```

The IR code is organized in so-called **basic blocks**. A well-formed basic block is a linear sequence of instructions, which begins with an optional label and ends with a terminator instruction, for example, a branch or return instruction. Each basic block thus has one entry point and one exit point. LLVM allows malformed basic blocks at construction time. The label of the first basic block is `entry`. The code in the block is simple: the first instruction compares the parameter `%b` against `0`. The second instruction branched to label `return` if the condition was `true` and to label `while.body` if the condition was `false`.

Another characteristic of the IR code is that it is in a **SSA** form. The code uses an unlimited number of virtual registers, but each register is only written once. The result of the comparison is assigned to the named virtual register, `%cmp`. This register is subsequently used, but it is never written again. Optimizations such as constant propagation and common subexpression elimination work very well with the SSA form and all modern compilers are using it.

The next basic block is the body of the `while` loop:

```
while.body:
  %b.addr.010 = phi i32 [ %rem, %while.body ],
```

```
                           [ %b, %entry ]
   %a.addr.09 = phi i32 [ %b.addr.010, %while.body ],
                           [ %a, %entry ]
   %rem = urem i32 %a.addr.09, %b.addr.010
   %cmp1 = icmp eq i32 %rem, 0
   br i1 %cmp1, label %return, label %while.body
```

Inside the loop of gcd, the a and b parameters are assigned new values. If a register can be only written once, then this is not possible. The solution is to use the special phi instruction. The phi instruction has a list of basic blocks and values as parameters. A basic block presents the incoming edge from that basic block, and the value is the values from those basic blocks. At runtime, the phi instruction compares the label of the previously executed basic block with the labels in the parameter list.

The value of the instruction is then the value associated with the label. For the first phi instruction, the value is to register %rem if the previously executed basic block was while.body. The value is %b, if entry was the previously executed basic block. The values are the ones at the start of the basic block. The register %b.addr.010 gets a value from the first phi instruction. The same register is used in the parameter list of the second phi instruction, but the value is assumed to be the one before it is changed through the first phi instruction.

After the loop body, the return value must be chosen:

```
return:
   %retval.0 = phi i32 [ %a, %entry ],
                       [ %b.addr.010, %while.body ]
   ret i32 %retval.0
}
```

Again, a phi instruction is used to select the desired value. The ret instruction does not only end this basic block, but also denotes the end of this function at runtime. It has the return value as a parameter.

There are some restrictions regarding the use of phi instructions. They must be the first instructions of a basic block. The first basic block is special: it has no previously executed block. Therefore, it cannot begin with a phi instruction.

The IR code itself looks a lot like a mix of C and assembly language. Despite this familiar style, it is not clear how we can easily generate IR code from an AST. In particular, the phi instruction looks difficult to generate. But don't be scared. In the next section, we will implement a simple algorithm to do just that!

Knowing the load-and-store approach

All local optimizations in LLVM are based on the SSA form shown here. For global variables, memory references are used. The IR language knows load-and-store instructions, which are used to fetch and store those values. You can use this for local variables, too. These instructions are not in SSA form, and LLVM knows how to convert them into the required SSA form. Therefore, you can allocate memory slots for each local variable and use load-and-store instructions to change their value. All you need to remember is the pointer to the memory slot where a variable is stored. In fact, the clang compiler uses this approach.

Let's look at the IR code with loads and stores. Compile gcd.c again, this time without enabling optimization:

```
$ clang --target=aarch64-linux-gnu -S -emit-llvm gcd.c
```

The gcd function now looks different. This is the first basic block:

```
define i32 @gcd(i32, i32) {
  %3 = alloca i32, align 4
  %4 = alloca i32, align 4
  %5 = alloca i32, align 4
  %6 = alloca i32, align 4
  store i32 %0, i32* %4, align 4
  store i32 %1, i32* %5, align 4
  %7 = load i32, i32* %5, align 4
  %8 = icmp eq i32 %7, 0
  br i1 %8, label %9, label %11
```

The IR code now relays the automatic numbering of registers and labels. The names of the parameters are not specified. Implicitly, they are %0 and %1. The basic block has no label, so it gets 2 assigned. The first instructions allocate memory for four 32-bit values. After that, the parameters %0 and %1 are stored in the memory slots pointed to by registers %4 and %5. To perform the comparison of parameter %1 against 0, the value is explicitly loaded from the memory slot. With this approach, you do not need to use the phi instruction! Instead, you load a value from a memory slot, perform a calculation on it and store the new value back in the memory slot. The next time you read the memory slot, you get the last computed value. All the other basic blocks for the gcd function follow this pattern.

The advantage of using load-and-store instructions in this way is that it is fairly easy to generate the IR code. The disadvantage is that you generate a lot of IR instructions that LLVM will remove with the mem2reg pass in the very first optimization step, after converting the basic block to SSA form. Therefore, we generate the IR code in SSA form directly.

We begin the development of IR code generation with the mapping of the control flow to basic blocks.

Mapping the control flow to basic blocks

As mentioned in the previous section, a well-formed basic block is just a *linear sequence of instructions*. A basic block can begin with phi instructions and must end with a branch instruction. Inside a basic block, neither phi nor branch instructions are allowed. Each basic block has exactly one label, marking the first instruction of the basic block. Labels are the targets of branch instructions. You can view branches as directed edges between two basic blocks, resulting in the **Control Flow Graph** (**CFG**). A basic block can have **predecessors** and **successors**. The first basic block of a function is special in the sense that no predecessors are allowed.

As a consequence of these restrictions, control statements of the source language, such as WHILE or IF, produce several basic blocks. Let's look at the WHILE statement. The condition of the WHILE statement controls whether the loop body or the next statement is executed. The condition must be generated in a basic block of its own because there are two predecessors:

- The basic block resulting from the statement before the WHILE loop
- The branch from the end of the loop body back to the condition

There are also two successors:

- The beginning of the loop body
- The basic block resulting from the statement following the WHILE loop

The loop body itself has at least one basic block:

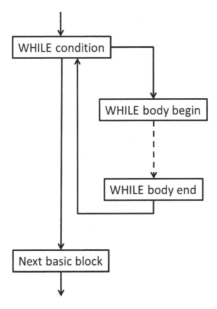

Figure 5.1 – Basic blocks of a WHILE statement

The IR code generation follows this structure. We store a pointer to the current basic block in the CGProcedure class and use an instance of llvm::IRBuilder<> for inserting instructions into the basic block. First, we create the basic blocks:

```
void emitStmt(WhileStatement *Stmt) {
  llvm::BasicBlock *WhileCondBB = llvm::BasicBlock::Create(
      getLLVMCtx(), "while.cond", Fn);
  llvm::BasicBlock *WhileBodyBB = llvm::BasicBlock::Create(
      getLLVMCtx(), "while.body", Fn);
  llvm::BasicBlock *AfterWhileBB =
    llvm::BasicBlock::Create(
      getLLVMCtx(), "after.while", Fn);
```

The Fn variable denotes the current function, and getLLVMCtx() returns the LLVM context. Both are set later. We end the current basic block with a branch to the basic block, which will hold the condition:

```
  Builder.CreateBr(WhileCondBB);
```

The basic block for the condition becomes the new current basic block. We generate the condition and end the block with a conditional branch:

```
setCurr(WhileCondBB);
llvm::Value *Cond = emitExpr(Stmt->getCond());
Builder.CreateCondBr(Cond, WhileBodyBB, AfterWhileBB);
```

Next, we generate the loop body. As a final instruction, we add a branch back to the basic block of the condition:

```
setCurr(WhileBodyBB);
emit(Stmt->getWhileStmts());
Builder.CreateBr(WhileCondBB);
```

This ends the generation of the WHILE statement. The empty basic block for statements following the WHILE statement becomes the new current basic block:

```
setCurr(AfterWhileBB);
}
```

Following this schema, you can create an emit() method for each statement of the source language.

Using AST numbering to generate IR code in SSA form

In order to generate IR code in SSA form from the AST, we use an approach called **AST numbering**. The basic idea is that for each basic block, we store the current value of local variables written to in this basic block.

Although it is simple, we will still need several steps. We will introduce the required data structure first, after which we will implement the reading and writing of values local to a basic block. We will then handle values that are used in several basic blocks and conclude by optimizing the phi instructions created.

Defining the data structure to hold values

We use `struct BasicBlockDef` to hold the information for a single block:

```
struct BasicBlockDef {
llvm::DenseMap<Decl *, llvm::TrackingVH<llvm::Value>> Defs;
// ...
};
```

The LLVM class, `llvm::Value`, represents a value in SSA form. The `Value` class acts like a label on the result of a computation. It is created once, usually through an IR instruction, and then subsequently used. There can be changes during various optimizations. For example, if the optimizer detects that the values `%1` and `%2` are always the same, then it can replace uses of `%2` with `%1`. Basically, this changes the label, but not the computation. To be aware of such changes, we cannot use the `Value` class directly. Instead, we need a value handle. There are value handles with different functionalities. To track replacements, we use the `llvm::TrackingVH<>` class. As a result, the `Defs` member maps a declaration of the AST (a variable or a formal parameter) to its current value. We now need to store this information for each basic block:

```
llvm::DenseMap<llvm::BasicBlock *, BasicBlockDef>
  CurrentDef;
```

With this data structure, we are now able to handle local values.

Reading and writing values local to a basic block

To store the current value of a local variable in a basic block, we just create an entry in the maps:

```
void writeLocalVariable(llvm::BasicBlock *BB, Decl *Decl,
                        llvm::Value *Val) {
  CurrentDef[BB].Defs[Decl] = Val;
}
```

The lookup of a variable's value is a bit more complicated, because the value might not be in the basic block. In this case, we need to extend the search to the predecessors using a possible recursive search:

```
llvm::Value *
readLocalVariable(llvm::BasicBlock *BB, Decl *Decl) {
  auto Val = CurrentDef[BB].Defs.find(Decl);
```

```
  if (Val != CurrentDef[BB].Defs.end())
    return Val->second;
  return readLocalVariableRecursive(BB, Decl);
}
```

The real work is searching the predecessors, which is implemented in the next section.

Searching the predecessor blocks for a value

If the current basic block we are looking at has only one predecessor, then we search there for the value of the variable. If the basic block has several predecessors, then we need to search for the value in all these blocks and combine the results. To illustrate this situation, you can look at the basic block with the condition of the WHILE statement from the previous section.

This basic block has two predecessors – the one resulting from the statement before the WHILE loop, and the one resulting from the branch for the end of the body of the WHILE loop. A variable used in the condition should have an initial value and will most likely be changed in the body of the loop. So, we need to collect these definitions and create a phi instruction from it. The basic blocks created from the WHILE statement contain a cycle.

Because we recursively search the predecessor blocks, we must break this cycle. To do so, we use a simple trick. We insert an empty phi instruction and record this as the current value of the variable. If we see this basic block again in our search, then we find that the variable has a value, which we use. The search stops at this point. After we have collected all the values, we must update the phi instruction.

We will still face a problem. At the time of the lookup, not all predecessors of a basic block may be known. How can this happen? Look at the creation of the basic blocks for the WHILE statement. The IR for the condition of the loop is generated first. But the branch from the end of the body back to the basic block containing the condition can only be added after the IR for the body is generated, because this basic block is not known earlier. If we need to read the value of a variable in the condition, then we are stuck, because not all predecessors are known.

To solve this situation, we must do a little bit more:

1. First, we attach a flag to the basic block.
2. Then, we define a basic block as sealed if we know all the predecessors of the basic block. If the basic block is not sealed and we need to look up the value of the variable not yet defined in this basic block, then we insert an empty phi instruction and use it as the value.

3. We also need to remember this instruction. If the block is later sealed, then we need to update the instruction with the real values. To implement this, we add two more members to `struct BasicBlockDef`: The `IncompletePhis` map records the `phi` instructions that we need to later update, and the `Sealed` flag indicates whether the basic block is sealed:

```
llvm::DenseMap<llvm::PHINode *, Decl *>
   IncompletePhis;
unsigned Sealed : 1;
```

4. Then, the method can be implemented as described:

```
llvm::Value *readLocalVariableRecursive(
                            llvm::BasicBlock *BB,
                            Decl *Decl) {
   llvm::Value *Val = nullptr;
   if (!CurrentDef[BB].Sealed) {
     llvm::PHINode *Phi = addEmptyPhi(BB, Decl);
     CurrentDef[BB].IncompletePhis[Phi] = Decl;
     Val = Phi;
   } else if (auto *PredBB = BB
                            ->getSinglePredecessor()) {
     Val = readLocalVariable(PredBB, Decl);
   } else {
     llvm::PHINode *Phi = addEmptyPhi(BB, Decl);
     Val = Phi;
     writeLocalVariable(BB, Decl, Val);
     addPhiOperands(BB, Decl, Phi);
   }
   writeLocalVariable(BB, Decl, Val);
   return Val;
}
```

5. The `addEmptyPhi()` method inserts an empty `phi` instruction at the beginning of the basic block:

```
llvm::PHINode *addEmptyPhi(llvm::BasicBlock *BB, Decl
*Decl) {
   return BB->empty()
```

```
          ? llvm::PHINode::Create(mapType(Decl), 0,
            "", BB)
          : llvm::PHINode::Create(mapType(Decl), 0,
            "", &BB->front());
  }
```

6. To add the missing operands to the `phi` instruction, we first search all the predecessors of the basic block and add the operand pair value and basic block to the `phi` instruction. Then, we try to optimize the instruction:

```
void addPhiOperands(llvm::BasicBlock *BB, Decl *Decl,
                    llvm::PHINode *Phi) {
  for (auto I = llvm::pred_begin(BB),
         E = llvm::pred_end(BB);
       I != E; ++I) {
    Phi->addIncoming(readLocalVariable(*I, Decl), *I);
  }
  optimizePhi(Phi);
}
```

This algorithm can generate unwanted `phi` instructions. An approach to optimize these is implemented in the next section.

Optimizing the generated phi instructions

How can we optimize a `phi` instruction and why should we do it? Although the SSA form is advantageous for many optimizations, the `phi` instruction is often not interpreted by the algorithms and thereby hinders optimization in general. Therefore, the fewer `phi` instructions we generate, the better:

1. If the instruction has only one operand or all operands have the same value, then we replace the instruction with this value. If the instruction has no operand, then we replace the instruction with the special value, `Undef`. Only if the instruction has two or more distinct operands do we have to keep the instruction:

```
void optimizePhi(llvm::PHINode *Phi) {
  llvm::Value *Same = nullptr;
  for (llvm::Value *V : Phi->incoming_values()) {
```

```
    if (V == Same || V == Phi)
      continue;
    if (Same && V != Same)
      return;
    Same = V;
  }
  if (Same == nullptr)
    Same = llvm::UndefValue::get(Phi->getType());
```

2. Removing a `phi` instruction may lead to optimization opportunities in other `phi` instructions. We search for all uses of the value in other `phi` instructions and then try to optimize these instructions, too:

```
  llvm::SmallVector<llvm::PHINode *, 8> CandidatePhis;
  for (llvm::Use &U : Phi->uses()) {
    if (auto *P =
            llvm::dyn_cast<llvm::PHINode>(U.getUser()))
      CandidatePhis.push_back(P);
  }
  Phi->replaceAllUsesWith(Same);
  Phi->eraseFromParent();
  for (auto *P : CandidatePhis)
    optimizePhi(P);
}
```

If desired, this algorithm can be improved further. Instead of always iterating the list of values for each `phi` instruction, we could pick and remember two distinct values. In the `optimize` function, we could then check whether these two values are still in the list of the `phi` instruction. If yes, then we know that there is nothing to optimize. But even without this optimization, this algorithm runs very fast, so we are not going to implement this now.

We are almost done. Only the operation to seal a basic block has not yet been implemented, which we will do in the next section.

Sealing a block

As soon as we know that all predecessors of a block are known, we can seal the block. If the source language contains only structured statements, such as `tinylang`, then it is easy to determine that place where a block can be sealed. Look again at the basic blocks generated for the `WHILE` statement. The basic block containing the condition can be sealed after the branch from the end of the body is added, because this was the last missing predecessor. To seal a block, we simply add the missing operands to the incomplete `phi` instructions and set the flag:

```
void sealBlock(llvm::BasicBlock *BB) {
  for (auto PhiDecl : CurrentDef[BB].IncompletePhis) {
    addPhiOperands(BB, PhiDecl.second, PhiDecl.first);
  }
  CurrentDef[BB].IncompletePhis.clear();
  CurrentDef[BB].Sealed = true;
}
```

With these methods, we are now ready to generate the IR code for expressions.

Creating IR code for expressions

In general, you translate expressions as already shown in *Chapter 3, The Structure of a Compiler*. The only interesting part is how to access variables. The previous section covered local variables, but there are other kinds of variables. Let's discuss briefly what we need to do:

- For a local variable of the procedure, we use the `readLocalVariable()` and `writeLocalVariable()` methods from the previous section.

- For a local variable in an enclosing procedure, we require a pointer to the frame of the enclosing procedure. This is handled in a later section.

- For a global variable, we generate load-and-store instructions.

- For a formal parameter, we have to differentiate between passing by value and passing by reference (the `VAR` parameter in `tinylang`). A parameter passed by value is treated as a local variable, and a parameter passed by reference is treated as a global variable.

Putting it all together, we get the following code for reading a variable or formal parameter:

```
llvm::Value *CGProcedure::readVariable(llvm::BasicBlock
                                       *BB,
                                       Decl *D) {
  if (auto *V = llvm::dyn_cast<VariableDeclaration>(D)) {
    if (V->getEnclosingDecl() == Proc)
      return readLocalVariable(BB, D);
    else if (V->getEnclosingDecl() ==
             CGM.getModuleDeclaration()) {
      return Builder.CreateLoad(mapType(D),
                                CGM.getGlobal(D));
    } else
      llvm::report_fatal_error(
          "Nested procedures not yet supported");
  } else if (auto *FP =
                 llvm::dyn_cast<FormalParameterDeclaration>(
                     D)) {
    if (FP->isVar()) {
      return Builder.CreateLoad(
          mapType(FP)->getPointerElementType(),
          FormalParams[FP]);
    } else
      return readLocalVariable(BB, D);
  } else
    llvm::report_fatal_error("Unsupported declaration");
}
```

Writing to a variable or formal parameter is symmetrical; we just need to exchange the method to read with the one to write and use a `store` instruction instead of a `load` instruction.

Next, these functions are applied while generating the IR code for functions, which we implement next.

Emitting the IR code for a function

Most of the IR code will live in a function. A function in IR code resembles a function in C. It specifies the name, and the types of the parameters and of the return value and other attributes. To call a function in a different compilation unit, you need to declare the function. This is similar to a prototype in C. If you add basic blocks to the function, then you define the function. We will do all this in the next sections, beginning with a discussion regarding the visibility of symbol names.

Controlling visibility with linkage and name mangling

Functions (and also global variables) have a linkage style attached. With the linkage style, we define the visibility of a symbol name and what should happen if more than one symbol has the same name. The most basic linkage styles are `private` and `external`. A symbol with `private` linkage is only visible in the current compilation unit, while a symbol with `external` linkage is globally available.

For a language without a proper module concept, such as C, this is certainly adequate. With modules, we need to do more. Assume that we have a module called `Square` providing a `Root()` function and a `Cube` module also providing a `Root()` function. If the functions are private, then there is obviously no problem. The function gets the name `Root` and private linkage. The situation is different if the function is exported, so that it can be called in other modules. Using the function name alone is not enough, because this name is not unique.

The solution is to tweak the name to make it globally unique. This is called name mangling. How this is done depends on the requirements and characteristics of the language. In our case, the base idea is to use a combination of the module and the function name to create a global unique name. Using `Square.Root` as a name looks like an obvious solution, but may lead to problems with assemblers, as the dot may have a special meaning. Instead of using a delimiter between the name components, we can get a similar effect with prefixing the name components with their length: `6Square4Root`. This is no legal identifier for LLVM, but we can fix this by prefixing the whole name with `_t` (t for `tinylang`): `_t6Square4Root`. In this way, we can create unique names for exported symbols:

```
std::string CGModule::mangleName(Decl *D) {
  std::string Mangled;
  llvm::SmallString<16> Tmp;
  while (D) {
    llvm::StringRef Name = D->getName();
    Tmp.clear();
```

```
    Tmp.append(llvm::itostr(Name.size()));
    Tmp.append(Name);
    Mangled.insert(0, Tmp.c_str());
    D = D->getEnclosingDecl();
  }
  Mangled.insert(0, "_t");
  return Mangled;
}
```

If your source language supports type overloading, then you need to extend this scheme with type names. For example, to distinguish between the C++ functions `int root(int)` and `double root(double)`, the type of the parameter and the return value are added to the function name.

You also need to think about the length of the generated name, because some linkers place restrictions on the length. With nested namespaces and classes in C++, the mangled names can be rather long. There, C++ defines a compression scheme to avoid repeating name components over and over again.

Next, we look at how to treat the parameter types.

Converting types from an AST description to LLVM types

The parameters of a function also require some consideration. First, we need to map the types of the source language to an LLVM type. As `tinylang` currently only has two types, this is easy:

```
llvm::Type *convertType(TypeDeclaration *Ty) {
  if (Ty->getName() == "INTEGER")
    return Int64Ty;
  if (Ty->getName() == "BOOLEAN")
    return Int1Ty;
  llvm::report_fatal_error("Unsupported type");
}
```

`Int64Ty`, `Int1Ty`, and later `VoidTy` are class members holding the type representation of LLVM types, `i64`, `i1`, and `void`.

For a formal parameter that passes by reference, this is not enough. The LLVM type of this parameter is a pointer. We generalize the function and take formal parameters into account:

```
llvm::Type *mapType(Decl *Decl) {
  if (auto *FP = llvm::
    dyn_cast<FormalParameterDeclaration>(
        Decl)) {
    llvm::Type *Ty = convertType(FP->getType());
    if (FP->isVar())
      Ty = Ty->getPointerTo();
    return Ty;
  }
  if (auto *V = llvm::dyn_cast<VariableDeclaration>(Decl))
    return convertType(V->getType());
  return convertType(llvm::cast<TypeDeclaration>(Decl));
}
```

With these helpers at hand, we create the LLVM IR function next.

Creating the LLVM IR function

To emit a function in LLVM IR, a function type is needed, which is similar to a prototype in C. Creating the function type involves mapping the types and then calling the factory method to create the function type:

```
llvm::FunctionType *createFunctionType(
    ProcedureDeclaration *Proc) {
  llvm::Type *ResultTy = VoidTy;
  if (Proc->getRetType()) {
    ResultTy = mapType(Proc->getRetType());
  }
  auto FormalParams = Proc->getFormalParams();
  llvm::SmallVector<llvm::Type *, 8> ParamTypes;
  for (auto FP : FormalParams) {
    llvm::Type *Ty = mapType(FP);
    ParamTypes.push_back(Ty);
  }
```

```
    return llvm::FunctionType::get(ResultTy, ParamTypes,
                            /* IsVarArgs */ false);
}
```

Based on the function type, we also create the LLVM function. This associates the function type with the linkage and the mangled name:

```
llvm::Function *
createFunction(ProcedureDeclaration *Proc,
               llvm::FunctionType *FTy) {
    llvm::Function *Fn = llvm::Function::Create(
        Fty, llvm::GlobalValue::ExternalLinkage,
        mangleName(Proc), getModule());
```

The `getModule()` method returns the current LLVM module, which we will set up a bit later.

With the function created, we can add some more information to it. First, we can give the parameter's names. This makes the IR more readable. Second, we can add attributes to the function and to the parameters to specify some characteristics. As an example, we do this for parameters passed by reference.

At the LLVM level, these parameters are pointers. But from the source language design, these are very restricted pointers. Analog to references in C++, we always need to specify a variable for a VAR parameter. So, we know by design that this pointer will never be null and that it is always dereferenceable, meaning that we can read the value pointed to by risking a general protection fault. Also by design, this pointer cannot be passed around. In particular, there are no copies of the pointer that outlive the call to the function. Therefore, the pointer is said to not be captured.

The `llvm::AttributeBuilder` class is used to build the set of attributes for a formal parameter. To get the storage size of a parameter type, we can simply ask the data layout:

```
    size_t Idx = 0;
    for (auto I = Fn->arg_begin(), E = Fn->arg_end(); I != E;
         ++I, ++Idx) {
        llvm::Argument *Arg = I;
        FormalParameterDeclaration *FP =
            Proc->getFormalParams()[Idx];
        if (FP->isVar()) {
            llvm::AttrBuilder Attr;
```

```
        llvm::TypeSize Sz =
            CGM.getModule()
                ->getDataLayout().getTypeStoreSize(
                    CGM.convertType(FP->getType()));
        Attr.addDereferenceableAttr(Sz);
        Attr.addAttribute(llvm::Attribute::NoCapture);
        Arg->addAttrs(Attr);
      }
      Arg->setName(FP->getName());
    }
    return Fn;
}
```

We now have created the IR function. In the next section, we add the basic blocks of the function body to the function.

Emitting the function body

We are almost done with emitting the IR code for a function! We only need to put the pieces together to emit a function, including its body:

1. Given a procedure declaration from tinylang, we first create the function type and the function:

    ```
    void run(ProcedureDeclaration *Proc) {
        this->Proc = Proc;
        Fty = createFunctionType(Proc);
        Fn = createFunction(Proc, Fty);
    ```

2. Next, we create the first basic block of the function and make it the current one:

    ```
    llvm::BasicBlock *BB = llvm::BasicBlock::Create(
        CGM.getLLVMCtx(), "entry", Fn);
    setCurr(BB);
    ```

3.　Then we step through all formal parameters. To handle VAR parameters correctly, we need to initialize the `FormalParams` member (used in `readVariable()`). In contrast to local variables, formal parameters have a value in the first basic block, so we make these values known:

```
size_t Idx = 0;
auto &Defs = CurrentDef[BB];
for (auto I = Fn->arg_begin(), E = Fn->arg_end(); I !=
     E; ++I, ++Idx) {
  llvm::Argument *Arg = I;
  FormalParameterDeclaration *FP = Proc->
    getParams()[Idx];
  FormalParams[FP] = Arg;
  Defs.Defs.insert(
      std::pair<Decl *, llvm::Value *>(FP, Arg));
}
```

4.　Following this setup, we can call the `emit()` method to start generating the IR code for statements:

```
auto Block = Proc->getStmts();
emit(Proc->getStmts());
```

5.　The last block after generating the IR code may not yet be sealed, so we call `sealBlock()` now. A procedure in `tinylang` may have an implicit return, so we also check whether the last basic block has a proper terminator, and add one if not:

```
sealBlock(Curr);
if (!Curr->getTerminator()) {
  Builder.CreateRetVoid();
}
}
```

This finishes the generation of IR code for functions. We still need to create the LLVM module, which holds all the IR code together. We do this in the next section.

Setting up the module and the driver

We collect all functions and global variables of a compilation unit in an LLVM module. To facilitate IR generation, we wrap all the functions from the previous sections in a code generator class. To get a working compiler, we also need to define the target architecture for which we want to generate code, and also add the passes that emit the code. We implement all this in the next chapters, starting with the code generator.

Wrapping everything in the code generator

The IR module is the brace around all elements we generate for a compilation unit. At the global level, we iterate through the declarations at the module level and create global variables and call the code generation for procedures. A global variable in `tinylang` is mapped to an instance of the `llvm::GobalValue` class. This mapping is saved in `Globals` and made available to the code generation for procedures:

```
void CGModule::run(ModuleDeclaration *Mod) {
  for (auto *Decl : Mod->getDecls()) {
    if (auto *Var =
           llvm::dyn_cast<VariableDeclaration>(Decl)) {
      llvm::GlobalVariable *V = new llvm::GlobalVariable(
         *M, convertType(Var->getType()),
         /*isConstant=*/false,
         llvm::GlobalValue::PrivateLinkage, nullptr,
         mangleName(Var));
      Globals[Var] = V;
    } else if (auto *Proc =
                 llvm::dyn_cast<ProcedureDeclaration>(
                    Decl)) {
      CGProcedure CGP(*this);
      CGP.run(Proc);
    }
  }
}
```

The module also holds the `LLVMContext` class and caches the most commonly used LLVM types. The latter ones need to be initialized, for example, for the 64-bit integer type:

```
Int64Ty = llvm::Type::getInt64Ty(getLLVMCtx());
```

The `CodeGenerator` class initializes the LLVM IR module and calls the code generation for the module. Most importantly, this class must know for which target architecture we like to generate code. This information is passed in the `llvm::TargetMachine` class, which is set up in the driver:

```
void CodeGenerator::run(ModuleDeclaration *Mod, std::string
FileName) {
  llvm::Module *M = new llvm::Module(FileName, Ctx);
  M->setTargetTriple(TM->getTargetTriple().getTriple());
  M->setDataLayout(TM->createDataLayout());
  CGModule CGM(M);
  CGM.run(Mod);
}
```

For ease of use, we also introduce a factory method for the code generator:

```
CodeGenerator *CodeGenerator::create(llvm::TargetMachine *TM) {
  return new CodeGenerator(TM);
}
```

The `CodeGenerator` class provides a small interface to create IR code, which is ideal for use in the compiler driver. Before we integrate it, we need to implement support for machine code generation.

Initializing the target machine class

Now, only the creation of the target machine is missing. With the target machine, we define the CPU architecture for which we like to generate code. For each CPU, there are also features available that can be used to influence code generation. For example, a newer CPU of a CPU architecture family can support vector instructions. With features, we can toggle the use of vector instructions on or off. To support setting all these options from the command line, LLVM provides some supporting code. In the `Driver` class, we add the following `include` variable:

```
#include "llvm/CodeGen/CommandFlags.h"
```

This `include` variable adds common command-line options to our compiler driver. Many LLVM tools also use these command-line options, which have the benefit of providing a common interface to the user. Only the option to specify a target triple is missing. As this is very useful, we add this on our own:

```
static cl::opt<std::string>
    MTriple("mtriple",
            cl::desc("Override target triple for module"));
```

Let's create the **target** machine:

1. For the purpose of displaying error messages, the name of the application must be passed to the function:

    ```
    llvm::TargetMachine *
    createTargetMachine(const char *Argv0) {
    ```

2. We first collect all the information provided by the command line. These are options for the code generator, the name of the CPU, possible features that should be activated or deactivated, and the triple of the target:

    ```
    llvm::Triple = llvm::Triple(
        !MTriple.empty()
            ? llvm::Triple::normalize(MTriple)
            : llvm::sys::getDefaultTargetTriple());

    llvm::TargetOptions =
        codegen::InitTargetOptionsFromCodeGenFlags(Triple);
    std::string CPUStr = codegen::getCPUStr();
    std::string FeatureStr = codegen::getFeaturesStr();
    ```

3. Then we look up the target in the target registry. If an error occurs, then we display the error message and bail out. A possible error would be an unsupported triple specified by the user:

    ```
    std::string Error;
    const llvm::Target *Target =
        llvm::TargetRegistry::lookupTarget(
                        codegen::getMArch(), Triple,
                        Error);
    ```

```
  if (!Target) {
    llvm::WithColor::error(llvm::errs(), Argv0) <<
                         Error;
    return nullptr;
  }
```

4. With the help of the `Target` class, we configure the target machine using all the known options requested by the user:

```
llvm::TargetMachine *TM = Target->
  createTargetMachine(
    Triple.getTriple(), CPUStr, FeatureStr,
    TargetOptions,
    llvm::Optional<llvm::Reloc::Model>(
                      codegen::getRelocModel())));
  return TM;
}
```

With the target machine instance, we can generate IR code targeting a CPU architecture of our choice. What is missing is the translation to assembly text or the generation of object code files. We add this support in the next section.

Emitting assembler text and object code

In LLVM, the IR code is run through a pipeline of passes. Each pass performs a single task, for example, removing dead code. We will learn more about passes in *Chapter 8, Optimizing IR*. Outputting assembler code or an object file is implemented as a pass, too. Let's add basic support for it!

We need to include even more LLVM header files. We need the `llvm::legacy::PassManager` class for holding the passes to emit code to a file. We also want to be able to output LLVM IR code, so we also need a pass to emit this. And last, we use the `llvm::ToolOutputFile` class for file operations:

```
#include "llvm/IR/IRPrintingPasses.h"
#include "llvm/IR/LegacyPassManager.h"
#include "llvm/Support/ToolOutputFile.h"
```

Another command-line option for outputting LLVM IR is also required:

```
static cl::opt<bool>
    EmitLLVM("emit-llvm",
             cl::desc("Emit IR code instead of assembler"),
             cl::init(false));
```

The first task in the new `emit()` method is to deal with the name of the output file. If the input is read from `stdin`, indicated by the use of the minus symbol, `-`, then we output the result to `stdout`. The `ToolOutputFile` class knows how to handle the special filename, `-`:

```
bool emit(StringRef Argv0, llvm::Module *M,
          llvm::TargetMachine *TM,
          StringRef InputFilename) {
  CodeGenFileType FileType = codegen::getFileType();
  std::string OutputFilename;
  if (InputFilename == "-") {
    OutputFilename = "-";
  }
```

Otherwise, we drop a possible extension of the input filename and append `.ll`, `.s`, or `.o` as an extension, depending on the command-line options given by the user. The `FileType` option is defined in the `llvm/CodeGen/CommandFlags.inc` header file, which we included earlier. This option has no support for emitting IR code, and so we added the new option, `-emit-llvm`, which only takes effect if used together with the assembly file type:

```
  else {
    if (InputFilename.endswith(".mod"))
      OutputFilename = InputFilename.drop_back(4).str();
    else
      OutputFilename = InputFilename.str();
    switch (FileType) {
    case CGFT_AssemblyFile:
      OutputFilename.append(EmitLLVM ? ".ll" : ".s");
      break;
    case CGFT_ObjectFile:
      OutputFilename.append(".o");
```

```
      break;
   case CGFT_Null:
      OutputFilename.append(".null");
      break;
   }
}
```

Some platforms distinguish between text and binary files, and so we have to provide the right open flags when opening the output file:

```
std::error_code EC;
sys::fs::OpenFlags = sys::fs::OF_None;
if (FileType == CGFT_AssemblyFile)
   OpenFlags |= sys::fs::OF_Text;
auto Out = std::make_unique<llvm::ToolOutputFile>(
      OutputFilename, EC, OpenFlags);
if (EC) {
   WithColor::error(errs(), Argv0) << EC.message() <<
      '\n';
   return false;
}
```

Now we can add the required passes to `PassManager`. The `TargetMachine` class has a utility method, which adds the requested classes. Therefore, we only need to check whether the user requests to output LLVM IR code:

```
legacy::PassManager PM;
if (FileType == CGFT_AssemblyFile && EmitLLVM) {
   PM.add(createPrintModulePass(Out->os()));
} else {
   if (TM->addPassesToEmitFile(PM, Out->os(), nullptr,
                                 FileType)) {
      WithColor::error() << "No support for file type\n";
      return false;
   }
}
```

With all this preparation done, emitting the file boils down to a single function call:

```
PM.run(*M);
```

The `ToolOutputFile` class automatically deletes the file if we do not explicitly request that we want to keep it. This makes error handling easier, as there are potentially many places where we need to handle errors and only one place that is reached in case everything went well. We successfully emitted the code, so we want to keep the file:

```
Out->keep();
```

And finally, we report success to the caller:

```
    return true;
}
```

Calling the `emit()` method with the `llvm::Module` we created, with a call to the `CodeGenerator` class, emits the code as requested.

Suppose you have the greatest common divisor algorithm in `tinylang` stored in the `gcd.mod` file. To translate this to a `gcd.os` object file, you type the following:

```
$ tinylang -filetype=obj gcd.mod
```

If you would like to inspect the generated IR code directly on screen, then you can type the following:

```
$ tinylang -filetype=asm -emit-llvm -o - gcd.mod
```

Let's celebrate! At this point, we have created a complete compiler, from reading the source language up to emitting assembler code or an object file.

Summary

In this chapter, you learned how to implement your own code generator for LLVM IR code. Basic blocks are an important data structure, holding all the instructions and expressing branches. You learned how to create basic blocks for the control statements of the source language and how to add instructions to a basic block. You applied a modern algorithm to handle local variables in functions, leading to less IR code. The goal of a compiler is to generate assembler text or an object file for the input, so you also added a simple compilation pipeline. With this knowledge, you will be able to generate LLVM IR and, subsequently, assembler text or object code for your own language compiler.

In the next chapter, you will learn how to deal with aggregate data structures and how to ensure that function calls comply with the rules of your platform.

6

IR Generation for High-Level Language Constructs

High-level languages today usually make use of aggregate data types and **object-oriented programming** (**OOP**) constructs. **LLVM IR** has some support for aggregate data types, and we must implement OOP constructs such as classes on our own. Adding aggregate types gives rise to the question of how parameters of an aggregate type are passed. Different platforms have different rules, and this is also reflected in the IR. Being compliant with the calling convention ensures that system functions can be called.

In this chapter, you will learn how to translate aggregate data types and pointers to LLVM IR, and how to pass parameters to a function in a system-compliant way. You'll also learn how to implement classes and virtual functions in LLVM IR.

This chapter will cover the following topics:

- Working with arrays, structs, and pointers
- Getting the application binary interface right
- Creating IR code for classes and virtual functions

By the end of the chapter, you will have acquired the knowledge to create LLVM IR for aggregate data types and OOP. You will also know how to pass aggregate data types according to the rules of the platform.

Technical requirements

The code files for the chapter are available at `https://github.com/PacktPublishing/Learn-LLVM-12/tree/master/Chapter06/tinylang`

You can find the code in action videos at `https://bit.ly/3nllhED`

Working with arrays, structs, and pointers

For almost all applications, basic types such as `INTEGER` are not sufficient. For example, to represent mathematical objects such as a matrix or a complex number, you must construct new data types based on existing data types. These new data types are generally called **aggregate** or **composite types**.

Arrays are a sequence of elements of the same type. In LLVM, arrays are always static: the number of elements is constant. The `tinylang` type of `ARRAY [10] OF INTEGER`, or the C type of `long[10]`, is expressed in IR as follows:

```
[10 x i64]
```

Structures are composites of different types. In programming languages, they are often expressed with named members. For example, in `tinylang`, a structure is written as `RECORD x, y: REAL; color: INTEGER; END;` and the same structure in C is `struct { float x, y;  long color; };`. In LLVM IR, only the type names are listed:

```
{ float, float, i64 }
```

To access a member, a numerical index is used. Like arrays, the first element has the index number 0.

The members of this structure are laid out in memory according to the specification in the data layout string. If necessary, unused padding bytes are inserted. If you need to take control of the memory layout, then you can use a packed structure, in which all elements have a 1-byte alignment. The syntax is slightly different:

```
<{ float, float, i64 }>
```

Loaded into a register, arrays and structs are treated as a unit. It is not possible to refer to a single element of the %x array-valued register as %x[3], for example. This is due to the **SSA** form because it is not possible to tell whether %x[i] and %x[j] refer to the same element or not. Instead, we need special instructions to extract and insert single-element values into an array. To read the second element, we use the following:

```
%el2 = extractvalue [10 x i64] %x, 1
```

We can also update an element, for example, the first one:

```
%xnew = insertvalue [10 x i64] %x, i64 %el2, 0
```

Both instructions work on the structure, too. For example, to access the color member from the %pt register, you write the following:

```
%color = extractvalue { float, float, i64 } %pt, 2
```

There is an important limitation on both instructions: the index must be a constant. For structures, this is easily explainable. The index number is only a substitute for the name, and languages such as C have no notion of dynamically computing the name of a struct member. For arrays, it is simply that it can't be implemented efficiently. Both instructions have value in specific cases when the number of elements is small and known. For example, a complex number could be modeled as an array of two floating-point numbers. It's reasonable to pass this array around and it is always clear which part of the array must be accessed during a computation.

For general use in the frontend, we have to resort to pointers to memory. All global values in LLVM are expressed as pointers. Let's declare a global variable, @arr, as an array of eight i64 elements, the equivalent of the long arr[8] C declaration:

```
@arr = common global [8 x i64] zeroinitializer
```

To access the second element of the array, an address calculation must be performed to determine the address of the indexed element. Then, the value can then be loaded from that address. Put into a @second function, this looks like this:

```
define i64 @second() {
  %1 = getelementptr [8 x i64], [8 x i64]* @arr, i64 0, i64
      1
  %2 = load i64, i64* %1
  ret i64 %2
}
```

The getelementptr instruction is the workhorse for address calculations. As such, it needs some more explanation. The first operand, [8 x i64], is the base type the instruction is operating on. The second operand, [8 x i64]* @arr, specifies the base pointer. Please note the subtle difference here: we declared an array of eight elements, but because all global values are treated as pointers, we have a pointer to the array. In C syntax, we work with long (*arr) [8]! The consequence is that we first have to dereference the pointer before we can index the element, such as arr[0][1] in C. The third operand, i64 0, dereferences the pointer and the fourth operand, i64 1, is the element index. The result of this computation is the address of the indexed element. Please note that no memory is touched by this instruction.

Except for structs, the index parameters do not need to be constant. Therefore, the getelementptr instruction can be used in a loop to retrieve the elements of an array. Structs are treated differently here: only constants can be used, and the type must be i32.

With this knowledge, arrays are easily integrated into the code generator from *Chapter 5, Basics of IR Generation*. The convertType() method must be extended to create the type. If the Arr variable holds the type denoter of an array, then we can add the following to the method:

```
llvm::Type *Component = convertType(Arr->getComponentType());
uint64_t NumElements = Arr->getNumElem();
return llvm::ArrayType::get(Component, NumElements);
```

This type can be used to declare global variables. For local variables, we need to allocate memory for the array. We do this in the first basic block of the procedure:

```
for (auto *D : Proc->getDecls()) {
  if (auto *Var =
        llvm::dyn_cast<VariableDeclaration>(D)) {
    llvm::Type *Ty = mapType(Var);
    if (Ty->isAggregateType()) {
      llvm::Value *Val = Builder.CreateAlloca(Ty);
      Defs.Defs.insert(
        std::pair<Decl *, llvm::Value *>(Var, Val));
    }
  }
}
```

To read and write an element, we have to generate the `getelemtptr` instruction. This is added to the `emitExpr()` (reading a value) and `emitAssign()` (writing a value) methods. To read an element of an array, the value of the variable is read first. Then the selectors of the variable are processed. For each index, the expression is evaluated and the value is stored. Based on this list, the address of the referenced element is calculated and the value is loaded:

```
auto &Selectors = Var->getSelectorList();
for (auto *I = Selectors.begin(),
          *E = Selectors.end();
     I != E;) {
  if (auto *Idx = llvm::dyn_cast<IndexSelector>(*I)) {
    llvm::SmallVector<llvm::Value *, 4> IdxList;
    IdxList.push_back(emitExpr(Idx->getIndex()));
    for (++I; I != E;) {
      if (auto *Idx2 =
              llvm::dyn_cast<IndexSelector>(*I)) {
        IdxList.push_back(emitExpr(Idx2->getIndex()));
        ++I;
      } else
        break;
    }
    Val = Builder.CreateGEP(Val, IdxList);
    Val = Builder.CreateLoad(
        Val->getType()->getPointerElementType(), Val);
  } else {
    llvm::report_fatal_error("Unsupported selector");
  }
}
```

Writing to an array element uses the same code, with the exception that you do not generate a `load` instruction. Instead, you use the pointer as the target in a `store` instruction. For records, you use a similar approach. The selector for a record member contains the constant field index, named `Idx`. You convert this constant into a constant LLVM value with the following:

```
llvm::Value *FieldIdx = llvm::ConstantInt::get(Int32Ty, Idx);
```

Then, you can use value in the `Builder.CreateGEP()` methods as for arrays.

Now you have the knowledge to translate aggregate data types to LLVM IR. Passing values of those types in a system-compliant way requires some care, and you will learn how to implement it correctly in the next section.

Getting the application binary interface right

With the latest addition of arrays and records to the code generator, you may notice that sometimes the generated code does not execute as expected. The reason is that we have ignored the calling conventions of the platform so far. Each platform defines its own rules for how one function can call another function in the same program or a library. These rules are summarized in the **application binary interface** (**ABI**) documentation. Typical information includes the following:

- Are machine registers used for parameter passing? If yes, which?

- How are aggregates such as arrays and structs passed to a function?

- How are return values handled?

There is a wide variety of rules in use. On some platforms, aggregates are always passed indirectly, meaning that a copy of the aggregate is placed on the stack and only a pointer to the copy is passed as a parameter. On other platforms, a small aggregate (say 128- or 256-bit-wide) is passed in registers and only above that threshold is indirect parameter passing used. Some platforms also use floating-point and vector registers for parameter passing, while others demand that floating-point values are passed in integer registers.

Of course, this is all interesting, low-level stuff. Unfortunately, it leaks into LLVM IR. At first, this is surprising. After all, we define the types of all parameters of a function in LLVM IR! It turns out that this is not enough. To understand this, let's consider complex numbers. Some languages have built-in data types for complex numbers; for example, C99 has `float _Complex` (among others). Older versions of C do not have complex number types, but you can easily define `struct Complex { float re, im; }` and create arithmetic operations on this type. Both types can be mapped to the `{ float, float }` LLVM IR type. If the ABI now states that values of a built-in complex number type are passed in two floating-point registers, but user-defined aggregates are always passed indirectly, then the information given with the function is not enough for LLVM to decide how to pass this particular parameter. The unfortunate consequence is that we need to provide more information to LLVM, and this information is highly ABI-specific.

There are two ways to specify this information to LLVM: parameter attributes and type rewriting. What you need to use depends on the target platform and the code generator. The most commonly used parameter attributes are the following:

- `inreg` specifies that the parameter is passed in a register.
- `byval` specifies that the parameter is passed by value. The parameter must be a pointer type. A hidden copy is made of the pointed-to data and this pointer is passed to the called function.
- `zeroext` and `signext` specify that the passed integer value should be zero- or sign-extended.
- `sret` specifies that this parameter holds a pointer to memory that is used to return an aggregate type from the function.

While all code generators support the `zeroext`, `signext`, and `sret` attributes, only some support `inreg` and `byval`. An attribute can be added to the argument of a function with the `addAttr()` method. For example, to set the `inreg` attribute on the `Arg` argument, you call the following:

```
Arg->addAttr(llvm::Attribute::InReg);
```

To set multiple attributes, you can use the `llvm::AttrBuilder` class.

The other way to provide additional information is to use type rewriting. With this approach, you disguise the original types. You can do the following:

- Split the parameter; for example, instead of passing one complex argument, you can pass two floating-point arguments.
- Cast the parameter into a different representation, for example, a struct of size 64 bits or less into an `i64` integer.

To cast between types without changing the bits of the value, you use the `bitcast` instruction. The `bitcast` instruction does not operate on aggregate types, but this is not a restriction as you can always use pointers. If a point is modeled as a struct with two `int` members, expressed as type `{ i32, i32 }` in LLVM, then this can be `bitcast` to `i64` in the following way:

```
%intpoint = bitcast { i32, i32}* %point to i64*
```

This converts the pointer to the struct into a pointer to an `i64` integer value. Subsequently, you can load this value and pass it as a parameter. You must only make sure that both types have the same size.

Adding attributes to an argument or changing the type is not complicated. But how do you know what you need to implement? First of all, you should get an overview of the calling convention used on your target platform. For example, the ELF ABI on Linux is documented for each supported CPU platform. Just look up the document and make yourself comfortable with it. There is documentation about the requirements of the LLVM code generators. The source of information is the Clang implementation, in the `https://github.com/llvm/llvm-project/blob/main/clang/lib/CodeGen/TargetInfo.cpp` file. This single file contains the ABI-specific actions for all supported platforms. It is also the single place where all information is collected.

In this section, you learned how to generate the IR for function calls to be compliant with the ABI of your platform. The next section covers the different ways to create IR for classes and virtual functions.

Creating IR code for classes and virtual functions

Many modern programming languages support object orientation using classes. A **class** is a high-level language construct, and in this section, we explore how we can map a class construct into LLVM IR.

Implementing single inheritance

A class is a collection of data and methods. A class can inherit from another class, potentially adding more data fields and methods or overriding existing virtual methods. Let's illustrate this with classes in Oberon-2, which is also a good model for `tinylang`. A `Shape` class defines an abstract shape with a color and an area:

```
TYPE Shape = RECORD
             color: INTEGER;
             PROCEDURE (VAR s: Shape) GetColor():
                 INTEGER;
             PROCEDURE (VAR s: Shape) Area(): REAL;
        END;
```

The `GetColor` method only returns the color number:

```
PROCEDURE (VAR s: Shape) GetColor(): INTEGER;
BEGIN RETURN s.color; END GetColor;
```

The area of an abstract shape cannot be calculated, so this is an abstract method:

```
PROCEDURE (VAR s: Shape) Area(): REAL;
BEGIN HALT; END;
```

The `Shape` type can be extended to represent a `Circle` class:

```
TYPE Circle = RECORD (Shape)
                radius: REAL;
                PROCEDURE (VAR s: Circle) Area(): REAL;
            END;
```

For a circle, the area can be calculated:

```
PROCEDURE (VAR s: Circle) Area(): REAL;
BEGIN RETURN 2 * radius * radius; END;
```

The type can also be queried at runtime. If `shape` is a variable of the `Shape` type, then we can formulate a type test in this way:

```
IF shape IS Circle THEN (* … *) END;
```

The different syntax aside, this works much like in C++. One notable difference to C++ is that the Oberon-2 syntax makes the implicit `this` pointer explicit, calling it the receiver of a method.

The basic problems to solve are how to lay out a class in memory and how to implement the dynamic call of methods and runtime type checking. For the memory layout, this is quite easy. The `Shape` class has only one data member, and we can map it to a corresponding LLVM structure type:

```
@Shape = type { i64 }
```

The `Circle` class adds another data member. The solution is to append the new data member at the end:

```
@Circle = type { i64, float }
```

The reason is that a class can have many subclasses. With this strategy, the data member of the common base class always has the same memory offset and also uses the same index to access the field via the `getelementptr` instruction.

To implement a dynamic call of a method, we must further extend the LLVM structure. If the Area() function is called on a Shape object, then the abstract method is called, causing the application to halt. If it is called on a Circle object, then the corresponding method to calculate the area of a circle is called. The GetColor() function can be called for objects of both classes. The basic idea to implement this is to associate a table with function pointers with each object. Here, the table would have two entries: one for the GetColor() method and one for the Area() function. The Shape class and the Circle class each have such a table. The tables differ in the entry for the Area() function, which calls different code depending on the type of the object. This table is called the **virtual method table**, often abbreviated as the **vtable**.

The vtable alone is not useful. We must connect it with an object. To do so, we add a pointer to the vtable always as the first data member to the structure. At the LLVM level, the @Shape type then becomes the following:

```
@Shape = type { [2 x i8*]*, i64 }
```

The @Circle type is similarly extended. The resulting memory structure is shown in *Figure 6.1*:

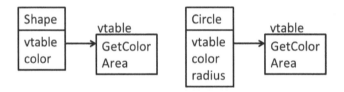

Figure 6.1 – Memory layout of the classes and the virtual method tables

LLVM does not have void pointers and pointers to bytes are used instead. With the introduction of the hidden vtable field, there is now also the need to have a way to initialize it. In C++, this is part of calling the constructor. In Oberon-2, the field is initialized automatically when the memory is allocated.

A dynamic call to a method is then executed with the following steps:

1. Calculate the offset of the vtable pointer via the getelementptr instruction.
2. Load the pointer to the vtable.
3. Calculate the offset of the function in the vtable.
4. Load the function pointer.
5. Indirectly call the function via the pointer with the call instruction.

This does not sound very efficient, but in fact, most CPU architectures can perform this dynamic call in just two instructions. So, it is really the LLVM level that is verbose.

To turn a function into a method, a reference to the object's data is required. This is implemented by passing the pointer to the data as the first parameter of the method. In Oberon-2, this is the explicit receiver. In languages similar to C++, it is the implicit this pointer.

With the vtable, we have a unique address in memory for each class. Does this help with the runtime type test, too? The answer is that it helps only in a limited way. To illustrate the problem, let's extend the class hierarchy with an Ellipse class, which inherits from the Circle class. (This is not the classical *is-a* relationship in the mathematical sense.) If we have the shape variable of the Shape type, then we could implement the shape IS Circle type test as a comparison of the vtable pointer stored in the shape variable with the vtable pointer of the Circle class. This comparison only results in true if shape has the exact Circle type. But if shape is indeed of the Ellipse type, then the comparison returns false, even if an object of the Ellipse type can be used in all places where only an object of the Circle type is required.

Clearly, we need to do more. The solution is to extend the virtual method table with runtime type information. How much information you need to store depends on the source language. To support the runtime type check, it is enough to store a pointer to the vtable of the base class, which then looks as in *Figure 6.2*:

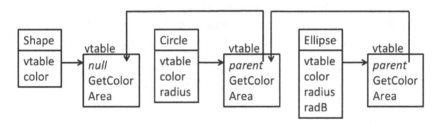

Figure 6.2 – Class and vtable layout supporting simple type tests

If the test fails as described earlier, then the test is repeated with the pointer to the vtable of the base class. This is repeated until the test yields true or, if there is no base class, false. In contrast to calling a dynamic function, the type test is a costly operation, because in the worst case, the inheritance hierarchy is walked up to the root class.

If you know the whole class hierarchy, then an efficient approach is possible: you number each member of the class hierarchy in depth-first order. Then, the type test becomes a comparison against a number or an interval, which can be done in constant time. In fact, that is the approach of LLVM's own runtime type test, which we learned about in the previous chapter.

Coupling runtime type information with the vtable is a design decision, either mandated by the source language or just an implementation detail. For example, if you need detailed runtime type information, because the source language supports reflection at runtime, and you have data types without a vtable, then coupling both is not a good idea. In C++, the coupling results in the fact that a class with virtual functions (and therefore no vtable) has no runtime type data attached to it.

Often, programming languages support interfaces, which are a collection of virtual methods. Interfaces are important because they add a useful abstraction. We will look at possible implementations of interfaces in the next section.

Extending single inheritance with interfaces

Languages such as **Java** support interfaces. An interface is a collection of abstract methods, comparable to a base class with no data members and only abstract methods defined. Interfaces pose an interesting problem because each class implementing an interface can have the corresponding method at a different position in the vtable. The reason is simply that the order of function pointers in the vtable is derived from the order of the functions in the class definition in the source language. The definition in the interface is independent of this, and different orders are the norm.

Because the methods defined in an interface can have a different order, we attach a table for each implemented interface to the class. For each method of the interface, this table can specify either the index of the method in the vtable or can be a copy of the function pointer stored in the vtable. If a method is called on the interface, then the corresponding vtable of the interface is searched, then the pointer to the function is fetched and the method is called. Adding two interfaces, I1 and I2, to the Shape class results in the following layout:

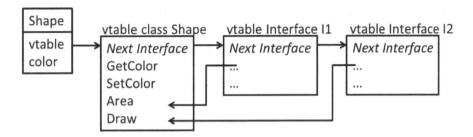

Figure 6.3 – Layout of vtables for interfaces

The caveat lies in the fact that we have to find the right vtable. We can use an approach similar to the *runtime type test*: we can perform a linear search through the list of interface vtables. We can assign a unique number to each interface (for example, a memory address) and identify the vtable using this number. The disadvantage of this scheme is obvious: calling a method through an interface takes much more time than calling the same method on the class. There is no easy mitigation for this problem.

A good approach is to replace the linear search with a hash table. At compile time, the interface that a class implements is known. Therefore, we can construct a perfect hash function, which maps the interface number to the vtable for the interface. A known unique number identifying an interface may be needed for the construction, so memory does not help. But there are other ways to compute a unique number. If the symbol names in the source are unique, then it is always possible to compute a cryptographic hash such as the MD5 of the symbol and use the hash as the number. The calculation occurs at compile time and therefore has no runtime cost.

The result is much faster than the linear search and only takes constant time. Still, it involves several arithmetic operations on a number and is slower than the method call of a class type.

Usually, interfaces also take part in runtime type tests, making the list to search even longer. Of course, if the hash table approach is implemented, then it can also be used for the runtime type test.

Some languages allow more than one parent class. This has some interesting challenges for the implementation, and we master this in the next section.

Adding support for multiple inheritance

Multiple inheritance adds another challenge. If a class inherits from two or more base classes, then we need to combine the data members in such a way that they are still accessible from the methods. Like in the single inheritance case, the solution is to append all data members, including the hidden vtable pointers. The Circle class is not only a geometric shape but also a graphic object. To model this, we let the Circle class inherit from the Shape class and the GraphicObj class. In the class layout, the fields from the Shape class come first. Then, we append all fields of the GraphicObj class, including the hidden vtable pointer. After that, we add the new data members of the Circle class, resulting in the overall structure shown in *Figure 6.4*:

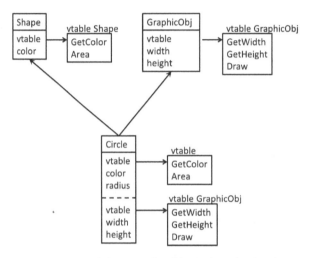

Figure 6.4 – Layout of classes and vtables with multiple inheritance

This approach has several implications. There can now be several pointers to the object. A pointer to the Shape or Circle class points to the top of the object, while a pointer to a GraphicObj class points to inside this object, to the beginning of the embedded GraphicObj object. This has to be taken into account when comparing pointers.

Calling a virtual method is also affected. If a method is defined in the GraphicObj class, then this method expects the class layout of the GraphicObj class. If this method is not overridden in the Circle class, then there are two possibilities. The easy case is if the method call is done with a pointer to a GraphicObj instance: in this case, you look up the address of the method in the vtable of the GraphicObj class and call the function. The more complicated case is if you call the method with a pointer to the Circle class. Again, you can look up the address of the method in the vtable of the Circle class. The called method expects a this pointer to an instance of the GraphicObj class, so we have to adjust that pointer, too. We can do this because we know the offset of the GraphicObj class inside the Circle class.

If a method of GrapicObj is overridden in the Circle class, then nothing special needs to be done if the method is called through a pointer to the Circle class. However, if the method is called through a pointer to a GraphicObj instance, then we need to make another adjustment because the method needs a this pointer pointing to a Circle instance. At compile time, we cannot compute this adjustment, because we do not know whether this GraphicObj instance is part of a multiple inheritance hierarchy or not. To solve this, we store the adjustment we need to make to the this pointer before calling the method together with each function pointer in the vtable, as in *Figure 6.5*:

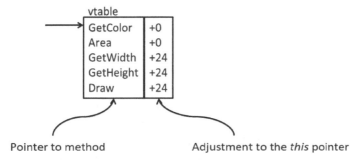

Figure 6.5 – vtable with adjustments to the this pointer

The method call now becomes the following:

1. Look up the function pointer in the vtable.

2. Adjust the this pointer.

3. Call the method.

This approach can also be used for implementing interfaces. Because an interface has only methods, each implemented interface adds a new vtable pointer to the object. This is easier to implement and most likely faster, but it adds overhead to each object instance. In the worst case, if your class has a single 64-bit data field but implements 10 interfaces, then your object requires 96 bytes in memory: 8 bytes for the vtable pointer of the class itself, 8 bytes for the data member, and 10 * 8 bytes for the vtable pointers of each interface.

To support meaningful comparisons to objects and to perform runtime type tests, it is needed to normalize a pointer to an object first. If we add an additional field to the vtable, containing an offset at the top of the object, then we can always adjust the pointer to point to the real object. In the vtable of the Circle class, this offset is 0, but not in the vtable of the embedded GraphicObj class. Of course, whether this needs to be implemented depends on the semantics of the source language.

LLVM itself does not favor a special implementation of object-oriented features. As seen in this section, we can implement all approaches with the available LLVM data types. If you want to try a new approach, then a good way is to do a prototype in C first. The required pointer manipulations are quickly translated to LLVM IR, but reasoning about the functionality is easier in a higher-level language.

With the knowledge acquired in this section, you can implement the lowering of all OOP constructs commonly found in programming languages into LLVM IR in your own code generator. You have recipes on how to represent single inheritance, single inheritance with an interface, or multiple inheritance in memory, and also how to implement type tests and how to look up virtual functions, which are the core concepts of OOP languages.

Summary

In this chapter, you learned how to translate aggregate data types and pointers to LLVM IR code. You also learned about the intricacies of the ABI. Finally, you learned about the different approaches to translating classes and virtual functions to LLVM IR. With the knowledge of this chapter, you will be able to create an LLVM IR code generator for most real programming languages.

In the next chapter, you will learn about some advanced techniques. Exception handling is fairly common in modern programming languages, and LLVM has some support for it. Attaching type information to pointers can help with certain optimizations, so we will add this, too. Last but not least, the ability to debug an application is essential for many developers, so we will add the generation of debug metadata to our code generator.

7

Advanced IR Generation

With the **intermediate representation** (**IR**) generation introduced in the previous chapters, you can already implement most of the functionality required in a compiler. In this chapter, we will look at some advanced topics that often arise in terms of real-world compilers. For example, many modern languages make use of exception handling, and we look at how to translate this to **low-level virtual machine** (**LLVM**) IR.

To support the LLVM optimizer in producing better code in certain situations, we add additional type metadata to the IR code, and attaching debug metadata enables the compiler's user to take advantage of source-level debug tools.

In this chapter, you will learn about the following topics:

- In *Throwing and catching exceptions*, you will learn how to implement exception handling in your compiler.

- In *Generating metadata for type-based alias analysis*, you attach additional metadata to LLVM IR, which helps LLVM to better optimize the code.

- In *Adding debug metadata*, you implement the support classes needed to add debug information to the generated IR code.

By the end of the chapter, you will acquire knowledge about exception handling and about metadata for type-based alias analysis and debug information.

Technical requirements

The code files for this chapter is available at `https://github.com/PacktPublishing/Learn-LLVM-12/tree/master/Chapter07`

You can find the code in action videos at `https://bit.ly/3nllhED`.

Throwing and catching exceptions

Exception handling in LLVM IR is closely tied to the platform's support. Here, we will look at the most common type of exception handling using `libunwind`. Its full potential is used by C++, so we will look at an example in C++ first, where the `bar()` function can throw an `int` or a `double` value, as follows:

```
int bar(int x) {
    if (x == 1) throw 1;
    if (x == 2) throw 42.0;
    return x;
}
```

The `foo()` function calls `bar()`, but only handles a thrown `int` value. It also declares that it only throws `int` values, as follows:

```
int foo(int x) throw(int) {
    int y = 0;
    try {
        y = bar(x);
    }
    catch (int e) {
        y = e;
    }
    return y;
}
```

Throwing an exception requires two calls into the runtime library. First, memory for the exception is allocated with a call to __cxa_allocate_exception(). This function takes the number of bytes to allocate as a parameter. The exception payload (the int or the double value in the example) is copied to the allocated memory. The exception is then raised with a call to __cxa_throw(). This function takes three arguments: a pointer to the allocated exception; type information about the payload; and a pointer to a destructor, if the exception payload has one. The __cxa_throw() function initiates the stack-unwinding process and never returns. In LLVM IR, this is done for the int value, as follows:

```
%eh = tail call i8* @__cxa_allocate_exception(i64 4)
%payload = bitcast i8* %eh to i32*
store i32 1, i32* %payload
tail call void @__cxa_throw(i8* %eh,
                    i8* bitcast (i8** @_ZTIi to i8*), i8*
                  null)
unreachable
```

_ZTIi is the type information describing an int type. For a double type, it would be _ZTId. The call to __cxa_throw() is marked as a tail call because it is the final call in this function, possibly enabling reuse of the current stack frame.

So far, nothing LLVM-specific has been done. This changes in the foo() function, because the call to bar() could possibly raise an exception. If it is an int-type exception, then the control flow must be transferred to the IR code of the catch clause. To accomplish this, an invoke instruction must be used instead of a call instruction, as illustrated in the following code snippet:

```
%y = invoke i32 @_Z3bari(i32 %x) to label %next
                            unwind label %lpad
```

The difference between both instructions is that invoke has two labels associated. The first label is where execution continues if the called function ended normally, usually with a ret instruction. In the preceding code example, this label is called %next. If an exception occurs, then execution continues at a so-called *landing pad*, with a %lpad label.

The landing pad is a basic block that must begin with a landingpad instruction. The landingpad instruction gives LLVM information about the handled exception types. For the foo() functions, it gives the following information:

```
lpad:
%exc = landingpad { i8*, i32 }
        cleanup
        catch i8* bitcast (i8** @_ZTIi to i8*)
        filter [1 x i8*] [i8* bitcast (i8** @_ZTIi to
            i8*)]
```

There are three possible types of action here, outlined as follows:

- cleanup: This denotes that code to clean up the current state is present. Usually, this is used to call destructors of local objects. If this marker is present, then the landing pad is always called during stack unwinding.

- catch: This is a list of type-value pairs and denotes the exception types that can be handled. The landing pad is called if the thrown exception type is found in this list. In the case of the foo() function, the value is a pointer to the C++ runtime type information for the int type, similar to the parameter of the __cxa_throw() function.

- filter: This specifies an array of exception types. The landing pad is called if the exception type of the current exception is not found in the array. This is used to implement the throw() specification. For the foo() function, the array has only one member—the type information for the int type.

The result type of the landingpad instruction is a { i8*, i32 } structure. The first element is a pointer to the thrown exception, while the second element is a type selector. Let's extract both elements from the structure, as follows:

```
%exc.ptr = extractvalue { i8*, i32 } %exc, 0
%exc.sel = extractvalue { i8*, i32 } %exc, 1
```

A *type selector* is a number that helps us to identify the cause of *why the landing pad is called*. It has a positive value if the current exception type matches one of the exception types given in the `catch` part of the `landingpad` instruction. If the current exception type does not match any of the values given in the `filter` part, then the value is negative, and it is 0 if the cleanup code should be called.

Basically, the type selector is offset into a type information table, constructed from the values given in the `catch` and `filter` parts of the `landingpad` instruction. During optimization, multiple landing pads can be combined into one, which means that the structure of this table is not known at the IR level. To retrieve the type selector for a given type, we need to call the `@llvm.eh.typeid.for` intrinsic function. We need this to check if the type selector value corresponds to the type information for `int`, to be able to execute the code in the `catch (int e) {}` block, as follows:

```
%tid.int = tail call i32 @llvm.eh.typeid.for(
                        i8* bitcast (i8** @_ZTIi to
                        i8*))
%tst.int = icmp eq i32 %exc.sel, %tid.int
 br i1 % tst.int, label %catchint, label %filterorcleanup
```

The handing of an exception is framed by calls to `__cxa_begin_catch()` and `__cxa_end_catch()`. The `__cxa_begin_catch()` function needs one argument: the current exception. That is one of the values returned by the `landingpad` instruction. It returns a pointer to the exception payload—an `int` value, in our case. The `__cxa_end_catch()` function marks the end of exception handling and deallocates the memory allocated with `__cxa_allocate_exception()`. Please note that the runtime behavior is much more complicated if another exception is thrown inside the `catch` block. The handling of the exception is done like this:

```
catchint:
%payload = tail call i8* @__cxa_begin_catch(i8* %exc.ptr)
%payload.int = bitcast i8* %payload to i32*
%retval = load i32, i32* %payload.int
tail call void @__cxa_end_catch()
br label %return
```

If the type of the current exception does not match the list in the throws() declaration, the unexpected exception handler is called. First, we need to check the type selector again, as follows:

```
filterorcleanup:
%tst.blzero = icmp slt i32 %exc.sel, 0
br i1 %tst.blzero, label %filter, label %cleanup
```

If the value of the type selector is lower than 0 we then call the handler, as follows:

```
filter:
tail call void @__cxa_call_unexpected(i8* %exc.ptr) #4
unreachable
```

Again, the handler is not expected to come back.

There is no cleanup work needed in this case, so all the cleanup code does is resume the execution of the stack unwinder, as follows:

```
cleanup:
resume { i8*, i32 } %exc
```

One piece is still missing: libunwind drives the stack unwinding, but it is not tied to a single language. Language-dependent handling is done in the personality function. For C++ on Linux, the personality function is called __gxx_personality_v0(). Depending on the platform or compiler, this name can vary. Each function that needs to take part in stack unwinding has a personality function attached. The personality function analyzes if the function catches an exception, has a non-matching filter list, or needs a cleanup call. It gives this information back to the unwinder, which acts accordingly. In LLVM IR, the pointer to the personality function is given as part of the function definition, as illustrated in the following code snippet:

```
define i32 @_Z3fooi(i32) personality i8* bitcast
                    (i32 (...)* @__gxx_personality_v0 to
                 i8*)
```

With this, the exception-handling facility is complete.

To use exception handling in the compiler for your programming language, the simplest strategy is to piggyback onto the existing C++ runtime functions. This has also the advantage that your exceptions are interoperable with C++. A disadvantage is that you tie some of the C++ runtime into the runtime of your language—most notably, memory management. If you want to avoid this, then you need to create your own equivalents of the _cxa_ functions. Still, you will want to use libunwind, which provides the stack-unwinding mechanism.

1. Let's look at how to create this IR. We created the calc expression compiler in *Chapter 3, The Structure of a Compiler*. We will now extend the code generator of the expression compiler to raise and handle an exception if a division by 0 is performed. The generated IR will check if the divisor of a division is 0. If true, then an exception will be raised. We will also add a landing pad to the function, which catches the exception, prints Divide by zero! to the console, and ends the calculation. Using exception handling is not really necessary in this simple case, but it allows us to concentrate on the code generation. We add all code to the CodeGenerator.cpp file. We begin by adding required new fields and some helper methods. We need to store the LLVM declaration of the __cxa_allocate_exception() and __cxa_throw() functions, consisting of the function type and the function itself. A GlobalVariable instance is needed to hold the type information. We also need references to the basic blocks holding the landing pad and a basic block containing just an unreachable instruction, as illustrated in the following code snippet:

```
GlobalVariable *TypeInfo = nullptr;
FunctionType *AllocEHFty = nullptr;
Function *AllocEHFn = nullptr;
FunctionType *ThrowEHFty = nullptr;
Function *ThrowEHFn = nullptr;
BasicBlock *LPadBB = nullptr;
BasicBlock *UnreachableBB = nullptr;
```

2. We also add a new helper function to create the IR for comparing two values. The createICmpEq() function takes the Left and Right value to compare as parameters. It creates a compare instruction, testing for equality of the values, and a branch instruction to two basic blocks, for the equal and unequal cases. The two basic blocks are returned via references in the TrueDest and FalseDest parameters. A label for the new basic blocks can be given in the TrueLabel and FalseLabel parameters. The code is shown in the following snippet:

```
void createICmpEq(Value *Left, Value *Right,
                  BasicBlock *&TrueDest,
```

```
                              BasicBlock *&FalseDest,
                          const Twine &TrueLabel = "",
                          const Twine &FalseLabel = "") {
    Function *Fn =
        Builder.GetInsertBlock()->getParent();
    TrueDest = BasicBlock::Create(M->getContext(),
                                  TrueLabel, Fn);
    FalseDest = BasicBlock::Create(M->getContext(),
                                   FalseLabel, Fn);
    Value *Cmp = Builder.CreateCmp(CmpInst::ICMP_EQ,
                                   Left, Right);
    Builder.CreateCondBr(Cmp, TrueDest, FalseDest);
}
```

3. To use the functions from the runtime, we need to create several function declarations. In LLVM, a function type giving the signature—as well as the function itself—must be constructed. We use the `createFunc()` method to create both objects. The functions need references to `FunctionType` and `Function` pointers, the name of the newly declared function, and the result type. The parameter-type list is optional, and the flag to indicate a variable parameter list is set to `false`, indicating that there is no variable part in the parameter list. The code can be seen in the following snippet:

```
void createFunc(FunctionType *&Fty, Function *&Fn,
                const Twine &N, Type *Result,
                ArrayRef<Type *> Params = None,
                bool IsVarArgs = false) {
    Fty = FunctionType::get(Result, Params, IsVarArgs);
    Fn = Function::Create(
        Fty, GlobalValue::ExternalLinkage, N, M);
}
```

With these preparations done, we continue to generate the IR to raise an exception.

Raising an exception

To generate the IR code to raise an exception, we add an `addThrow()` method. This new method needs to initialize the new fields, and then generates the IR to raise an exception via the `__cxa_throw` function. The payload of the raised exception is of an `int` type and can be set to an arbitrary value. Here is what we need to code:

1. The new `addThrow()` method begins with checking if the `TypeInfo` field has been initialized. If not, then a global external constant of an `i8*` type and a `_ZTIi` name is created. This represents the C++ metadata describing the C++ `int` type. The code is illustrated in the following snippet:

```
void addThrow(int PayloadVal) {
    if (!TypeInfo) {
        TypeInfo = new GlobalVariable(
            *M, Int8PtrTy,
            /*isConstant=*/true,
            GlobalValue::ExternalLinkage,
            /*Initializer=*/nullptr, "_ZTIi");
```

2. The initialization continues with creating the IR declaration for `__cxa_allocate_exception()` and `__cxa_throw functions()` using our `createFunc()` helper method, as follows:

```
createFunc(AllocEHFty, AllocEHFn,
            "__cxa_allocate_exception",
            Int8PtrTy,
            {Int64Ty});
createFunc(ThrowEHFty, ThrowEHFn, "__cxa_throw",
            VoidTy,
            {Int8PtrTy, Int8PtrTy, Int8PtrTy});
```

3. A function using exception handling needs a `personality` function, which helps with the stack unwinding. We add the IR code to declare a `__gxx_personality_v0()` personality function from the C++ library, and set it as the `personality` routine of the current function. The current function is not stored as a field but we can use a `Builder` instance to query the current basic block, which has the function stored as a `parent` field, as illustrated in the following code snippet:

```
FunctionType *PersFty;
Function *PersFn;
```

```
createFunc(PersFty, PersFn,
           "__gxx_personality_v0", Int32Ty, None,
           true);
Function *Fn =
    Builder.GetInsertBlock()->getParent();
Fn->setPersonalityFn(PersFn);
```

4. Next, we create and populate the basic block for the landing pad. First, we need to save the pointer to the current basic block. Then, we create a new basic block, set it inside the builder to use as the basic block to insert instructions, and call the `addLandingPad()` method. This method generates the IR code for handling an exception and is described in the next section, *Catching an exception*. The following code populates the basic block for the landing pad:

```
BasicBlock *SaveBB = Builder.GetInsertBlock();
LPadBB = BasicBlock::Create(M->getContext(),
                            "lpad", Fn);
Builder.SetInsertPoint(LPadBB);
addLandingPad();
```

5. The initialization part has finished with creating the basic block holding an `unreachable` instruction. Again, we create a basic block and set it as an insertion point at the builder. Then, we add an `unreachable` instruction to it. Lastly, we set the insertion point of the builder back to the saved `SaveBB` instance so that the following IR is added to the right basic block. The code is illustrated in the following snippet:

```
UnreachableBB = BasicBlock::Create(
    M->getContext(), "unreachable", Fn);
Builder.SetInsertPoint(UnreachableBB);
Builder.CreateUnreachable();
Builder.SetInsertPoint(SaveBB);
}
```

6. To raise an exception, we need to allocate memory for the exception and the payload via a call to the `__cxa_allocate_exception()` function. Our payload is of a C++ `int` type, which usually has a size of 4 bytes. We create a constant unsigned value for the size, and call the function with it as a parameter. The function type and the function declaration are already initialized, so we only need to create a `call` instruction, as follows:

```
Constant *PayloadSz =
    ConstantInt::get(Int64Ty, 4, false);
CallInst *EH = Builder.CreateCall(
    AllocEHFty, AllocEHFn, {PayloadSz});
```

7. Next, we store the `PayloadVal` value into the allocated memory. To do so, we need to create an LLVM IR constant with a call to the `ConstantInt::get()` function. The pointer to the allocated memory is of an `i8*` type, but to store a value of an `i32` type we need to create a `bitcast` instruction to cast the type, as follows:

```
Value *PayloadPtr =
    Builder.CreateBitCast(EH, Int32PtrTy);
Builder.CreateStore(
    ConstantInt::get(Int32Ty, PayloadVal, true),
    PayloadPtr);
```

8. Finally, we raise an exception with a call to the `__cxa_throw` function. Because this function actually raises an exception that is also handled in the same function, we need to use an `invoke` instruction instead of a `call` instruction. Unlike with a `call` instruction, an `invoke` instruction ends a basic block because it has two successor basic blocks. Here, these are the `UnreachableBB` and `LPadBB` basic blocks. If the function raises no exception, the control flow is transferred to the `UnreachableBB` basic block. Due to the design of the `__cxa_throw()` function, this will never happen. The control flow is transferred to the `LPadBB` basic block to handle the exception. This finishes the implementation of the `addThrow()` method, as illustrated in the following code snippet:

```
Builder.CreateInvoke(
    ThrowEHFty, ThrowEHFn, UnreachableBB, LPadBB,
    {EH, ConstantExpr::getBitCast(TypeInfo,
        Int8PtrTy),
    ConstantPointerNull::get(Int8PtrTy)});
}
```

Next, we add the code to generate the IR for handling an exception.

Catching an exception

To generate the IR code to catch an exception, we add an addLandingPad() method. The generated IR extracts the type information from the exception. If it matches the C++ int type, then the exception is handled by printing Divide by zero! to the console and returning from the function. If the type does not match, we simply execute a resume instruction, which transfers control back to the runtime. Because there are no other functions in the call hierarchy to handle this exception, the runtime will terminate the application. These are the steps we need to take to generate the IR to catch an exception:

1. In the generated IR, we need to call the __cxa_begin_catch() and _cxa_end_catch() functions from the C++ runtime library. To print an error message, we will generate a call to the puts() function from the C runtime library, and to get the type information from the exception, we must generate a call to the llvm.eh.typeid.for instrinsic. We need FunctionType and Function instances for all of them, and we take advantage of our createFunc() method to create them, as follows:

```
void addLandingPad() {
  FunctionType *TypeIdFty; Function *TypeIdFn;
  createFunc(TypeIdFty, TypeIdFn,
             "llvm.eh.typeid.for", Int32Ty,
             {Int8PtrTy});
  FunctionType *BeginCatchFty; Function
      *BeginCatchFn;
  createFunc(BeginCatchFty, BeginCatchFn,
             "__cxa_begin_catch", Int8PtrTy,
             {Int8PtrTy});
  FunctionType *EndCatchFty; Function *EndCatchFn;
  createFunc(EndCatchFty, EndCatchFn,
             "__cxa_end_catch", VoidTy);
  FunctionType *PutsFty; Function *PutsFn;
  createFunc(PutsFty, PutsFn, "puts", Int32Ty,
             {Int8PtrTy});
```

2. The `landingpad` instruction is the first instruction we generate. The result type is a structure containing fields of `i8*` and `i32` types. This structure is generated with a call to the `StructType::get()` function. We handle an exception of a C++ `int` type, and we must add this as a clause to the `landingpad` instruction. The clause must be a constant of the `i8*` type, therefore we need to generate a `bitcast` instruction to convert the `TypeInfo` value to this type. We store the value returned from the instruction for later use in an `Exc` variable, as follows:

```
LandingPadInst *Exc = Builder.CreateLandingPad(
        StructType::get(Int8PtrTy, Int32Ty), 1, "exc");
Exc->addClause(ConstantExpr::getBitCast(TypeInfo,
                Int8PtrTy));
```

3. Next, we extract the type selector from the returned value. With a call to the `llvm.eh.typeid.for` intrinsic, we retrieve the type ID for the `TypeInfo` field, representing the C++ `int` type. With this IR, we now have generated the two values we need to compare to decide if we can handle the exception, as illustrated in the following code snippet:

```
Value *Sel = Builder.CreateExtractValue(Exc, {1},
                "exc.sel");
CallInst *Id =
        Builder.CreateCall(TypeIdFty, TypeIdFn,
                        {ConstantExpr::getBitCast(
                          TypeInfo, Int8PtrTy)});
```

4. To generate the IR for the comparison, we call our `createICmpEq()` function. This function also generates two basic blocks, which we store in the `TrueDest` and `FalseDest` variables, as illustrated in the following code snippet:

```
BasicBlock *TrueDest, *FalseDest;
createICmpEq(Sel, Id, TrueDest, FalseDest,
            "match",
            "resume");
```

5. If the two values do not match, the control flow continues at the `FalseDest` basic
    block. This basic block only contains a `resume` instruction, to give control back to
    the C++ runtime. This is illustrated in the following code snippet:

    ```
    Builder.SetInsertPoint(FalseDest);
    Builder.CreateResume(Exc);
    ```

6. If the two values are equal, the control flow continues at the `TrueDest` basic
    block. We first generate the IR code to extract the pointer to the exception from the
    return value of the `landingpad` instruction, stored in the `Exc` variable. Then, we
    generate a call to the `__cxa_begin_catch ()` function, passing the pointer to
    the exception as a parameter. This indicates the start of the exception being handled
    to the runtime, as illustrated in the following code snippet:

    ```
    Builder.SetInsertPoint(TrueDest);
    Value *Ptr =
        Builder.CreateExtractValue(Exc, {0},
            "exc.ptr");
    Builder.CreateCall(BeginCatchFty, BeginCatchFn,
                       {Ptr});
    ```

7. We handle the exception by calling the `puts ()` function, to print a message
    to the console. For this, we first generate a pointer to the string with a call to
    the `CreateGlobalStringPtr ()` function, and then pass this pointer as a
    parameter in the generated call to the `puts ()` function, as follows:

    ```
    Value *MsgPtr = Builder.CreateGlobalStringPtr(
        "Divide by zero!", "msg", 0, M);
    Builder.CreateCall(PutsFty, PutsFn, {MsgPtr});
    ```

8. This finishes the handling of the exception, and we generate a call to the
    `__cxa_end_catch()` function to inform the runtime about it. Lastly, we
    return from the function with a `ret` instruction, as follows:

    ```
    Builder.CreateCall(EndCatchFty, EndCatchFn);
    Builder.CreateRet(Int32Zero);
    }
    ```

With the `addThrow ()` and `addLandingPad ()` functions, we can generate the IR to
raise an exception and to handle an exception. We still need to add the IR to check if the
divisor is `0`, which is the topic of the next section.

Integrating the exception-handling code into the application

The IR for the division is generated inside the visit (BinaryOp&) method. Instead of just generating a sdiv instruction, we first generate the IR to compare the divisor with 0. If the divisor is 0, then the control flow continues in a basic block raising the exception. Otherwise, the control flow continues in a basic block with the sdiv instruction. With the help of the createICmpEq() and addThrow() functions, we can code this very easily, as follows:

```
case BinaryOp::Div:
    BasicBlock *TrueDest, *FalseDest;
    createICmpEq(Right, Int32Zero, TrueDest,
                 FalseDest, "divbyzero", "notzero");
    Builder.SetInsertPoint(TrueDest);
    addThrow(42); // Arbitrary payload value.
    Builder.SetInsertPoint(FalseDest);
    V = Builder.CreateSDiv(Left, Right);
    break;
```

The code-generation part is now complete. To build the application, you change into the build directory and run the ninja tool, as follows:

```
$ ninja
```

After the build is finished, you can check the generated IR—for example, with the with a: 3/a expression, as follows:

```
$ src/calc "with a: 3/a"
```

You will see the additional IR needed to raise and catch the exception.

The generated IR now depends on the C++ runtime. The easiest way to link against the required libraries is to use the clang++ compiler. Rename the rtcalc.c file with the runtime functions for the expression calculator as rtcalc.cpp, and add extern "C" in front of each function inside the file. Then we can use the llc tool to turn the generated IR into an object file and use the clang++ compiler to create an executable, as follows:

```
$ src/calc "with a: 3/a" | llc -filetype obj -o exp.o
$ clang++ -o exp exp.o ../rtcalc.cpp
```

Then, we can run the generated application with different values, as follows:

```
$ ./exp
Enter a value for a: 1
The result is: 3
$ ./exp
Enter a value for a: 0
Divide by zero!
```

In the second run the input is 0, and this raises an exception. It works as expected!

We have learned how to raise and catch exceptions. The code to generate the IR can be used as a blueprint for other compilers. Of course, the used type information and the number of catch clauses depends on the input to the compiler, but the IR we need to generate still follows the pattern presented in this section.

Adding metadata is a way to provide further information to LLVM. In the next section, we add type metadata to support the LLVM optimizer in certain situations.

Generating metadata for type-based alias analysis

Two pointers may point to the same memory cell, and they then alias each other. Memory is not typed in the LLVM model, which makes it difficult for the optimizer to decide if two pointers alias each other or not. If the compiler can prove that two pointers do not alias each other, then more optimizations are possible. In the next section, we will have a closer look at the problem and investigate how adding additional metadata will help, before we implement this approach.

Understanding the need for additional metadata

To demonstrate the problem, let's look at the following function:

```
void doSomething(int *p, float *q) {
  *p = 42;
  *q = 3.1425;
}
```

The optimizer cannot decide if the p and q pointers point to the same memory cell or not. During optimization this is an important analysis, called an **alias analysis**. If p and q point to the same memory cell, then they are aliases. If the optimizer can prove that both pointers never alias each other, this enables additional optimization opportunities. For example, in the doSomething() function, the stores can be reordered without altering the result in this case.

It depends on the definition of the source language as to whether a variable of one type can be an alias of another variable of a different type. Please note that languages may also contain expressions that break the type-based alias assumption—for example, typecasts between unrelated types.

The solution chosen by the LLVM developers is to add metadata to load and store instructions. The metadata has two purposes, outlined as follows:

- First, it defines the type hierarchy based on which type may alias another type
- Secondly, it describes the memory access in a load or store instruction

Let's have a look at the type hierarchy in C. Each type of hierarchy starts with a root node, either **named** or **anonymous**. LLVM assumes that root nodes with the same name describe the same type of hierarchy. You can use different type hierarchies in the same LLVM modules, and LLVM makes the safe assumption that these types may alias. Beneath the root node, there are nodes for scalar types. Nodes for aggregate types are not attached to the root node, but they refer to scalar types and other aggregate types. Clang defines the hierarchy for C as follows:

- The root node is called Simple C/C++ TBAA.
- Beneath the root node is the node for char types. This is a special type in C because all pointers can be converted to a pointer to char.
- Beneath the char node are nodes for the other scalar types and a type for all pointers, called any pointer.

Aggregate types are defined as a sequence of member types and offsets.

These metadata definitions are used in access tags attached to the load and store instructions. An access tag is made up of three parts: a base type, an access type, and an offset. Depending on the base type, there are two possible ways the access tag describes memory access, outlined here:

1. If the base type is an aggregate type, then the access tag describes the memory access of a struct member, having the access type and being located at a given offset.
2. If the base type is a scalar type, then the access type must be the same as the base type and the offset must be 0.

With these definitions, we can now define a relation on the access tags, which is used to evaluate if two pointers may alias each other or not. The immediate parent of a tuple (base type, offset) is determined by the base type and the offset, as follows:

- If the base type is a scalar type and the offset is 0, then the immediate parent is (parent type, 0), with parent type being the type of the parent node as defined in the type hierarchy. If the offset is not 0, then the immediate parent is undefined.

- If the base type is an aggregate type, then the immediate parent of tuple (base type, offset) is the tuple (new type, new offset), with the new type being the type of the member at the offset. The new offset is the offset of the new type, adjusted to its new start.

The transitive closure of this relation is the parent relation. Two-memory access types—for example, (base type 1, access type 1, offset 1) and (base type 2, access type 2, offset 2) —may alias if (base type 1, offset 1) and (base type 2, offset 2) or vice versa are related in the parent relation.

Let's illustrate this in an example, as follows:

```
struct Point { float x, y; }
void func(struct Point *p, float *x, int *i, char *c) {
    p->x = 0; p->y = 0; *x = 0.0; *i = 0; *c = 0;
}
```

Using the preceding memory-access tag definition for scalar types, the access tag for parameter i is (int, int, 0), and for parameter c it is (char, char, 0). In the type hierarchy, the parent of the node for the int type is the char node, therefore the immediate parent of (int, 0) is (char, 0), and both pointers can alias. The same is true for parameter x and parameter c. But parameter x and i are not related, and hence they do not alias each other. The access for the y member of struct Point is (Point, float, 4), with 4 being the offset of the y member in the struct. The immediate parent of (Point, 4) is (float, 0), therefore access to p->y and x may alias, and—with the same reasoning—also with parameter c.

To create the metadata, we use the llvm::MDBuilder class, which is declared in the llvm/IR/MDBuilder.h header file. The data itself is stored in instances of the llvm::MDNode and llvm::MDString classes. Using the builder class shields us from the internal details of the construction.

A root node is created with a call to the `createTBAARoot()` method, which expects the name of the type hierarchy as a parameter and returns the root node. An anonymous unique root node can be created with the `createAnonymousTBAARoot()` method.

A scalar type is added to the hierarchy with the `createTBAAScalarTypeNode()` method, which takes the name of the type and the parent node as a parameter. Adding a type node for an aggregate type is slightly more complex. The `createTBAAStructTypeNode()` method takes the name of the type and a list of the fields as parameters. The fields are given as a `std::pair<llvm::MDNode*, uint64_t>` instance. The first element indicates the type of the member and the second element indicates the offset in the `struct` type.

An access tag is created with the `createTBAAStructTagNode()` method, which takes the base type, the access type, and the offset as parameters.

Lastly, the metadata must be attached to a `load` or `store` instruction. The `llvm::Instruction` class has a `setMetadata()` method, which is used to add various metadata. The first parameter must be `llvm::LLVMContext::MD_tbaa` and the second must be the access tag.

Equipped with this knowledge, we will add metadata for **type-based alias analysis** (**TBAA**) to `tinylang` in the next section.

Adding TBAA metadata to tinylang

To support TBAA, we add a new `CGTBAA` class. This class is responsible for generating the metadata nodes. We make it a member of the `CGModule` class, calling it `TBAA`. Every `load` and `store` instruction could be possibly annotated, and we place a new function for this purpose in the `CGModule` class too. The function tries to create the tag-access information. If this is successful, the metadata is attached to the instruction. This design also allows us to turn off the metadata generation if we do not need it—for example, in builds with the optimization turned off. The code is illustrated in the following snippet:

```
void CGModule::decorateInst(llvm::Instruction *Inst,
                            TypeDenoter *TyDe) {
  if (auto *N = TBAA.getAccessTagInfo(TyDe))
    Inst->setMetadata(llvm::LLVMContext::MD_tbaa, N);
}
```

We put the declaration of the new CGTBAA class into the include/tinylang/ CodeGen/CGTBAA.h header file and put the definition into the lib/CodeGen/ CGTBAA.cpp file. Besides the **abstract syntax tree** (**AST**) definitions, the header file needs to include the files defining the metadata nodes and builder, as illustrated in the following code snippet:

```
#include "tinylang/AST/AST.h"
#include "llvm/IR/MDBuilder.h"
#include "llvm/IR/Metadata.h"
```

The CGTBAA class needs to store some data members. So, let's see how to do this step by step, as follows:

1. First of all, we need to cache the root of the type hierarchy, like this:

    ```
    class CGTBAA {
      llvm::MDNode *Root;
    ```

2. To construct the metadata nodes, we need an instance of the MDBuilder class, as follows:

    ```
    llvm::MDBuilder MDHelper;
    ```

3. Lastly, we store the metadata generated for a type to reuse, as follows:

    ```
    llvm::DenseMap<TypeDenoter *, llvm::MDNode *>
      MetadataCache;
    // …
    };
    ```

After defining the variables required for the construction, we now add the methods required to create the metadata, as follows:

1. The constructor initializes the data members, like this:

    ```
    CGTBAA::CGTBAA(llvm::LLVMContext &Ctx)
        : MDHelper(llvm::MDBuilder(Ctx)), Root(nullptr) {}
    ```

2. We lazily instantiate the root of the type hierarchy, which we name Simple tinylang TBAA, as illustrated in the following code snippet:

    ```
    llvm::MDNode *CGTBAA::getRoot() {
      if (!Root)
    ```

```
        Root = MDHelper.createTBAARoot("Simple tinylang
                                        TBAA");
    return Root;
}
```

3. For a scalar type, we create a metadata node with the help of the `MDBuilder` class based on the name of the type. The new metadata node is stored in the cache, as illustrated in the following code snippet:

```
llvm::MDNode *
CGTBAA::createScalarTypeNode(TypeDeclaration *Ty,
                             StringRef Name,
                             llvm::MDNode *Parent) {
  llvm::MDNode *N =
      MDHelper.createTBAAScalarTypeNode(Name, Parent);
  return MetadataCache[Ty] = N;
}
```

4. The method to create the metadata for a record is more complicated, as we have to enumerate all the fields of the record. The code is shown in the following snippet:

```
llvm::MDNode *CGTBAA::createStructTypeNode(
    TypeDeclaration *Ty, StringRef Name,
    llvm::ArrayRef<std::pair<llvm::MDNode *,
        uint64_t>>
        Fields) {
  llvm::MDNode *N =
      MDHelper.createTBAAStructTypeNode(Name, Fields);
  return MetadataCache[Ty] = N;
}
```

5. To return the metadata for a `tinylang` type, we need to create the type hierarchy. Because the type system of `tinylang` is very restricted, we can use a simple approach. Each scalar type is mapped to a unique type attached to the root node, and we map all pointers to a single type. Structured types then refer to these nodes. If we cannot map a type we then return `nullptr`, as follows:

```
llvm::MDNode *CGTBAA::getTypeInfo(TypeDeclaration *Ty) {
  if (llvm::MDNode *N = MetadataCache[Ty])
```

```
    return N;


  if (auto *Pervasive =
          llvm::dyn_cast<PervasiveTypeDeclaration>(Ty)) {
    StringRef Name = Pervasive->getName();
    return createScalarTypeNode(Pervasive, Name,
        getRoot());
  }
  if (auto *Pointer =
          llvm::dyn_cast<PointerTypeDeclaration>(Ty)) {
    StringRef Name = "any pointer";
    return createScalarTypeNode(Pointer, Name,
        getRoot());
  }
  if (auto *Record =
          llvm::dyn_cast<RecordTypeDeclaration>(Ty)) {
    llvm::SmallVector<std::pair<llvm::MDNode *,
        uint64_t>,
                        4>
        Fields;
    auto *Rec =
        llvm::cast<llvm::StructType>(
            CGM.convertType(Record));
    const llvm::StructLayout *Layout =
        CGM.getModule()->getDataLayout()
            .getStructLayout(Rec);


    unsigned Idx = 0;
    for (const auto &F : Record->getFields()) {
      uint64_t Offset = Layout->getElementOffset(Idx);
      Fields.emplace_back(getTypeInfo(F.getType()),
          Offset);
      ++Idx;
    }
    StringRef Name = CGM.mangleName(Record);
    return createStructTypeNode(Record, Name, Fields);
```

```
    }
    return nullptr;
}
```

6. A general method to get the metadata is `getAccessTagInfo()`. As we only need to look for a pointer type, we check for it. Otherwise, we return a `nullptr`, as illustrated in the following code snippet:

```
llvm::MDNode *CGTBAA::getAccessTagInfo(TypeDenoter *TyDe)
{
    if (auto *Pointer = llvm::dyn_cast<PointerType>(TyDe))
    {
        return getTypeInfo(Pointer->getTyDen());
    }
    return nullptr;
}
```

To enable the generation of TBAA metadata, we now simply need to attach the metadata to the `load` and `store` instructions we generate. For example, in `CGProcedure::writeVariable()`, a store to a global variable, use a `store` instruction, as follows:

```
Builder.CreateStore(Val, CGM.getGlobal(D));
```

To decorate the instruction, we need to replace the preceding line with the following lines:

```
auto *Inst = Builder.CreateStore(Val,
                                 CGM.getGlobal(Decl));
CGM.decorateInst(Inst, V->getTypeDenoter());
```

With these changes in place, we have finished the generation of TBAA metadata.

In the next section, we look at a very similar topic: the generation of debug metadata.

Adding debug metadata

To allow source-level debugging, we have to add debug information. Support for debug information in LLVM uses debug metadata to describe the types of the source language and other static information, and an intrinsic to track variable values. The LLVM core libraries generate debug information in DWARF format on Unix systems and in **Protein Data Bank (PDB)** format for Windows. We take a look at the general structure in the next section.

Understanding the general structure of debug metadata

To describe the static structure, LLVM uses metadata in a similar way to the metadata for type-based analysis. The static structure describes the file, the compilation unit, functions, lexical blocks, and the used data types.

The main class we use is `llvm::DIBuilder`, and we need to use the `llvm/IR/DIBuilder` include file to get the class declaration. This builder class provides an easy-to-use interface to create the debug metadata. The metadata is later either added to LLVM objects such as global variables or is used in calls to debug intrinsics. Important metadata that the builder class can create is listed here:

- `lvm::DIFile`: This describes a file using the filename and the absolute path of the directory containing the file. You use the `createFile()` method to create it. A file can contain the main compilation unit or it could contain imported declarations.

- `llvm::DICompileUnit`: This is used to describe the current compilation unit. Among other things, you specify the source language, a compiler-specific producer string, whether optimizations are enabled or not, and—of course—the `DIFile` in which the compilation unit resides. You create it with a call to `createCompileUnit()`.

- `llvm::DISubprogram`: This describes a function. Important information is the scope (usually a `DICompileUnit` or a `DISubprogram` for a nested function), the name of the function, the mangled name of the function, and the function type. It is created with a call to `createFunction()`.

- `llvm::DILexicalBlock`: This describes a lexical block that models the block scoping found in many high-level languages. You create this with a call to `createLexicalBlock()`.

LLVM makes no assumptions about the language your compiler translates. As a consequence, it has no information about the data types of the language. To support source-level debugging, especially displaying variable values in a debugger, type information must be added too. Important constructs are listed here:

- The `createBasicType()` function, returning a pointer to the `llvm::DIBasicType` class, creates the metadata to describe a basic type such as `INTEGER` in `tinylang` or `int` in C++. Besides the name of the type, the required parameters are the size in bits and the encoding—for example, whether it is a signed or unsigned type.

- There are several ways to construct the metadata for composite data types, represented by the `llvm::DIComposite` class. You use `createArrayType()`, `createStructType()`, `createUnionType()`, and `createVectorType()` functions to instantiate the metadata for `array`, `struct`, `union`, and `vector` data types. The functions require the parameter you expect—for example, the base type and the number of subscriptions for an array type, or a list of the field members of a `struct` type.

- There are also methods to support enumerations, templates, classes, and so on.

The list of functions shows you that you have to add every detail of the source language to the debug information. Let's assume your instance of the `llvm::DIBuilder` class is called `DBuilder`. Assume further that you have some `tinylang` source in a file called `File.mod` in the `/home/llvmuser` folder. Inside the file is a `Func():INTEGER` function at *line 5*, which contains a `VAR i:INTEGER` local declaration at *line 7*. Let's create the metadata for this, beginning with the information for the file. You need to specify the filename and the absolute path of the folder in which the file resides, as illustrated in the following code snippet:

```
llvm::DIFile *DbgFile = DBuilder.createFile("File.mod",
                                            "/home/llvmuser");
```

The file is a module in `tinylang` and therefore is the compilation unit for LLVM. This carries a lot of information, as can be seen in the following code snippet:

```
bool IsOptimized = false;
llvm::StringRef CUFlags;
unsigned ObjCRunTimeVersion = 0;
llvm::StringRef SplitName;
llvm::DICompileUnit::DebugEmissionKind EmissionKind =
        llvm::DICompileUnit::DebugEmissionKind::FullDebug;
```

```
llvm::DICompileUnit *DbgCU = DBuilder.createCompileUnit(
    llvm::dwarf::DW_LANG_Modula2, DbgFile, „tinylang",
    IsOptimized, CUFlags, ObjCRunTimeVersion, SplitName,
    EmissionKind);
```

The debugger needs to know the source language. The DWARF standard defines an enumeration with all the common values. A disadvantage is that you cannot simply add a new source language. To do that, you have to create a request through the DWARF committee. Be aware that the debugger and other debug tools also need support for a new language—just adding a new member to the enumeration is not enough.

In many cases, it is sufficient to choose a language that is close to your source language. In the case of tinylang this is Modula-2, and we use DW_LANG_Modula2 for language identification. A compilation unit resides in a file, which is identified by the DbgFile variable we created before. The debug information can carry information about the producer. This can be the name of the compiler and the version information. Here, we just pass a tinylang string. If you do not want to add this information, then you can simply use an empty string as a parameter.

The next set of information includes an IsOptimized flag, which should indicate if the compiler has turned optimization on or not. Usually, this flag is derived from the -O command-line switch. You can pass additional parameter settings to the debugger with the CUFlags parameter. This is not used here, and we pass an empty string. We do not use Objective-C, so we pass 0 as the Objective-C runtime version. Normally, debug information is embedded in the object file we are creating. If we want to write the debug information into a separate file, then the SplitName parameter must contain the name of this file; otherwise, just pass an empty string. And lastly, you can define the level of debug information that should be emitted. The default setting is full debug information, indicated by the use of the FullDebug enum value. You can also choose the LineTablesOnly value if you want to emit only line numbers, or the NoDebug value for no debug information at all. For the latter, it is better to not create debug information in the first place.

Our minimalistic source uses only the INTEGER data type, which is a signed 32-bit value. Creating the metadata for this type is straightforward, as can be seen in the following code snippet:

```
llvm::DIBasicType *DbgIntTy =
                    DBuilder.createBasicType("INTEGER", 32,
                            llvm::dwarf::DW_ATE_signed);
```

To create the debug metadata for the function, we have to create a type for the signature first, and then the metadata for the function itself. This is similar to the creation of IR for a function. The signature of the function is an array with all the types of the parameters in source order and the return type of the function as the first element at index 0. Usually, this array is constructed dynamically. In our case, we can also construct the metadata statically. This is useful for internal functions—for example, for module initializing. Typically, the parameters of these functions are always known, and the compiler writer can hardcode them. The code is shown in the following snippet:

```
llvm::Metadata *DbgSigTy = {DbgIntTy};
llvm::DITypeRefArray DbgParamsTy =
                    DBuilder.getOrCreateTypeArray(DbgSigTy);
llvm::DISubroutineType *DbgFuncTy =
                    DBuilder.createSubroutineType(DbgParamsTy);
```

Our function has an INTEGER return type and no further parameters, so the DbgSigTy array contains only the pointer to the metadata for this type. This static array is turned into a type array, which is then used to create the type for the function.

The function itself requires more data, as follows:

```
unsigned LineNo = 5;
unsigned ScopeLine = 5;
llvm::DISubprogram *DbgFunc = DBuilder.createFunction(
      DbgCU, "Func", "_t4File4Func", DbgFile, LineNo,
      DbgFuncTy, ScopeLine,
      llvm::DISubprogram::FlagPrivate,
      llvm::DISubprogram::SPFlagLocalToUnit);
```

A function belongs to a compilation unit, in our case stored in the DbgCU variable. We need to specify the name of the function in the source file, which is Func, and the mangled name is stored in the object file. This information helps the debugger to locate the machine code of the function later on. The mangled name, based on the rules of tinylang, is _ t4File4Func. We also have to specify the file that contains the function.

This may sound surprising at first, but think of the include mechanism in C and C++: a function can be stored in a different file, which is then included with #include in the main compilation unit. Here, this is not the case, and we use the same file as the one the compilation unit uses. Next, the line number of the function and the function type are passed. The line number of the function may not be the line number where the lexical scope of the function begins. In this case, you can specify a different ScopeLine. A function also has protection, which we specify here with the FlagPrivate value to indicate a private function. Other possible values are FlagPublic and FlagProtected, for public and protected functions.

Besides the protection level, there are other flags that can be specified here. For example, FlagVirtual indicates a virtual function, and FlagNoReturn indicates that the function does not return to the caller. You can find a complete list of possible values in the llvm/include/llvm/IR/DebugInfoFlags.def LLVM include file. And lastly, flags specific to a function can be specified. The most used one is the SPFlagLocalToUnit value, which indicates that the function is local to this compilation unit. Also often used is the MainSubprogram value, indicating that this function is the main function of the application. You can also find all possible values in the LLVM include file mentioned previously.

So far, we only created the metadata referring to static data. Variables are dynamic in nature, and we explore how to attach the static metadata to the IR code for accessing variables in the next section.

Tracking variables and their values

To be useful, the type metadata described in the last section needs to be associated with the variables of the source program. For a global variable, this is pretty easy. The createGlobalVariableExpression() function of the llvm::DIBuilder class creates the metadata to describe a global variable. This includes the name of the variable in the source, the mangled name, the source file, and so on. A global variable in LLVM IR is represented by an instance of the GlobalVariable class. This class has an addDebugInfo() method, which associates the metadata node returned from createGlobalVariableExpression() with the global variable.

For local variables, we need to take another approach. LLVM IR does not know a class representing a local variable; it knows only about values. The solution the LLVM community developed is to insert calls to intrinsic functions into the IR code of a function. An intrinsic function is a function that LLVM knows about and therefore can do some magic with it. In most cases, intrinsic functions do not result in a subroutine call at the machine level. Here, the function call is a convenient vehicle to associate the metadata with a value.

The most important intrinsic functions for debug metadata are `llvm.dbg.declare` and `llvm.dbg.value`. The former is called once to declare the address of a local variable, while the latter is called whenever a local variable is set to a new value.

> **Future LLVM versions will replace llvm.dbg.declare with the llvm.dbg.addr intrinsic**
>
> The `llvm.dbg.declare` intrinsic function makes a very strong assumption: the address of the variable described in the call to the intrinsic is valid throughout the lifetime of the function. This assumption makes it very hard to preserve debug metadata during optimization because the real storage address can change. To solve this, a new intrinsic called `llvm.dbg.addr` was designed. This intrinsic takes the same parameters as `llvm.dbg.declare`, but it has less strict semantics. It still describes the address of a local variable, and a frontend should generate exactly one call to it.
>
> During optimization, passes can replace this intrinsic with (possibly multiple) calls to `llvm.dbg.value` and/or `llvm.dbg.addr` in order to preserve the debug information.
>
> The `llvm.dbg.declare` intrinsic will be deprecated and later removed when work on `llvm.dbg.addr` is finished.

How does it work? The LLVM IR representation and the programmatic creation via the `llvm::DIBuilder` class differ a bit, so we look at both. Continuing our example from the previous section, we allocate local storage for the `i` variable inside the `Func` function with the `alloca` instruction, as follows:

```
@i = alloca i32
```

After that, we add a call to the `llvm.dbg.declare` intrinsic, like this:

```
call void @llvm.dbg.declare(metadata i32* %i,
                        metadata !1, metadata
                        !DIExpression())
```

The first parameter is the address to the local variable. The second parameter is the metadata describing the local variable, created by a call to either `createAutoVariable()` for a local variable or `createParameterVariable()` for a parameter of the `llvm::DIBuilder` class. The third parameter describes an address expression, which I explain later.

Let's implement the IR creation. You allocate the storage for the @i local variable with a call to the CreateAlloca() method of the llvm::IRBuilder<> class, as follows:

```
llvm::Type *IntTy = llvm::Type::getInt32Ty(LLVMCtx);
llvm::Value *Val = Builder.CreateAlloca(IntTy, nullptr, "i");
```

The LLVMCtx variable is the used context class, and Builder is the used instance of the llvm::IRBuilder<> class.

A local variable also needs to be described by metadata, as follows:

```
llvm::DILocalVariable *DbgLocalVar =
  DBuilder.createAutoVariable(DbgFunc, "i", DbgFile,
                              7, DbgIntTy);
```

Using the values from the previous section, we specify that the variable is part of the DbgFunc function, has the name i, is defined in the file named by DbgFile at *line 7*, and has a DbgIntTy type.

Finally, we associate the debug metadata with the address of the variable using the llvm.dbg.declare intrinsic. Using llvm::DIBuilder shields you from all of the details of adding a call. The code is shown in the following snippet:

```
llvm::DILocation *DbgLoc =
                  llvm::DILocation::get(LLVMCtx, 7, 5,
                                        DbgFunc);
DBuilder.insertDeclare(Val, DbgLocalVar,
                       DBuilder.createExpression(), DbgLoc,
                       Val.getParent());
```

Again, we have to specify a source location for the variable. An instance of llvm::DILocation is a container to hold the line and column of a location associated with a scope. The insertDeclare() method adds a call to the intrinsic function to the LLVM IR. As parameters it requires the address of the variable, stored in Val, and the debug metadata for the variable, stored in DbgValVar. We also pass an empty address expression and the debug location created before. As with a normal instruction, we need to specify into which basic block the call is inserted. If we specify a basic block, then the call is inserted at the end. Alternatively, we can specify an instruction, and the call is inserted before that instruction. We have the pointer to the alloca instruction, which is the last one that we inserted into the underlying basic block. So, we use this basic block, and the call gets appended after the alloca instruction.

If a value of a local variable changes, then a call to `llvm.dbg.value` must be added to the IR. You use the `insertValue()` method of `llvm::DIBuilder` to do so. This works similarly for `llvm.dbg.addr`. The difference is that instead of the address of the variable, now the new value is specified.

When we implemented the IR generation for functions, we used an advanced algorithm that mainly used values and avoided allocating storage for local variables. For adding debug information, this only means that we use `llvm.dbg.value` much more often than you see in Clang-generated IR.

What can we do if the variable does not have dedicated storage space but is part of a larger aggregate type? One situation where this can arise is with the use of nested functions. To implement access to the stack frame of the caller, you collect all used variables in a structure and pass a pointer to this record to the called function. Inside the called function, you can refer to the variables of the caller as if they were local to the function. What is different is that these variables are now part of an aggregate.

In the call to `llvm.dbg.declare`, you use an empty expression if the debug metadata describes the whole memory the first parameter is pointing to. If it instead describes only a part of the memory, then you need to add an expression indicating which part of the memory the metadata applies to. In the case of the nested frame, you need to calculate the offset into the frame. You need access to a `DataLayout` instance, which you can get from the LLVM module into which you are creating the IR code. If the `llvm::Module` instance is named `Mod`, the variable holding the nested frame structure is named `Frame`, being of type `llvm::StructType`, and you access the third member of the frame. This then gives you the offset of the member, as illustrated in the following code snippet:

```
const llvm::DataLayout &DL = Mod->getDataLayout();
uint64_t Ofs = DL.getStructLayout(Frame)
                    ->getElementOffset(3);
```

The expression is created from a sequence of operations. To access the third member of the frame, the debugger needs to add the offset to the base pointer. You need to create an array and this information—for example, in this way:

```
llvm::SmallVector<int64_t, 2> AddrOps;
AddrOps.push_back(llvm::dwarf::DW_OP_plus_uconst);
AddrOps.push_back(Offset);
```

From this array, you can create an expression that you then pass to `llvm.dbg.declare` instead of the empty expression, as follows:

```
llvm::DIExpression *Expr = DBuilder.createExpression(AddrOps);
```

You are not limited to this offset operation. DWARF knows many different operators, and you can create fairly complex expressions. You can find a complete list of operators in the `llvm/include/llvm/BinaryFormat/Dwarf.def` LLVM include file.

You are now able to create debug information for variables. To enable the debugger to follow the control flow in the source, you also need to provide line-number information, which is the topic of the next section.

Adding line numbers

A debugger allows a programmer to step line by line through an application. For this, the debugger needs to know which machine instructions belong to which line in the source code. LLVM allows a source location to be added to each instruction. In the previous section, we created location information of the `llvm::DILocation` type. A debug location has more information than just the line, column, and scope. If needed, the scope into which this line is inlined can be specified. It is also possible to indicate that this debug location belongs to implicit code—that is, code that the frontend has generated but that is not in the source code.

Before it can be attached to an instruction, we must wrap the debug location in an `llvm::DebugLoc` object. To do so, you simply pass the location information obtained from the `llvm::DILocation` class to the `llvm::DebugLoc` constructor. With this wrapping, it is possible for LLVM to track the location information. While the location in the source obviously does not change, the generated machine code for a source-level statement or expression can be dropped during optimization. Encapsulation helps to deal with these possible changes.

Adding line-number information mostly boils down to retrieving the line-number information from the AST and adding it to the generated instructions. The `llvm::Instruction` class has the `setDebugLoc()` method, which attaches the location information to the instruction.

In the next section, we add the generation of debug information to our `tinylang` compiler.

Adding debug support to tinylang

We encapsulate the generation of debug metadata in the new `CGDebugInfo` class. We put the declaration into the `tinylang/CodeGen/CGDebugInfo.h` header file and the definition into the `tinylang/CodeGen/CGDebugInfo.cpp` file.

The `CGDebugInfo` class has five important members. We need a reference to the code generator for the module, `CGM`, because we need to convert types from AST representation to LLVM types. Of course, we also need an instance of the `llvm::DIBuilder` class, called `DBuilder`, as in the previous sections. A pointer to the instance of the compile unit is also needed, and we store it in a member called `CU`.

To avoid repeated creation of the debug metadata for types, we also add a map to cache this information. The member is called `TypeCache`. And lastly, we need a way to manage the scope information, for which we create a stack based on the `llvm::SmallVector<>` class, called `ScopeStack`. Thus we have the following code:

```
CGModule &CGM;
llvm::DIBuilder DBuilder;
llvm::DICompileUnit *CU;
llvm::DenseMap<TypeDeclaration *, llvm::DIType *>
    TypeCache;
llvm::SmallVector<llvm::DIScope *, 4> ScopeStack;
```

The following methods of the `CGDebugInfo` class all make use of these members:

1. First, we need to create the compile unit, which we do in the constructor. We also create a file containing the compile unit here. Later, we can refer to the file through the `CU` member. The code for the constructor is shown in the following snippet:

```
CGDebugInfo::CGDebugInfo(CGModule &CGM)
    : CGM(CGM), DBuilder(*CGM.getModule()) {
  llvm::SmallString<128> Path(
      CGM.getASTCtx().getFilename());
  llvm::sys::fs::make_absolute(Path);

  llvm::DIFile *File = DBuilder.createFile(
      llvm::sys::path::filename(Path),
      llvm::sys::path::parent_path(Path));

  bool IsOptimized = false;
  unsigned ObjCRunTimeVersion = 0;
  llvm::DICompileUnit::DebugEmissionKind EmissionKind =
      llvm::DICompileUnit::DebugEmissionKind::FullDebug;
  CU = DBuilder.createCompileUnit(
      llvm::dwarf::DW_LANG_Modula2, File, "tinylang",
```

```
        IsOptimized, StringRef(), ObjCRunTimeVersion,
        StringRef(), EmissionKind);
}
```

2. Very often, we need to provide a line number. This can be derived from the source manager location, which is available is most AST nodes. The source manager can convert this into a line number, as follows:

```
unsigned CGDebugInfo::getLineNumber(SMLoc Loc) {
    return CGM.getASTCtx().getSourceMgr().FindLineNumber(
        Loc);
}
```

3. Information about a scope is held on a stack. We need methods to open and close a scope and to retrieve the current scope. The compilation unit is the global scope, which we add automatically, as follows:

```
llvm::DIScope *CGDebugInfo::getScope() {
    if (ScopeStack.empty())
        openScope(CU->getFile());
    return ScopeStack.back();
}

void CGDebugInfo::openScope(llvm::DIScope *Scope) {
    ScopeStack.push_back(Scope);
}

void CGDebugInfo::closeScope() {
    ScopeStack.pop_back();
}
```

4. We create a method for each category of the type we need to transform. The getPervasiveType() method creates the debug metadata for basic types. Note in the following code snippet the use of the encoding parameter, declaring the INTEGER type as a signed type and the BOOLEAN type encoded as a Boolean type:

```
llvm::DIType *
CGDebugInfo::getPervasiveType(TypeDeclaration *Ty) {
    if (Ty->getName() == "INTEGER") {
```

```
      return DBuilder.createBasicType(
          Ty->getName(), 64, llvm::dwarf::DW_ATE_signed);
    }
    if (Ty->getName() == "BOOLEAN") {
      return DBuilder.createBasicType(
          Ty->getName(), 1,
              llvm::dwarf::DW_ATE_boolean);
    }
    llvm::report_fatal_error(
        "Unsupported pervasive type");
  }
```

5. If the type name is simply renamed, then we map this to a type definition. Here, we need to make the first use of the scope and line-number information, as follows:

```
llvm::DIType *
CGDebugInfo::getAliasType(AliasTypeDeclaration *Ty) {
  return DBuilder.createTypedef(
      getType(Ty->getType()), Ty->getName(),
      CU->getFile(), getLineNumber(Ty->getLocation()),
      getScope());
}
```

6. Creating the debug information for an array requires specification about the size and the alignment. We retrieve this data from the DataLayout class. We also need to specify the index range of the array. We can do this with the following code:

```
llvm::DIType *
CGDebugInfo::getArrayType(ArrayTypeDeclaration *Ty) {
  auto *ATy =
      llvm::cast<llvm::ArrayType>(CGM.convertType(Ty));
  const llvm::DataLayout &DL =
      CGM.getModule()->getDataLayout();

  uint64_t NumElements = Ty->getUpperIndex();
  llvm::SmallVector<llvm::Metadata *, 4> Subscripts;
  Subscripts.push_back(
      DBuilder.getOrCreateSubrange(0, NumElements));
```

```
    return DBuilder.createArrayType(
        DL.getTypeSizeInBits(ATy) * 8,
        DL.getABITypeAlignment(ATy),
        getType(Ty->getType()),
        DBuilder.getOrCreateArray(Subscripts));
}
```

7. Using all these single methods, we create a central method to create the metadata for a type. This metadata is also responsible for caching the data. The code can be seen in the following snippet:

```
llvm::DIType *
CGDebugInfo::getType(TypeDeclaration *Ty) {
  if (llvm::DIType *T = TypeCache[Ty])
    return T;

  if (llvm::isa<PervasiveTypeDeclaration>(Ty))
    return TypeCache[Ty] = getPervasiveType(Ty);
  else if (auto *AliasTy =
              llvm::dyn_cast<AliasTypeDeclaration>(Ty))
    return TypeCache[Ty] = getAliasType(AliasTy);
  else if (auto *ArrayTy =
              llvm::dyn_cast<ArrayTypeDeclaration>(Ty))
    return TypeCache[Ty] = getArrayType(ArrayTy);
  else if (auto *RecordTy =
              llvm ::dyn_cast<RecordTypeDeclaration>(
                Ty))
    return TypeCache[Ty] = getRecordType(RecordTy);
  llvm::report_fatal_error("Unsupported type");
  return nullptr;
}
```

8. We also need to add a method to emit metadata for global variables, as follows:

```
void CGDebugInfo::emitGlobalVariable(
    VariableDeclaration *Decl,
    llvm::GlobalVariable *V) {
  llvm::DIGlobalVariableExpression *GV =
```

```
        DBuilder.createGlobalVariableExpression(
            getScope(), Decl->getName(), V->getName(),
            CU->getFile(),
            getLineNumber(Decl->getLocation()),
            getType(Decl->getType()), false);
    V->addDebugInfo(GV);
}
```

9. To emit the debug information for procedures, we first need to create the metadata for the procedure type. For this, we need a list of the types of the parameter, with the return type being the first entry. If the procedure has no return type, then we use an unspecified type called void, as in C. If a parameter is a reference, then we need to add the reference type; otherwise, we add the type to the list. The code is illustrated in the following snippet:

```
llvm::DISubroutineType *
CGDebugInfo::getType(ProcedureDeclaration *P) {
    llvm::SmallVector<llvm::Metadata *, 4> Types;
    const llvm::DataLayout &DL =
        CGM.getModule()->getDataLayout();
    // Return type at index 0
    if (P->getRetType())
      Types.push_back(getType(P->getRetType()));
    else
      Types.push_back(
          DBuilder.createUnspecifiedType("void"));
    for (const auto *FP : P->getFormalParams()) {
      llvm::DIType *PT = getType(FP->getType());
      if (FP->isVar()) {
        llvm::Type *PTy = CGM.convertType(FP->getType());
        PT = DBuilder.createReferenceType(
            llvm::dwarf::DW_TAG_reference_type, PT,
            DL.getTypeSizeInBits(PTy) * 8,
            DL.getABITypeAlignment(PTy));
      }
      Types.push_back(PT);
    }
```

```
    return DBuilder.createSubroutineType(
        DBuilder.getOrCreateTypeArray(Types));
}
```

10. For the procedure itself, we can now create the debug information using the procedure type created in the last step. A procedure also opens a new scope, so we push the procedure onto the scope stack. We also associate the LLVM function object with the new debug information, as follows:

```
void CGDebugInfo::emitProcedure(
    ProcedureDeclaration *Decl, llvm::Function *Fn) {
  llvm::DISubroutineType *SubT = getType(Decl);
  llvm::DISubprogram *Sub = DBuilder.createFunction(
      getScope(), Decl->getName(), Fn->getName(),
      CU->getFile(), getLineNumber(Decl->getLocation()),
      SubT, getLineNumber(Decl->getLocation()),
      llvm::DINode::FlagPrototyped,
      llvm::DISubprogram::SPFlagDefinition);
  openScope(Sub);
  Fn->setSubprogram(Sub);
}
```

11. When the end of a procedure is reached, we must inform the builder to finalize the construction of debug information for this procedure. We also need to remove the procedure from the scope stack. We can do this with the following code:

```
void CGDebugInfo::emitProcedureEnd(
    ProcedureDeclaration *Decl, llvm::Function *Fn) {
  if (Fn && Fn->getSubprogram())
    DBuilder.finalizeSubprogram(Fn->getSubprogram());
  closeScope();
}
```

12. Lastly, when we are finished with adding the debug information, we need to add the finalize() method onto the builder. The generated debug information is then validated. This is an important step during development as it helps you to find wrongly generated metadata. The code can be seen in the following snippet:

```
void CGDebugInfo::finalize() { DBuilder.finalize(); }
```

Debug information should only be generated if the user requested it. We will need a new command-line switch for this. We will add this to the file of the CGModule class, and we will also use it inside this class, as follows:

```
static llvm::cl::opt<bool>
    Debug("g", llvm::cl::desc("Generate debug information"),
          llvm::cl::init(false));
```

The CGModule class holds an instance of the std::unique_ptr<CGDebugInfo> class. The pointer is initialized in the constructor, regarding the setting of the command-line switch, as follows:

```
  if (Debug)
    DebugInfo.reset(new CGDebugInfo(*this));
```

In the getter method we return the pointer, like this:

```
CGDebugInfo *getDbgInfo() {
  return DebugInfo.get();
}
```

A common pattern when generating the debug metadata is to retrieve the pointer and check if it is valid. For example, after we have created a global variable, we add the debug information in this way:

```
VariableDeclaration *Var = …;
llvm::GlobalVariable *V = …;
if (CGDebugInfo *Dbg = getDbgInfo())
  Dbg->emitGlobalVariable(Var, V);
```

In order to add line-number information, we need to add a getDebugLoc() conversion method into the CGDebugInfo class, which turns the location information from the AST into the debug metadata, as follows:

```
llvm::DebugLoc CGDebugInfo::getDebugLoc(SMLoc Loc) {
  std::pair<unsigned, unsigned> LineAndCol =
      CGM.getASTCtx().getSourceMgr().getLineAndColumn(Loc);
  llvm::DILocation *DILoc = llvm::DILocation::get(
      CGM.getLLVMCtx(), LineAndCol.first, LineAndCol.second,
      getCU());
  return llvm::DebugLoc(DILoc);
}
```

A utility function in the CGModule class can then be called to add the line-number information to an instruction, as follows:

```
void CGModule::applyLocation(llvm::Instruction *Inst,
                             llvm::SMLoc Loc) {
  if (CGDebugInfo *Dbg = getDbgInfo())
    Inst->setDebugLoc(Dbg->getDebugLoc(Loc));
}
```

In this way, you can add the debug information for your own compiler.

Summary

In this chapter, you learned how throwing and catching exceptions works in LLVM and about which IR code you need to generate to exploit this feature. To enhance the scope of IR, you learned how you can attach various metadata to instructions. Metadata for type-based aliases provides additional information to the LLVM optimizer and helps with certain optimizations to produce better machine code. Users always appreciate the possibility of using a source-level debugger, and through adding debug information to the IR code you are able to provide this important feature of a compiler.

Optimizing the IR code is a core task of LLVM. In the next chapter, we will learn how the pass manager works and how we can influence the optimization pipeline the pass manager governs.

8
Optimizing IR

LLVM uses a series of Passes to optimize the **intermediate representation** (**IR**). A Pass performs an operation on a unit of IR, either a function or a module. The operation can be a transformation, which changes the IR in a defined way, or an analysis, which collects information such as dependencies. A series of Passes is called the **Pass pipeline**. The Pass manager executes the Pass pipeline on the IR that our compiler produces. Therefore, it is important that we know what the Pass manager does and how to construct a Pass pipeline. The semantics of a programming language might require the development of new Passes, and we must add these Passes to the pipeline.

In this chapter, we will cover the following topics:

- Introducing the LLVM Pass manager
- Implementing a Pass using the new Pass manager
- Adapting a Pass for use with the old Pass manager
- Adding an optimization pipeline to your compiler

By the end of the chapter, you will know how to develop a new Pass and how to add it to a Pass pipeline. You will have also acquired the knowledge required to set up the Pass pipeline in your own compiler.

Technical requirements

The source code for this chapter is available at `https://github.com/PacktPublishing/Learn-LLVM-12/tree/master/Chapter08`

You can find the code in action videos at `https://bit.ly/3nllhED`

Introducing the LLVM Pass manager

The LLVM core libraries optimize the IR your compiler creates and turn it into object code. This giant task is broken down into separate steps, called **Passes**. These Passes need to be executed in the right order, which is the objective of the Pass manager.

But why not hardcode the order of the Passes? Well, the user of your compiler usually expects that your compiler provides a different level of optimization. Developers prefer a faster compilation speed over-optimization during development time. The final application should run as fast as possible, and your compiler should be able to perform sophisticated optimizations, with longer compilation times accepted. A different level of optimization means a different number of optimization Passes that need to be executed. And, as a compiler writer, you might want to provide your own Passes to take advantage of your knowledge of the source language. For example, you might want to replace well-known library functions with inline IR or, if possible, with the computed result of that function. For C, such a Pass is part of the LLVM core libraries, but for other languages, you will need to provide it yourself. And introducing your own Passes, you might need to reorder or add some Passes. For example, if you know that the operation of your Pass leaves some IR code unreachable, then you should also run the dead code removal Pass after your own Pass. The Pass manager helps you to organize these requirements.

A Pass is often categorized according to the scope in which it works:

- A *function Pass* takes a single function as input and performs its work on this function only.

- A *module Pass* takes a whole module as input. Such a Pass performs its work on the given module and can be used for intraprocedural operations inside this module.

- A *call graph* Pass traverses the functions of a call graph in bottom-up order.

Besides the IR code, a Pass might also consume, produce, or invalidate some analysis results. There are a lot of different analyses performed; for example, alias analysis or the construction of a dominator tree. The dominator tree helps move invariant code out of a loop, so a Pass performing such a transformation can only run after the dominator tree has been created. Another Pass might perform a transformation that could invalidate the existing dominator tree.

Under the hood, the Pass manager ensures the following:

- Analysis results are shared among Passes. This requires you to keep track of which Pass requires which analysis, and of the state of each analysis. The goal is to avoid needless recomputation of analyses and to free up the memory held by the analysis results as soon as possible.

- The Passes are executed in a pipeline fashion. For example, if several function Passes should be executed in sequence, then the Pass manager runs each of these function Passes on the first function. It will then run all function Passes on the second function, and so on. The underlying idea here is to improve the cache behavior, as the compiler performs transformations on only a limited set of data (that is, one IR function) and then moves on to the next limited set of data.

There are two Pass managers in LLVM, as follows:

- The old (or legacy) Pass manager
- The new Pass manager

The future belongs to the new Pass manager, but the transition is not yet complete. A number of crucial Passes, such as object code emission, have not yet been migrated to the new Pass manager, so it is important to understand both Pass managers.

The old Pass manager requires a Pass to inherit from a base class, for example, from the `llvm::FunctionPass` class for a function Pass. In contrast, the new Pass manager relies on a concept-based approach, requiring inheritance from the special `llvm::PassInfo<>` mixin class only. The dependence between Passes was not expressed explicitly with the old Pass manager. In the new Pass manager, it needs to be explicitly coded. The new Pass manager also features a different approach to handling analysis and allows the specification of an optimization pipeline through a textual representation on the command line. Some LLVM users reported a reduction of compile of up to 10% just by switching from the old to the new Pass manager, which is a very convincing argument for using the new Pass manager.

First, we will implement a Pass for the new Pass manager and explore how to add it to the optimization pipeline. Later, we will take a look at how to use a Pass with the old Pass manager, too.

Implementing a Pass using the new Pass manager

A Pass can perform arbitrary complex transformations on the LLVM IR. To illustrate the mechanics of adding a new Pass, our new Pass only counts the number of IR instructions and basic blocks. We name the Pass `countir`. Adding the Pass to the LLVM source tree or as a standalone Pass differs slightly, so we will do both in the following sections. Let's begin by adding a new Pass to the LLVM source tree.

Adding a Pass to the LLVM source tree

Let's start by adding the new Pass to the LLVM source. This is the right approach if we later want to publish the new Pass in the LLVM tree.

The source of Passes that perform transformations on the LLVM IR is located in the `llvm-project/llvm/lib/Transforms` folder, and the header files are in the `llvm-project/llvm/include/llvm/Transforms` folder. Because there are so many Passes, they are sorted into subfolders after the category they fit in.

For our new Pass, we create a new folder, called `CountIR`, in both locations. First, let's implement the `CountIR.h` header file:

1. As usual, we need to make sure that the file can be included multiple times. Additionally, we need to include the Pass manager definition:

    ```
    #ifndef LLVM_TRANSFORMS_COUNTIR_COUNTIR_H
    #define LLVM_TRANSFORMS_COUNTIR_COUNTIR_H

    #include "llvm/IR/PassManager.h"
    ```

2. Because we are inside the LLVM source, we put our new `CountIR` class into the `llvm` namespace. The class inherits from the `PassInfoMixin` template. This template only adds some boilerplate code, such as a `name()` method. It is not used the determine the type of Pass:

    ```
    namespace llvm {
    class CountIRPass : public PassInfoMixin<CountIRPass> {
    ```

3. At runtime, the `run()` method of the task will be called. The signature of the `run()` method determines the type of Pass. Here, the first argument is a reference to the `Function` type, so this is a function Pass:

```
public:
  PreservedAnalyses run(Function &F,
                          FunctionAnalysisManager &AM);
```

4. Finally, we need to close the class, the namespace, and the header guard:

```
};
} // namespace llvm
#endif
```

Of course, the definition of our new Pass is so simple because we have only performed a trivial task.

Let's continue with the implementation of the Pass inside the CountIIR.cpp file. LLVM supports the collection of statistical information about a Pass if compiled in debug mode. For our Pass, we will make use of this infrastructure.

5. We begin the source by including our own header file and the required LLVM header files:

```
#include "llvm/Transforms/CountIR/CountIR.h"
#include "llvm/ADT/Statistic.h"
#include "llvm/Support/Debug.h"
```

6. To shorten the source, we tell the compiler that we are using the llvm namespace:

```
using namespace llvm;
```

7. The built-in debug infrastructure of LLVM requires that we define a debug type, which is a string. This string is later shown in the printed statistic:

```
#define DEBUG_TYPE "countir"
```

8. We define two counter variables with the STATISTIC macro. The first parameter is the name of the counter variable, and the second parameter is the text that will be printed in the statistic:

```
STATISTIC(NumOfInst, "Number of instructions.");
STATISTIC(NumOfBB, "Number of basic blocks.");
```

9. Inside the `run()` method, we loop through all of the basic blocks of the function and increment the corresponding counter. We do the same for all instructions of a basic block. To prevent a compiler from warning us about unused variables, we insert a no-op use of the `I` variable. Because we only count and do not alter the IR, we tell the caller that we have preserved all existing analyses:

```
PreservedAnalyses
CountIRPass::run(Function &F,
                FunctionAnalysisManager &AM) {
  for (BasicBlock &BB : F) {
    ++NumOfBB;
    for (Instruction &I : BB) {
      (void)I;
      ++NumOfInst;
    }
  }
  return PreservedAnalyses::all();
}
```

So far, we have implemented the functionality of our new Pass. We will reuse this implementation later for an out-of-tree Pass. For the solution inside the LLVM tree, we must change several files in LLVM to announce the existence of the new Pass:

1. First, we need to add a `CMakeLists.txt` file to the source folder. This file contains the build instructions for a new LLVM library name, `LLVMCountIR`. The new library needs to link against the LLVM `Support` component because we use the debug and statistic infrastructure, and against the LLVM `Core` component, which contains the definition of the LLVM IR:

```
add_llvm_component_library(LLVMCountIR
  CountIR.cpp
  LINK_COMPONENTS Core Support )
```

2. In order to make this new library part of the build, we need to add the folder into the `CMakeLists.txt` file of the parent folder, which is the `llvm-project/llvm/lib/Transforms/CMakeList.txt` file. Then, add the following line:

```
add_subdirectory(CountIR)
```

3. The `PassBuilder` class needs to know about our new Pass. To do this, we add the following line into the `include` section of the `llvm-project/llvm/lib/Passes/PassBuilder.cpp` file:

```
#include "llvm/Transforms/CountIR/CountIR.h"
```

4. As the last step, we need to update the Pass registry, which is in the `llvm-project/llvm/lib/Passes/PassRegistry.def` file. Look for the section in which function Passes are defined, for example, by searching for the `FUNCTION_PASS` macro. Inside this section, you add the following line:

```
FUNCTION_PASS("countir", CountIRPass())
```

5. We have now made all the necessary changes. Follow the build instructions from *Chapter 1, Installing LLVM,* in the *Building with CMake* section, to recompile LLVM. To test the new Pass, we store the following IR code inside the `demo.11` file in our `build` folder. The code has two functions and, in sum, three instructions and two basic blocks:

```
define internal i32 @func() {
  ret i32 0
}

define dso_local i32 @main() {
  %1 = call i32 @func()
  ret i32 %1
}
```

6. We can use the new Pass with the `opt` utility. To run the new Pass, we will utilize the `--passes="countir"` option. To get the statistical output, we need to add the `--stats` option. Because we do not need the resulting bitcode, we also specify the `--disable-output` option:

```
$ bin/opt --disable-output --passes="countir" --stats
demo.11
===-------------------------------------------------------
--===
                 ... Statistics Collected ...
===-------------------------------------------------------
--===
```

```
2 countir - Number of basic blocks.
3 countir - Number of instructions.
```

7. We run our news Pass, and the output matches our expectations. We have successfully extended LLVM!

Running a single Pass helps with debugging. With the --passes option, you cannot only name a single Pass but describe a whole pipeline. For example, the default pipeline for optimization level 2 is named default<O2>. You can run the countir Pass before the default pipeline with the --passes="module(countir),default<O2>" argument. The Pass names in such a pipeline description must be of the same type. The default pipeline is a module Pass and our countir Pass is a function Pass. To create a module pipeline from both, first, we must create a module Pass containing the countir Pass. That is done with module(countir). You can add more function Passes to this module Pass by specifying them in a comma-separated list. In the same way, the module Passes can be combined. To study the effects of this, you can use the inline and countir Passes: running them in a different order, or as a module Pass, will give you a different statistical output.

Adding a new Pass to the LLVM source tree makes sense if you plan to publish your Pass as a part of LLVM. If you do not plan to do this, or if you want to distribute your Pass independently of LLVM, then you can create a Pass plugin. In the next section, we will view the steps to do this.

Adding a new Pass as a plugin

To provide a new Pass as a plugin, we will create a new project that uses LLVM:

1. Let's begin by creating a new folder, called countirpass, in our source folder. The folder will have the following structure and files:

```
|-- CMakeLists.txt
|-- include
|    `-- CountIR.h
|-- lib
     |-- CMakeLists.txt
     `-- CountIR.cpp
```

2. Note that we have reused the functionality from the previous section, with some small adaptions. The CountIR.h header file is now in a different location, so we change the name of the symbol that is used as a guard. We also do not use the llvm namespace, because we are now outside the LLVM source. As a result of this change, the header file becomes the following:

```
#ifndef COUNTIR_H
#define COUNTIR_H

#include "llvm/IR/PassManager.h"

class CountIRPass
    : public llvm::PassInfoMixin<CountIRPass> {
public:
  llvm::PreservedAnalyses
  run(llvm::Function &F,
      llvm::FunctionAnalysisManager &AM);
};

#endif
```

3. We can copy the CountIR.cpp implementation file from the previous section. Small changes are needed here, too. Because the path of our header file has changed, we need to replace the include directive with the following:

```
#include "CountIR.h"
```

4. We also need to register the new Pass at the Pass builder. This happens when the plugin is loaded. The Pass plugin manager calls the special function, llvmGetPassPluginInfo(), which performs the registration. For this implementation, we require two additional include files:

```
#include "llvm/Passes/PassBuilder.h"
#include "llvm/Passes/PassPlugin.h"
```

The user specifies the Passes to run on the command line with the `--passes` option. The `PassBuilder` class extracts the Pass names from the string. In order to create an instance of the named Pass, the `PassBuilder` class maintains a list of callbacks. Essentially, the callbacks are called with the Pass name and a Pass manager. If the callback knows the Pass name, then it adds an instance of this Pass to the Pass manager. For our Pass, we need to provide such a callback function:

```
bool PipelineParsingCB(
    StringRef Name, FunctionPassManager &FPM,
    ArrayRef<PassBuilder::PipelineElement>) {
  if (Name == "countir") {
    FPM.addPass(CountIRPass());
    return true;
  }
  return false;
}
```

5. Of course, we need to register this function as the `PassBuilder` instance. After the plugin is loaded, a registration callback is called for exactly this purpose. Our registration function is as follows:

```
void RegisterCB(PassBuilder &PB) {
  PB.registerPipelineParsingCallback(PipelineParsingCB);
}
```

6. Finally, each plugin needs to provide the mentioned `llvmGetPassPluginInfo()` function. This function returns a structure with four elements: the LLVM plugin API version used by our plugin, a name, the version number of the plugin, and the registration callback. The plugin API requires that the function uses the `extern "C"` convention. This is to avoid problems with C++ name mangling. The function is very simple:

```
extern "C" ::llvm::PassPluginLibraryInfo LLVM_ATTRIBUTE_
WEAK
llvmGetPassPluginInfo() {
  return {LLVM_PLUGIN_API_VERSION, "CountIR", "v0.1",
          RegisterCB};
}
```

The implementation of one separate function for each callback helps us to understand what is going on. If your plugin provides several Passes, then you can extend the `RegisterCB` callback function to register all of the Passes. Often, you can find a very compact approach. The following `llvmGetPassPluginInfo()` function combines `PipelineParsingCB()`, `RegisterCB()`, and `llvmGetPassPluginInfo()` from earlier into a single function. It does so by making use of lambda functions:

```
extern "C" ::llvm::PassPluginLibraryInfo LLVM_ATTRIBUTE_
WEAK
llvmGetPassPluginInfo() {
  return {LLVM_PLUGIN_API_VERSION, "CountIR", "v0.1",
          [](PassBuilder &PB) {
            PB.registerPipelineParsingCallback(
                [](StringRef Name, FunctionPassManager
                        &FPM,
                   ArrayRef<PassBuilder::PipelineElement>)
                {
                  if (Name == "countir") {
                    FPM.addPass(CountIRPass());
                    return true;
                  }
                  return false;
                });
          }};
}
```

7. Now, we only need to add the build files. The `lib/CMakeLists.txt` file contains just one command to compile the source file. The LLVM-specific command, `add_llvm_library()`, ensures that the same compiler flags that were used to build LLVM are utilized:

```
add_llvm_library(CountIR MODULE CountIR.cpp)
```

The top-level `CMakeLists.txt` file is more complex.

8. As usual, we set the required CMake version and the project name. Additionally, we set the `LLVM_EXPORTED_SYMBOL_FILE` variable to ON. This is necessary to make the plugin work on Windows:

```
cmake_minimum_required(VERSION 3.4.3)
project(countirpass)


set(LLVM_EXPORTED_SYMBOL_FILE ON)
```

9. Next, we look for the LLVM installation. We also print information about the found version to the console:

```
find_package(LLVM REQUIRED CONFIG)
message(STATUS "Found LLVM ${LLVM_PACKAGE_VERSION}")
message(STATUS "Using LLVMConfig.cmake in: ${LLVM_DIR}")
```

10. Now, we can add the `cmake` folder from LLVM to the search path. We include the LLVM-specific files, `ChooseMSVCCRT` and `AddLLVM`, which provide additional commands:

```
list(APPEND CMAKE_MODULE_PATH ${LLVM_DIR})
include(ChooseMSVCCRT)
include(AddLLVM)
```

11. The compiler needs to know about the required definitions and the LLVM paths:

```
include_directories("${LLVM_INCLUDE_DIR}")
add_definitions("${LLVM_DEFINITIONS}")
link_directories("${LLVM_LIBRARY_DIR}")
```

12. Finally, we add our own include and source folders:

```
include_directories(BEFORE include)
add_subdirectory(lib)
```

13. Having implemented all of the required files, we can now create the `build` folder beside the `countirpass` folder. First, change to the build directory and create the build files:

```
$ cmake -G Ninja ../countirpass
```

14. Then, you can compile the plugin, as follows:

```
$ ninja
```

15. You use the plugin with the `opt` utility, which is the **modular LLVM optimizer and analyzer**. Among other things, the `opt` utility produces an optimized version of the input file. To use the plugin with it, you need to specify an additional parameter to load the plugin:

```
$ opt --load-pass-plugin=lib/CountIR.so
--passes="countir"\
    --disable-output --stats demo.ll
```

The output is the same as the previous version. Congratulations; the Pass plugin works!

So far, we have only created a Pass for the new Pass manager. In the next section, we will also extend the Pass for the old Pass manager.

Adapting a Pass for use with the old Pass manager

The future belongs to the new Pass manager, and it makes no sense to develop a new Pass for the old Pass manager exclusively. However, during the ongoing transition phase, it would be useful if a Pass could work with both Pass managers, as most of the Passes in LLVM already do.

The old Pass manager requires a Pass that has been derived from certain base classes. For example, a function Pass must derive from the `FunctionPass` base class. There are more differences, too. The method run by the Pass manager is named `runOnFunction()`, and an `ID` for the Pass must also be provided. The strategy we follow here is to create a separate class that we can use with the old Pass manager and refactor the source code in a way that the functionality can be used with both Pass managers.

We use the Pass plugin as a base. In the `include/CountIR.h` header file, we add a new class definition, as follows:

1. The new class needs to derive from the `FunctionPass` class, so we include an additional header to get the class definition:

```
#include "llvm/Pass.h"
```

2. We name the new class `CountIRLegacyPass`. The class needs an ID for the internal LLVM machinery, and we initialize the parent class with it:

```
class CountIRLegacyPass : public llvm::FunctionPass {
public:
  static char ID;
  CountIRLegacyPass() : llvm::FunctionPass(ID) {}
```

3. In order to implement the Pass functionality, two functions must be overridden. The `runOnFunction()` method is called for every LLVM IR function and implements our counting functionality. The `getAnalysisUsage()` method is used to announce that all of the analysis results are saved:

```
  bool runOnFunction(llvm::Function &F) override;
  void getAnalysisUsage(llvm::AnalysisUsage &AU) const
    override;
};
```

4. With the changes to the header file now complete, we can enhance the implementation inside the `lib/CountIR.cpp` file. To reuse the counting functionality, we move the source code into a new function:

```
void runCounting(Function &F) {
  for (BasicBlock &BB : F) {
    ++NumOfBB;
    for (Instruction &I : BB) {
      (void)I;
      ++NumOfInst;
    }
  }
}
```

5. The method for the new Pass manager needs to be updated in order to use the new function:

```
PreservedAnalyses
CountIRPass::run(Function &F, FunctionAnalysisManager
&AM) {
  runCounting(F);
```

```
    return PreservedAnalyses::all();
}
```

6. In the same way, we implement the method for the old Pass manager. With the
    `false` return value, we indicate that the IR did not change:

```
bool CountIRLegacyPass::runOnFunction(Function &F) {
    runCounting(F);
    return false;
}
```

7. To preserve the existing analysis results, the `getAnalysisUsage()`
    method must be implemented in the following way. This is similar to the
    `PreservedAnalyses::all()` return value in the new Pass manager. If you do
    not implement this method, then all analysis results are thrown away by default:

```
void CountIRLegacyPass::getAnalysisUsage(
    AnalysisUsage &AU) const {
  AU.setPreservesAll();
}
```

8. The `ID` field can be initialized with an arbitrary value because LLVM uses the
    address of the field. The common value is `0`, so we use it too:

```
char CountIRLegacyPass::ID = 0;
```

9. Only the Pass registration is missing now. To register the new Pass, we need to
    provide a static instance of the `RegisterPass<>` template. The first argument is
    the name of the command-line option to invoke the new Pass. The second argument
    is the name of the Pass, which is used, among other things, as information for the
    user when invoking the `-help` option:

```
static RegisterPass<CountIRLegacyPass>
    X("countir", "CountIR Pass");
```

10. These changes are enough to allow us to invoke our new Pass under the old Pass
    manager and the new Pass manager. To test the addition, change back into the
    `build` folder and compile the Pass:

```
$ ninja
```

11. To load the plugin for use with the old Pass manager, we need to use the `--load` option. Our new Pass is invoked with the `--countir` option:

```
$ opt --load lib/CountIR.so --countir --stats\
  --disable-output demo.ll
```

> **Tip**
> Please also check, in the command line from the previous section, that the invocation of our Pass with the new Pass manager still works fine!

Being able to run our new Pass with an LLVM-provided tool is nice, but ultimately, we want to run it inside our compiler. In the next section, we will explore how to set up an optimization pipeline and how to customize it.

Adding an optimization pipeline to your compiler

Our `tinylang` compiler, which was developed in the previous chapters, performs no optimizations on the created IR code. In the following sections, we will add an optimization pipeline to the compiler to perform this exactly.

Creating an optimization pipeline with the new Pass manager

Central to the setup of the optimization pipeline is the `PassBuilder` class. This class knows about all of the registered Passes and can construct a Pass pipeline from a textual description. We use this class to either create the Pass pipeline from a description given on the command line or use a default pipeline based on the requested optimization level. We also support the use of Pass plugins, such as the `countir` Pass plugin, which we discussed in the previous section. With this, we mimic part of the functionality of the `opt` tool and also use similar names for the command-line options.

The `PassBuilder` class populates an instance of a `ModulePassManager` class, which is the Pass manager to hold the constructed Pass pipeline and actually run it. The code generation Passes still use the old Pass manager; therefore, we have to retain the old Pass manager for this purpose.

For the implementation, we extend the `tools/driver/Driver.cpp` file from our `tinylang` compiler:

1. We use new classes, so we begin by adding new `include` files. The `llvm/Passes/PassBuilder.h` file provides the definition of the `PassBuilder` class. The `llvm/Passes/PassPlugin.h` file is required for plugin support. Finally, the `llvm/Analysis/TargetTransformInfo.h` file provides a Pass that connects IR-level transformations with target-specific information:

    ```
    #include "llvm/Passes/PassBuilder.h"
    #include "llvm/Passes/PassPlugin.h"
    #include "llvm/Analysis/TargetTransformInfo.h"
    ```

2. To use certain features of the new Pass manager, we add three command-line options, using the same names as the `opt` tool. The `--passes` option enables the textual specification of the Pass pipeline, and the `--load-pass-plugin` option enables the use of Pass plugins. If the `--debug-pass-manager` option is given, then the Pass manager prints out information about the executed Passes:

    ```
    static cl::opt<bool>
        DebugPM("debug-pass-manager", cl::Hidden,
                cl::desc("Print PM debugging
                         information"));
    static cl::opt<std::string> PassPipeline(
        "passes",
        cl::desc("A description of the pass pipeline"));
    static cl::list<std::string> PassPlugins(
        "load-pass-plugin",
        cl::desc("Load passes from plugin library"));
    ```

3. The user influences the construction of the Pass pipeline with the optimization level. The `PassBuilder` class supports six different optimization levels: one level with no optimization, three levels for optimizing the speed, and two levels for reducing the size. We capture all of these levels in one command-line option:

    ```
    static cl::opt<signed char> OptLevel(
        cl::desc("Setting the optimization level:"),
        cl::ZeroOrMore,
        cl::values(
            clEnumValN(3, "O", "Equivalent to -O3"),
    ```

```
            clEnumValN(0, "O0", "Optimization level 0"),
            clEnumValN(1, "O1", "Optimization level 1"),
            clEnumValN(2, "O2", "Optimization level 2"),
            clEnumValN(3, "O3", "Optimization level 3"),
            clEnumValN(-1, "Os",
                          "Like -O2 with extra
                          optimizations "
                          "for size"),
            clEnumValN(
                -2, "Oz",
                "Like -Os but reduces code size further")),
       cl::init(0));
```

4. The plugin mechanism of LLVM supports a static plugin registry, which is created during the configuration of the project. To make use of this registry, we include the `llvm/Support/Extension.def` database file to create the prototype for the functions, which returns the plugin information:

```
#define HANDLE_EXTENSION(Ext)                                    \
  llvm::PassPluginLibraryInfo get##Ext##PluginInfo();
#include "llvm/Support/Extension.def"
```

5. We replace the existing `emit()` function with a new version. We declare the required `PassBuilder` instance at top of the function:

```
bool emit(StringRef Argv0, llvm::Module *M,
          llvm::TargetMachine *TM,
          StringRef InputFilename) {
  PassBuilder PB(TM);
```

6. To implement the support for the Pass plugins given on the command line, we loop through the list of plugin libraries given by the user and try to load the plugin. We emit an error message if this fails; otherwise, we register the Passes:

```
for (auto &PluginFN : PassPlugins) {
  auto PassPlugin = PassPlugin::Load(PluginFN);
  if (!PassPlugin) {
    WithColor::error(errs(), Argv0)
        << "Failed to load passes from '"
```

```
            << PluginFN
            << "'. Request ignored.\n";
        continue;
    }

    PassPlugin->registerPassBuilderCallbacks(PB);
}
```

7. The information from the static plugin registry is used in a similar way to register those plugins with our `PassBuilder` instance:

```
#define HANDLE_EXTENSION(Ext)                              \
    get##Ext##PluginInfo().RegisterPassBuilderCallbacks( \
        PB);
#include "llvm/Support/Extension.def"
```

8. We need to declare variables for the different analysis managers. The only parameter is the debug flag:

```
    LoopAnalysisManager LAM(DebugPM);
    FunctionAnalysisManager FAM(DebugPM);
    CGSCCAnalysisManager CGAM(DebugPM);
    ModuleAnalysisManager MAM(DebugPM);
```

9. Next, we populate the analysis managers with calls to the respective `register` method on the `PassBuilder` instance. Through this call, the analysis manager is populated with the default analysis Passes and also runs registration callbacks. We also make sure that the function analysis manager uses the default alias-analysis pipeline and that all analysis managers know about each other:

```
    FAM.registerPass(
        [&] { return PB.buildDefaultAAPipeline(); });
    PB.registerModuleAnalyses(MAM);
    PB.registerCGSCCAnalyses(CGAM);
    PB.registerFunctionAnalyses(FAM);
    PB.registerLoopAnalyses(LAM);
    PB.crossRegisterProxies(LAM, FAM, CGAM, MAM);
```

10. The MPM module Pass manager holds the Pass pipeline that we construct. The instance is initialized with the debug flag:

```
ModulePassManager MPM(DebugPM);
```

11. We implement two different ways to populate the module Pass manager with the Pass pipeline. If the user provided a Pass pipeline on the command line, that is, they used the --passes option, then we use this as the Pass pipeline:

```
if (!PassPipeline.empty()) {
    if (auto Err = PB.parsePassPipeline(
            MPM, PassPipeline)) {
      WithColor::error(errs(), Argv0)
          << toString(std::move(Err)) << "\n";
      return false;
    }
}
```

12. Otherwise, we use the chosen optimization level to determine the Pass pipeline to construct. The name of the default Pass pipeline is default, and it takes the optimization level as a parameter:

```
else {
    StringRef DefaultPass;
    switch (OptLevel) {
    case 0: DefaultPass = "default<O0>"; break;
    case 1: DefaultPass = "default<O1>"; break;
    case 2: DefaultPass = "default<O2>"; break;
    case 3: DefaultPass = "default<O3>"; break;
    case -1: DefaultPass = "default<Os>"; break;
    case -2: DefaultPass = "default<Oz>"; break;
    }
    if (auto Err = PB.parsePassPipeline(
            MPM, DefaultPass)) {
      WithColor::error(errs(), Argv0)
          << toString(std::move(Err)) << "\n";
      return false;
    }
}
```

13. The Pass pipeline to run transformations on the IR code is now set up. We need an open file to write the result to. The system assembler and LLVM IR output are text based, so we should set the `OF_Text` flag for both of them:

```
std::error_code EC;
sys::fs::OpenFlags OpenFlags = sys::fs::OF_None;
CodeGenFileType FileType = codegen::getFileType();
if (FileType == CGFT_AssemblyFile)
  OpenFlags |= sys::fs::OF_Text;
auto Out = std::make_unique<llvm::ToolOutputFile>(
    outputFilename(InputFilename), EC, OpenFlags);
if (EC) {
  WithColor::error(errs(), Argv0)
      << EC.message() << '\n';
  return false;
}
```

14. For the code generation, we have to use the old Pass manager. We simply declare the `CodeGenPM` instances and add the Pass that makes target-specific information available at the IR transformation level:

```
legacy::PassManager CodeGenPM;
CodeGenPM.add(createTargetTransformInfoWrapperPass(
    TM->getTargetIRAnalysis()));
```

15. To output the LLVM IR, we add a Pass that just prints the IR into a stream:

```
if (FileType == CGFT_AssemblyFile && EmitLLVM) {
  CodeGenPM.add(createPrintModulePass(Out->os()));
}
```

16. Otherwise, we let the `TargetMachine` instance add the required code generation Passes, directed by the `FileType` value that we Pass as an argument:

```
else {
  if (TM->addPassesToEmitFile(CodeGenPM, Out->os(),
                              nullptr, FileType)) {
    WithColor::error()
```

```
        << "No support for file type\n";
      return false;
    }
  }
```

17. After all of this preparation, we are now ready to execute the Passes. First, we run the optimization pipeline on the IR module. Next, the code generation Passes are run. Of course, after all this work, we want to keep the output file:

```
    MPM.run(*M, MAM);
    CodeGenPM.run(*M);
    Out->keep();
    return true;
}
```

18. That was a lot of code, but it was straightforward. Of course, we also have to update the dependencies in the `tools/driver/CMakeLists.txt` build file. Besides adding the target components, we add all the transformation and code generation components from LLVM. The names roughly resemble the directory names where the source is located. The component name is translated to the link library name during the configuration process:

```
set(LLVM_LINK_COMPONENTS ${LLVM_TARGETS_TO_BUILD}
   AggressiveInstCombine Analysis AsmParser
   BitWriter CodeGen Core Coroutines IPO IRReader
   InstCombine Instrumentation MC ObjCARCOpts Remarks
   ScalarOpts Support Target TransformUtils Vectorize
   Passes)
```

19. Our compiler driver supports plugins, and we announce the following support:

```
add_tinylang_tool(tinylang Driver.cpp SUPPORT_PLUGINS)
```

20. In the same way as before, we have to link against our own libraries:

```
target_link_libraries(tinylang
   PRIVATE tinylangBasic tinylangCodeGen
   tinylangLexer tinylangParser tinylangSema)
```

These are necessary additions to the source code and the build system.

21. To build the extended compiler, change into your `build` directory and type in the following:

```
$ ninja
```

Changes to the files of the build system are automatically detected, and `cmake` is run before we compile and link our changed source. In case you need to rerun the configuration step, please follow the instructions located in *Chapter 2, Touring the LLVM Source,* in the *Compiling the tinylang application* section.

Since we have used the options for the `opt` tool as a blueprint, you should try running `tinylang` with the options to load a Pass plugin and run the Pass, as we did in the previous sections.

With the current implementation, we can either run a default Pass pipeline or construct one ourselves. The latter is very flexible but, in almost all cases, overkill. The default pipeline runs very well for C-like languages. What is missing is a way to extend the Pass pipeline. In the next section, we will explain how to implement this.

Extending the Pass pipeline

In the previous section, we used the `PassBuilder` class to create a Pass pipeline, either from a user-provided description or a predefined name. Now, we will look at another way to customize the Pass pipeline: using **extension points**.

During the construction of the Pass pipeline, the Pass builder allows you to add Passes contributed by the user. These places are called extension points. A number of extension points exist, such as the following:

- The pipeline start extension point allows you to add Passes at the beginning of the pipeline.

- The peephole extension point allows you to add Passes after each instance of the instruction combiner Pass.

Other extension points exist, too. To employ an extension point, you register a callback. During the construction of the Pass pipeline, your callback is run at the defined extension point and can add a Pass to the given Pass manager.

To register a callback for the pipeline start extension point, you call the `registerPipelineStartEPCallback()` method of the `PassBuilder` class. For example, to add our `CountIRPass` Pass to the beginning of the pipeline, you need to adapt the Pass to be used as a module Pass with a call to the `createModuleToFunctionPassAdaptor()` template function, and then add the Pass to the module Pass manager:

```
PB.registerPipelineStartEPCallback(
    [](ModulePassManager &MPM) {
        MPM.addPass(
            createModuleToFunctionPassAdaptor(
                CountIRPass());
    });
```

You can add this snippet in the Pass pipeline setup code at any point before the pipeline is created, that is, before the `parsePassPipeline()` method is called.

A very natural extension to what we have done in the previous section is to let the user Pass a pipeline description for an extension point on the command line. The `opt` tool allows this, too. Let's do this for the pipeline start extension point. First, we add the following code to the `tools/driver/Driver.cpp` file:

1. We add a new command line for the user to specify the pipeline description. Again, we take the option name from the `opt` tool:

```
static cl::opt<std::string> PipelineStartEPPipeline(
    "passes-ep-pipeline-start",
    cl::desc("Pipeline start extension point"));
```

2. Using a lambda function as a callback is the most convenient way. To parse the pipeline description, we call the `parsePassPipeline()` method of the `PassBuilder` instance. The Passes are added to the PM Pass manager and given as an argument to the lambda function. If there is an error, we print an error message without stopping the application. You can add this snippet after the call to the `crossRegisterProxies()` method:

```
PB.registerPipelineStartEPCallback(
    [&PB, Argv0](ModulePassManager &PM) {
        if (auto Err = PB.parsePassPipeline(
                PM, PipelineStartEPPipeline)) {
            WithColor::error(errs(), Argv0)
```

```
                   << "Could not parse pipeline "
                   << PipelineStartEPPipeline.ArgStr
                   << ": "
                   << toString(std::move(Err)) << "\n";
        }
     });
```

> **Tip**
>
> To allow the user to add Passes at every extension point, you need to add the preceding code snippet for each extension point.

3. It's now a good time to try out the different pass manager options. With the `--debug-pass-manager` option, you can follow which Passes are executed in which order. You can print the IR before or after each Pass is invoked using the `--print-before-all` and `--print-after-all` options. If you create your own Pass pipeline, then you can insert the `print` Pass in points of interest. For example, try the `--passes="print,inline,print"` option. You can also use the `print` Pass to explore the various extension points.

> **New print options in LLVM 12**
>
> LLVM 12 supports the `-print-changed` option, which will only print the IR code if it has changed, compared to the result from the earlier Pass. The greatly reduced output makes it much easier to follow IR transformations.

The `PassBuilder` class has a nested `OptimizationLevel` class to represent the six different optimization levels. Instead of using the `"default<O?>"` pipeline description as an argument to the `parsePassPipeline()` method, we can also call the `buildPerModuleDefaultPipeline()` method, which builds the default optimization pipeline for the request level – except for level `O0`. The optimization level, `O0`, means that no optimization is performed. Consequently, no Passes are added to the Pass manager. If we still want to run a certain Pass, then we can add it to the Pass manager manually. A simple Pass to run at this level is the `AlwaysInliner` Pass, which inlines a function marked with an `always_inline` attribute into the caller. After translating the command-line option value for the optimization level into the corresponding member of the `OptimizationLevel` class, we can implement this as follows:

```
     PassBuilder::OptimizationLevel OLevel = …;
     if (OLevel == PassBuilder::OptimizationLevel::O0)
```

```
        MPM.addPass(AlwaysInlinerPass());
    else
        MPM = PB.buildPerModuleDefaultPipeline(OLevel,
            DebugPM);
```

Of course, it is possible to add more than one Pass to the Pass manager in this fashion. The `PassBuilder` class also uses the `addPass()` method during the construction of the Pass pipeline.

> **New functionality in LLVM 12 – running extension point callbacks**
>
> Because the Pass pipeline is not populated for optimization level O0, the registered extension points are not called. If you use the extension points to register Passes, which should also run at the O0 level, this is problematic. In LLVM 12, the new `runRegisteredEPCallbacks()` method can be called to run the registered extension point callbacks, resulting in a Pass manager populated only with the Passes registered through the extension points.

With the addition of the optimization pipeline to `tinylang`, you can create an optimizing compiler such as clang. The LLVM community works on improving the optimizations and the optimization pipeline with each release. Because of this, it is very seldom that the default pipeline is not used. Most often, new Passes are added to implement certain semantics of the programming language.

Summary

In this chapter, you learned how to create a new Pass for LLVM. You ran the Pass using a Pass pipeline description and an extension point. You extended your compiler with the construction and execution of a Pass pipeline similar to clang, turning `tinylang` into an optimizing compiler. The Pass pipeline allows you to add Passes at extension points, and you learned how to register Passes at these points. This enables you to extend the optimization pipeline with your own developed Passes or existing Passes.

In the next chapter, we will explore how LLVM generates machine instructions from the optimized IR.

Section 3 – Taking LLVM to the Next Level

In this section, you will learn how instruction selection is implemented in LLVM, and you will apply this knowledge by adding support for a new machine instruction. LLVM has a **just-in-time** (**JIT**) compiler, and you will learn how you can use it and how to tailor it to your needs. You will also try out the various tools and libraries that help to identify bugs in applications. Finally, you will extend LLVM with a new backend, which will equip you with the knowledge required to take advantage of new architectures not yet supported by LLVM.

This section comprises the following chapters:

- *Chapter 9, Instruction Selection*
- *Chapter 10, JIT Compilation*
- *Chapter 11, Debugging Using LLVM Tools*
- *Chapter 12, Creating Your Own Backend*

9
Instruction Selection

The LLVM IR used so far still needs to be turned into machine instructions. This is called **instruction selection**, often abbreviated to **ISel**. Instruction selection is an important part of the target backend, and LLVM has three different approaches for selecting instructions: the selection DAG, fast instruction selection, and global instruction selection.

In this chapter, you will learn the following topics:

- Understanding the LLVM target backend structure, which introduces you to the task performed by the target backend, and you examine the machine passes to run.

- Using the **machine IR (MIR)** to test and debug the backend, which helps you to output MIR after a specified pass and run a pass on the MIR file.

- How instruction selection works, in which you learn about the different ways LLVM performs instruction selection.

- Supporting new machine instructions, in which you add a new machine instruction and make it available to the instruction selection.

By the end of the chapter, you will know how the target backends are structured and how instruction selection works. You will also acquire the knowledge to add currently unsupported machine instructions to the assembler and the instruction selection, and how to test your addition.

Technical requirements

To see the graph visualization, you must install the **Graphviz** software, which can be downloaded from `https://graphviz.org/`. The source code is available at `http://gitlab.com/graphviz/graphviz/`.

The source code for this chapter is available at `https://github.com/PacktPublishing/Learn-LLVM-12/tree/master/Chapter09`

You can find the code in action videos at `https://bit.ly/3nllhED`

Understanding the LLVM target backend structure

After the LLVM IR is optimized, the selected LLVM target is used to generate the machine code from it. Among others, the following tasks are performed in the target backend:

1. The **directed acyclic graph** (**DAG**) used for instruction selection, usually referred to as the **SelectionDAG**, is constructed.

2. Machine instructions corresponding to the IR code are selected.

3. The selected machine instructions are ordered in an optimal sequence.

4. Virtual registers are replaced with machine registers.

5. Prologue and epilogue code is added to functions.

6. Basic blocks are ordered in an optimal sequence.

7. Target-specific passes are run.

8. Object code or assembly is emitted.

All these steps are implemented as machine function passes, derived from the `MachineFunctionPass` class. This is a subclass of the `FunctionPass` class, one of the base classes used by the old pass manager. As of LLVM 12, the conversion of machine function passes to the new pass manager is still a work in progress.

During all these steps, an LLVM instruction undergoes a transformation. At the code level, an LLVM IR instruction is represented by an instance of the `Instruction` class. During the instruction selection phase, it is transformed into a `MachineInstr` instance. This is a representation much nearer to the actual machine level. It already contains the instructions that are valid for the target, but still operates on virtual registers (up to register allocation) and also can contain certain pseudo instructions. The passes after the instruction selection refine this, and in the end, an instance of `MCInstr` is created, which is a representation of the real machine instruction. The `MCInstr` instance can be written into an object file or printed as assembly code.

To explore the backend passes, you can create a small IR file with the following content:

```
define i16 @sum(i16 %a, i16 %b) {
  %res = add i16 %a, 3
  ret i16 %res
}
```

Save this code as sum.ll. Compile it for the MIPS architecture using llc, the LLVM static compiler. This tool compiles LLVM IR into assembly text or an object file. The target platform compile for can be overridden on the command line with the –mtriple option. Invoke the llc tool with the –debug-pass=Structure option:

```
$ llc -mtriple=mips-linux-gnu -debug-pass=Structure < sum.ll
```

Besides the generated assembly code, you will see a long list of machine passes to run. Among them, the MIPS DAG->DAG Pattern Instruction Selection pass performs the instruction selection, the Mips Delay Slot Filler is a target-specific pass, and the last pass before cleanup, Mips Assembly Printer, is responsible for printing the assembly code. Of all of these passes, the instruction selection pass is the most interesting one, and we look at it in detail in the next section.

Using MIR to test and debug the backend

You saw in the previous section that many passes are run in the target backend. However, most of these passes do not operate on LLVM IR, but on MIR. This is a target-dependent representation of the instructions, and therefore more low-level than LLVM IR. It can still contain references to virtual registers, so it is not yet the pure instruction of the target CPU.

To see the optimizations on the IR level, you can, for example, tell llc to dump the IR after each pass. This does not work with the machine passes in the backend, because they do not work on IR. Instead, MIR serves a similar purpose.

MIR is a textual representation of the current state of the machine instructions in the current module. It utilizes the YAML format, which allows for serialization and deserialization. The basic idea is that you can stop the pass pipeline at a point and inspect the state in YAML format. You can also modify the YAML file, or create your own, and pass on it, and inspect the result. This allows for easy debugging and testing.

Let's have a look at MIR. Run the `llc` tool with the `--stop-after=finalize-isel` option and the test input file we used earlier:

```
$ llc -mtriple=mips-linux-gnu \
       -stop-after=finalize-isel < sum.ll
```

This instructs `llc` to dump MIR after instruction selection is complete. The shortened output looks like this:

```
---
name:                    sum
body:                    |
  bb.0 (%ir-block.0):
      liveins: $a0, $a1

      %1:gpr32 = COPY $a1
      %0:gpr32 = COPY $a0
      %2:gpr32 = ADDu %0, %1
      $v0 = COPY %2
      RetRA implicit $v0

...
```

There are several properties you immediately note. First, there is a mix of virtual registers such as %0 and real machine registers such as $a0. The reason for this comes from ABI lowering. To be portable across different compilers and languages, functions adhere to a calling convention, which is part of the **application binary interface (ABI)**. The output is for a Linux system on a MIPS machine. With the calling convention used by the system, the first parameter is passed in register $a0. Because the MIR output was generated after the instruction selection but before register allocation, you still see the use of virtual registers.

Instead of the add instruction from LLVM IR, the machine instruction ADDu is used in the MIR file. You can also see that the virtual registers have a register call attached, in this case, gpr32. There are no 16-bit registers on the MIPS architecture, and therefore 32-bit registers must be used.

The bb.0 label refers to the first basic block, and the indented content after the label is part of the basic blocks. The first statement specifies the registers that are live on entry to the basic block. After that, the instructions follow. In this case, only $a0, and $a1, both parameters, are live on entry.

There are a lot of other details in the MIR file. You can read about them in the LLVM MIR documentation at `https://llvm.org/docs/MIRLangRef.html`.

One problem you encounter is how to find out the name of a pass, especially if you just need to examine the output after that pass without actively working on it. When using the `-debug-pass=Structure` option with `llc`, the options that activate the passes are printed on the top. For example, if you want to stop before the `Mips Delay Slot Filler` pass, then you need to look at the printed list, and hopefully find the `-mips-delay-slot-filler` option, which also gives you the name of the pass.

The main application of the MIR file format is to aid in testing machine passes in the target backend. Using `llc` with the `--stop-after` option, you get the MIR after the specified pass. Usually, you will use this as the base for your intended test case. The first thing you note is that the MIR output is very verbose. For example, many fields are empty. To reduce this clutter, you can add the `-simplify-mir` option to the `llc` command line.

You save and change the MIR as needed for your test case. The `llc` tool can run a single pass, and this is a perfect match for testing with the MIR file. Let's assume you like to test the `MIPS Delay Slot Filler` pass. The delay slot is a special property of RISC architectures such as MIPS or SPARC: the next instruction after a jump is always executed. Therefore, the compiler must make sure that there is a suitable instruction after each jump, and this pass performs this duty.

We generate the MIR before running the pass:

```
$ llc -mtriple=mips-linux-gnu \
      -stop-before=mips-delay-slot-filler -simplify-mir \
      < sum.ll   >delay.mir
```

The output is much smaller because we used the `-simplify-mir` option. The body of the function is now the following:

```
body:                           |
  bb.0 (%ir-block.0):
    liveins: $a0, $a1


    renamable $v0 = ADDu killed renamable $a0,
                              killed renamable $a1
    PseudoReturn undef $ra, implicit $v0
```

Most notably, you will see the ADDu instruction, followed by apseudo instruction for the return.

With the delay.ll file as input, we now run the delay slot filler pass:

```
$ llc -mtriple=mips-linux-gnu \
        -run-pass=mips-delay-slot-filler -o - delay.mir
```

Now compare the function in the output with the earlier one:

```
body:                           |
  bb.0 (%ir-block.0):
    PseudoReturn undef $ra, implicit $v0 {
        renamable $v0 = ADDu killed renamable $a0,
                             killed renamable $a1
    }
```

You see that ADDu and the pseudo instruction for the return have changed order, and the ADDu instruction is now nested inside the return: the pass identified the ADDu instruction as suitable for the delay slot.

In case the delay slot concept is new to you, you will also want to have a look at the generated assembly, which you easily generate with llc:

```
$ llc -mtriple=mips-linux-gnu < sum.ll
```

The output contains a lot of details, but with the help of the bb.0 name of the basic block, you can easily locate the generated assembly code for it:

```
# %bb.0:
        jr      $ra
        addu    $2, $4, $5
```

Indeed, the order of the instructions changed!

Equipped with this knowledge, we take a look at the heart of the target backend and examine how machine instruction selection is performed in LLVM.

How instruction selection works

The task of an LLVM backend is to create machine instructions from the LLVM IR. This process is called **instruction selection** or **lowering**. Motivated by the idea to automate this task as much as possible, the LLVM developers invented the TableGen language to capture all the details of a target description. We first look at this language before diving into the instruction selection algorithms.

Specifying the target description in the TableGen language

A machine instruction has a lot of properties: a mnemonic used by the assembler and disassembler, a bit pattern to represent the instruction in memory, input and output operands, and so on. The LLVM developers decided to capture all this information in a single place, the **target description**. A new language, the **TableGen language**, was invented for this purpose. The idea was to use a code generator to create various source fragments from the target description, which could then be used in different tools. Target descriptions are stored in files using the .td suffix.

In principle, the TableGen language is very simple. All you can do is define records. A **record** has a unique name and contains a list of values and a list of superclasses. A **definition** is a record in which all values are defined, while a **class** is a record that can have undefined values. The main purpose of classes is to have an abstract record that can be used to build other abstract or concrete records. For example, the Register class defines the common properties of a register, and you can define a concrete record for register R0:

```
class Register {
  string name;
}

def R0 : Register {
  let name = "R0";
  string altName = "$0";
}
```

You use the let keyword to override a value.

The TableGen language has a lot of syntactic sugar to make dealing with records easier. A class can have a template argument, for example:

```
class Register<string n> {
  string name = n;
}
```

```
def R0 : Register<"R0"> {
  string altName = "$0";
}
```

The TableGen language is statically typed, and you have to specify the type of each value. Some of the supported types are the following:

- `bit`: A single bit
- `int`: A 64-bit integer value
- `bits<n>`: An integral type consisting of *n* bits
- `string`: A character string
- `list<t>`: A list of elements of type `t`
- `dag`: A **directed acyclic graph** (**DAG**; used by the instruction selection)

The name of a class can also be used as a type. For example, `list<Register>` specifies a list of elements of the `Register` class.

The language allows the inclusion of other files with the `include` keyword. For conditional compiling, the preprocessor directives `#define`, `#ifdef`, and `#ifndef` are supported.

The TableGen library in LLVM can parse files written in the TableGen language and create an in-memory representation of the records. You can use this library to create your own generator.

LLVM comes with its own generator tool called `llvm-tblgen` and some `.td` files. The target description of a backend includes the `llvm/Target/Target.td` file first. This file defines classes such as `Register`, `Target`, or `Processor`. The `llvm-tblgen` tool knows about these classes and generates C++ code from the defined records.

Let's have a look at the MIPS backend as an example. The target description is in the `Mips.td` file in the `llvm/lib/Target/Mips` folder. This file includes the `Target.td` file mentioned first. It also defines target features, for example:

```
def FeatureMips64r2
  : SubtargetFeature<"mips64r2", "MipsArchVersion",
                     "Mips64r2", "Mips64r2 ISA Support",
                     [FeatureMips64, FeatureMips32r2]>;
```

Such features are later used to define CPU models, for example:

```
def : Proc<"mips64r2", [FeatureMips64r2]>;
```

Other files that define registers, instructions, scheduling models, and so on are also included.

The `llvm-tblgen` tool can show you the records defined by this target description. If you are in the `build` directory, then the following command will print the records to the console:

```
$ bin/llvm-tblgen \
  -I../llvm-project/llvm/lib/Target/Mips/ \
  -I../llvm-project/llvm/include \
  ../llvm-project/llvm/lib/Target/Mips/Mips.td
```

Like with Clang, the `-I` option adds a directory to search when including files. To see the records can be helpful for debugging. The real purpose of the tool is to generate C++ code from the records. For example, with the `-gen-subtarget` option, the data necessary to parse the `-mcpu=` and `-mtarget=` option of `llc` is emitted to the console:

```
$ bin/llvm-tblgen \
  -I../llvm-project/llvm/lib/Target/Mips/ \
  -I../llvm-project/llvm/include \
  ../llvm-project/llvm/lib/Target/Mips/Mips.td \
  -gen-subtarget
```

Save the generated code from that command in a file and explore how the feature and the CPU are used in generated code!

The encoding of instructions usually follows a handful of patterns. Therefore, the definition of instructions is split into classes defining the bit encoding and the concrete definition of instruction. The encoding for the MIPS instructions is in the file `llvm/Target/Mips/MipsInstrFormats.td`. Let's have a look at the definition of the `ADD_FM` format:

```
class ADD_FM<bits<6> op, bits<6> funct> : StdArch {
  bits<5> rd;
  bits<5> rs;
  bits<5> rt;

  bits<32> Inst;

  let Inst{31-26} = op;
  let Inst{25-21} = rs;
  let Inst{20-16} = rt;
  let Inst{15-11} = rd;
  let Inst{10-6}  = 0;
  let Inst{5-0}   = funct;
}
```

In the record body, several new bit fields are defined: `rd`, `rs`, and so on. They are used to override portions of the `Inst` field, which holds the bit pattern for the instruction. The `rd`, `rs`, and `rt` bit fields encode the registers the instruction operates on, and the `op` and `funct` parameters denote the opcode and a function number. The `StdArch` superclass only adds a field stating that this format follows a standard encoding.

Most instruction encoding in the MIPS target does not refer to the DAG nodes and do not specify the assembly mnemonic. A separate class is defined for that. One of the instructions in the MIPS architecture is the `nor` instruction, which computes the bitwise or of the first and second input register, inverts the bits of the result, and assigns the result to the output register. There are several variants of this instruction, and the following `LogicNOR` class helps with avoiding the same definitions multiple times:

```
class LogicNOR<string opstr, RegisterOperand RO>:
  InstSE<(outs RO:$rd), (ins RO:$rs, RO:$rt),
          !strconcat(opstr, "\t$rd, $rs, $rt"),
          [(set RO:$rd, (not (or RO:$rs, RO:$rt)))],
          II_NOR, FrmR, opstr> {
```

```
    let isCommutable = 1;
}
```

Wow, the simple concept of records now looks complicated. Let's dissect that definition. The class derives from the `InstSE` class, which is always used for instructions with standard encoding. If you follow the superclass hierarchy further, then you see that this class derives from `Instruction` class, which is the predefined class denoting an instruction of a target. The `(outs RO:$rd)` parameter defines the result of the final instruction as a DAG node. The `RO` part refers to the parameter of the same name of the `LogicNOR` class and denotes a register operand. The `$rd` is the register to use. This is the value that will be put later into the instruction encoding, in the `rd` field. The second parameter defines the values the instruction will operate on. In summary, this class is for an instruction that operates on three registers. The `!strconcat(opstr, "\t$rd, $rs, $rt")` parameter assembles the textual representation of the instruction. The `!strconcat` operator is a predefined functionality from TableGen, which concatenates two strings. You can look up all predefined operators in the TableGen programmer's guide at: `https://llvm.org/docs/TableGen/ProgRef.html`.

It follows a pattern definition, which resembles the textual description of the `nor` instruction and describes the computation of this instruction. The first element of the pattern is the operation, which is followed by a comma-separated list of operands. The operands refer to the register names in the DAG parameters and also specify an LLVM IR value type. LLVM has a set of predefined operators, such as `add` and `and`, which can be used in patterns. The operators are of the `SDNode` class, and can also be used as parameters. You can look up the predefined operators in the file `llvm/Target/TargetSelectionDAG.td`.

The `II_NOR` parameter specifies the itinerary class used in the scheduling model, and the `FrmR` parameter is a value defined to identify this instruction format. Finally, the `opstr` mnemonic is passed to the superclass. The body of this class is quite simple: it just specifies that the `nor` operation is commutative, which means that the order of the operands can be swapped.

Finally, this class is used to define a record for an instruction, as an example, for the `nor` instruction in 64-bit mode:

```
def NOR64 : LogicNOR<"nor", GPR64Opnd>, ADD_FM<0, 0x27>,
                        GPR_64;
```

This is the final definition, recognizable from the def keyword. It uses the LogicNOR class to define the DAG operands and pattern, and the ADD_FM class to specify the binary instruction encoding. The additional GPR_64 predicate makes sure that this instruction is only used if 64-bit registers are available.

The developers try hard to not repeat definitions multiple times, and one often-used approach is the use of multiclass classes. A multiclass class can define multiple records at once.

For example, the floating point unit of a MIPS CPU can perform addition with single- or double-precision floating point values. The definition of both instructions is very similar, therefore a multiclass class is defined to create two instructions at once:

```
multiclass ADDS_M<…> {
    def _D32 : ADDS_FT<…>, FGR_32;
    def _D64 : ADDS_FT<…>, FGR_64;
}
```

The ADDS_FT class defines the instruction format, similar to the LogicNOR class. The FGR_32 and FGR_64 predicates are used to decide at compile time which instruction can be used. The important part is the definition of _D32 and _D64 records. These are the templates for the records. The instruction records are then defined with the defm keyword:

```
defm FADD : ADDS_M<…>;
```

This defines the two records from the multiclass at once and assigns the names FADD_D32 and FADD_D64 to them. This is a very powerful way to avoid code repetition, and it is often used in the target descriptions, but combined with the other TableGen features it can lead to very cryptic definitions.

With the knowledge of how the target description is organized, we can now explore the instruction selection in the next section.

Instruction selection with the selection DAG

The standard way LLVM converts the IR to machine instructions is via a DAG. Using pattern matching with the patterns provided in the target description and using custom code, the IR instructions are transformed into machine instructions. This approach is not as straightforward as it sounds: the IR is mostly target-independent and can contain data types that are not supported on the target. For example, the i1 type representing a single bit is not a valid type on most targets.

The selectionDAG consists of nodes of `SDNode` type, defined in the file `llvm/CodeGen/SelectionDAGNodes.h`. The operation the node represents is called `OpCode`, and the target-independent codes are defined in the file `llvm/CodeGen/ISDOpcodes.h`. Besides the operation, the node stores the operands and the value it produces.

The values and operands of a node form a data flow dependency. A control flow dependency is represented by chain edges, which have the special type `MVT::Other`. This makes it possible to keep the order of instructions with side effects, for example, a load instruction.

Instruction selection using the selection DAG is performed with the following steps:

1. The DAG is constructed.
2. The DAG is optimized.
3. The types in the DAG are legalized.
4. The DAG is optimized.
5. The operations in the DAG are legalized.
6. The DAG is optimized.
7. The instructions are selected.
8. The instructions are ordered.

Let's examine how we can follow the changes each of the steps makes to the selection DAG.

How to follow the instruction selection process

You can see the work of the instruction selection in two different ways. If you pass the `-debug-only=isel` option to the `llc` tool, then the result of each step is printed in textual format. This is a great help if you need to investigate why a machine instruction was selected. For example, run the following command to see the output for the `sum.ll` file from the *Understanding the LLVM target backend structure* section:

```
$ llc -mtriple=mips-linux-gnu -debug-only=isel < sum.ll
```

This prints a lot of information. At the top of the output, you see the description of the initial created DAG for the input:

```
Initial selection DAG: %bb.0 'sum:'
SelectionDAG has 12 nodes:
  t0: ch = EntryToken
```

```
          t2: i32,ch = CopyFromReg t0, Register:i32 %0
       t5: i16 = truncate t2
          t4: i32,ch = CopyFromReg t0, Register:i32 %1
       t6: i16 = truncate t4
    t7: i16 = add t5, t6
  t8: i32 = any_extend t7
t10: ch,glue = CopyToReg t0, Register:i32 $v0, t8
t11: ch = MipsISD::Ret t10, Register:i32 $v0, t10:1
```

Like in the MIR output from the last section, you see here CopyFromReg instructions, which transfer the content of registers used by the ABI to virtual nodes. The truncate nodes are required because the example uses 16-bit values, but the MIPS architectures have only native support for 32-bit values. The add operation is performed on 16-bit virtual registers, and the result is extended and returned to the caller. Such a section is printed for each of the steps mentioned above.

LLVM can also generate a visualization of the selection DAG with the help of the *Graphviz* software. If you pass the —view-dag-combine1-dags option to the llc tool, then a window opens showing the constructed DAG. For example, run llc with the small file from the preceding:

```
$ llc -mtriple=mips-linux-gnu  -view-dag-combine1-dags sum.ll
```

Running on a Windows PC, you then see the DAG:

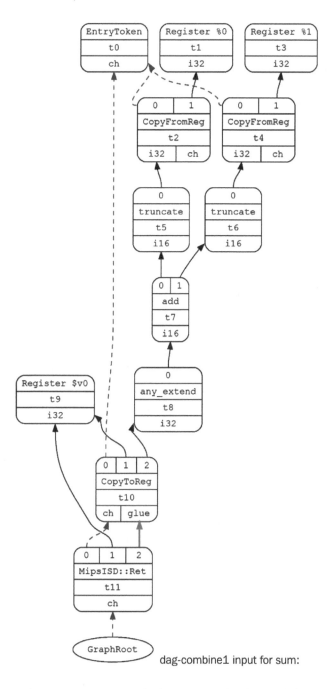

dag-combine1 input for sum:

Figure 9.1 – Constructed selection DAG for the sum.ll file

Be sure to compare that the textual representation and this graph contain the same information. The `EntryToken` is the start of the DAG, and the `GraphRoot` is the final node. The chain for the control flow is marked with the blue dashed arrows. The black arrows denote the data flow. The red arrows glue nodes together, preventing reordering them. The graph can get really big even for moderately sized functions. It does not contain more or other information than the textual output with the `-debug-only=isel` option, only the presentation is more comfortable. You can also generate the graph at other points in time, for example:

- Add the `--view-legalize-types-dags` option to see the DAG before type legalization.

- Add the `-view-isel-dags` option to see the selection instructions.

You can see all available options to view the DAG using the `--help-hidden` option. Because the DAG can get large and confusing, you can limit the rendering to one basic block using the `-filter-view-dags` option.

Examining the instruction selection

Knowing how to visualize the DAG, we can now dive into the details. The selection DAG is constructed from the IR. For each function in the IR, an instance of the `SelectionDAG` class is populated by the `SelectionDAGBuilder` class. There are no special optimizations done at this step. Nevertheless, a target needs to provide some functions to lower calls, argument handling, return jumps, and so on. To do so, the target has to implement the `TargetLowering` interface. Inside the folder of a target, the source is usually in the `XXXISelLowering.h` and `XXXISelLowering.cpp` files. The implementation of the `TargetLowering` interface provides all the information needed for the instruction process, for example, which data types and which operations are supported on the target.

The optimization step is run several times. The optimizer performs simple optimization, for example identifying rotates on targets that support these operations. The rationale here is that a cleaned-up DAG is produced, which simplifies the other steps.

During the type legalization step, types that are not supported on the target are replaced with supported ones. For example, if a target natively supports only 32-bit-wide integers, then smaller values must be converted to 32-bit through sign or zero extension. This is called **promoting**. If a 64-bit value can't be handled by this target, then the value must be split into a pair of 32-bit values. This is called **expanding**. Vector types are treated similarly. A vector type can be extended with additional elements, or it can be broken up into several values. For example, a vector with four values could be split into two vectors with two values each. If the splitting process ends with a single value, then no suitable vector could be found and scalar types are used instead. This is called **scalarizing**. The information about the supported types is configured in the target-specific implementation of the `TargetLowering` interface. After type legalization, the selection DAG has this textual representation for the `sum.ll` file:

```
Optimized type-legalized selection DAG: %bb.0 'sum:'
SelectionDAG has 9 nodes:
  t0: ch = EntryToken
        t2: i32,ch = CopyFromReg t0, Register:i32 %0
        t4: i32,ch = CopyFromReg t0, Register:i32 %1
     t12: i32 = add t2, t4
  t10: ch,glue = CopyToReg t0, Register:i32 $v0, t12
  t11: ch = MipsISD::Ret t10, Register:i32 $v0, t10:1
```

If you compare this with the initial constructed DAG, then here only 32-bit registers are used. The 16-bit values were promoted, because only 32-bit values are supported natively.

Operation legalization is similar to type legalization. This step is necessary because not all operations may be supported by a target, or even if a type is natively supported on a target, it may not valid for all operations. For example, not all targets have a native instruction for population count. In such cases, the operation is replaced by a sequence of operations to implement the functionality. If the type does not fit for the operation, then promoting the type to a larger one could be done. It is also possible for a backend author to provide custom code. If the legalization action is set to `Custom`, then the `LowerOperation()` method in the `TargetLowering` class is called for these operations. The method must create a legal version of the operation then. In the `sum.ll` example, the `add` operation is already legal, because addition of two 23-bit registers is supported on the platform, and nothing changed.

After types and operations are legalized, the instruction selection happens. A large part of the selection is automated. Remember from the previous section that you provided a pattern in the description of an instruction. From these descriptions, a pattern matcher is generated by the `llvm-tblgen` tool. Basically, the pattern matcher tries to find a pattern that matches the current DAG node. The instruction associated with the pattern will then be selected. The pattern matcher is implemented as a bytecode interpreter. The available codes for the interpreter are defined in the `llvm/CodeGen/SelectionDAGISel.h` header file. The `XXXISelDAGToDAG` class implements the instruction selection for a target. The `Select()` method is called for each DAG node. The default is to call the generated matcher, but you can also add code for cases not handled by it.

It is noteworthy that there is no one-to-one relationship between a selection DAG node and the selected instructions. A DAG node can expand into several instructions, and several DAG nodes can collapse into a single instruction. An example of the former is synthesizing immediate values. Especially on RISC architectures, the bit length of immediate values is restricted. A 32-bit target may only support an embedded immediate value of 16-bit length. To perform an operation that requires a 32-bit constant value, you usually split it into two 16-bit values and then generate two or more instructions that use the 16-bit values instead. Among others, you find patterns for this in the MIPS target. Bit-field instructions are a common example for the latter case: combinations of and, or, and `shift` DAG nodes can often be matched to special bit-field instructions, resulting in just one instruction for two or more DAG nodes.

Usually, you specify a pattern in the target description to combine two or more DAG nodes. For more complex cases, which are not easily handled with a pattern, you can mark the operation of the top node to require special DAG combine treatment. For these nodes, the `PerformDAGCombine()` method in the `XXXISelLowering` class is called. You can then check arbitrary complex patterns, and if you find your match, then you can return the operation representing the combined DAG nodes. This method is called before the generated matcher is run for the DAG node.

You can follow the instruction selection process in the printed output for the `sum.ll` file. For the add operation, you find there the following lines:

```
ISEL: Starting selection on root node: t12: i32 = add t2, t4
ISEL: Starting pattern match
  Initial Opcode index to 27835
  ...
  Morphed node: t12: i32 = ADDu t2, t4
ISEL: Match complete!
```

The index numbers point into the array of the generated matcher. The start is at index 27835 (an arbitrary value that can change from release to release), and after some steps, the ADDu instruction is selected.

> **Following the pattern matching**
>
> If you encounter a problem with a pattern, then you can also retrace the matching by reading the generated bytecode. You find the source in the `lib/Target/XXX/XXXGenDAGIsel.inc` file in the `build` directory. You open the file in a text editor and search for the index in the preceding output. Each line is prefixed with the index number, so you can easily find the right place in the array. The used predicates are also printed as comments, so they can help you to understand why a certain pattern was not selected.

Turning the DAG into instruction sequences

After instruction selection, the code is still a graph. This data structure needs to be flattened, which means that the instructions must be sequentially ordered. The graph contains data and control flow dependencies, but there are always several possibilities to order the instructions in such a way that these dependencies are fulfilled. What we want is an order that best utilizes the hardware. Modern hardware can issue several instructions in parallel, but restrictions always apply. A simple example of such a restriction is one instruction requiring the result of another instruction. In such a case, the hardware may not be able to issue both instructions and instead executes the instructions in sequence.

You can add a scheduling model to the target description, which describes the available units and their properties. For example, if a CPU has two integer arithmetic units, then this information is captured in the model. For each instruction, it is necessary to know which part of the model is used. There are different ways to do this. The newer, recommended approach is to define a scheduling model using the so-called machine-instruction scheduler. To do so, you need to define a `SchedMachineModel` record for each subtarget in the target description. Basically, the model consists of definitions for the input and output operands of instructions and processor resources. Both definitions are then associated together with latency values. You can look up the predefined types for this model in the `llvm/Target/TargetSched.td` file. Look at the Lanai target for a very simple model and in the SystemZ target for a complex scheduling model.

There is also an older model based on so-called itineraries. With this model, you define processor units as `FuncUnit` records. A step using such a unit is defined as an `InstrStage` record. Each instruction is associated with an itinerary class. For each itinerary class, the used processor pipeline composed of `InstrStage` records is defined, together with the number of processor cycles required for execution. You can find the predefined types for the itinerary model in the `llvm/Target/TargetItinerary.td` file.

Some targets use both models. One reason is due to development history. The itinerary-based model was the first one added to LLVM, and targets began using this model. When the new machine-instruction scheduler was added more than 5 years later, nobody cared enough to migrate the already existing models. Another reason is that with the itinerary model, you can not only model an instruction that uses multiple processor units, but you can also specify during which cycles the units are used. However, this detail level is rarely needed, and if it is needed, then you can refer to the machine-instruction scheduler model to the defined itineraries, basically pulling this information into the new model too.

If present, the scheduling model is used to order the instructions in an optimal way. After this step, the DAG is not needed anymore and is destroyed.

Performing instruction selection with the selection DAG produces almost optimal results, but it comes at a cost in terms of runtime and memory usage. Therefore, alternative approaches were developed, which we examine next. In the next section, we look at the fast instruction selection approach.

Fast instruction selection – FastISel

Using the selection DAG for instruction selection costs compile time. If you are developing an application, then the runtime of the compiler matters. You also do not care about the generated code so much, because it is more important that complete debug information is emitted. Because of these reasons, the LLVM developers decided to implement a special instruction selector that has a fast runtime but produces less optimal code, and which is used only for –O0 optimization level. This component is called fast instruction selection, or **FastISel** for short.

The implementation is in the `XXXFastISel` classes. Not every target supports this instruction selection method, in which case the selection DAG approach is used for –O0, too. The implementation is straightforward: a target-specific class is derived from a `FastISel` class and has to implement a couple of methods. The TableGen tool generates most of the required code from the target description. Nevertheless, there is some effort needed to implement this instruction selector. One of the root causes is that you need to get the calling convention right, which is usually complex.

The MIPS target features an implementation of fast instruction selection. You can enable use of fast instruction selection by passing the `-fast-isel` option to `llc` tool. Using the `sum.ll` example file from first section, an invocation looks like this:

```
$ llc -mtriple=mips-linux-gnu -fast-isel -O0 sum.ll
```

Fast instruction selection runs very quickly, but it is a completely different code path. Some LLVM developers decided to look for a solution that runs quickly but can also produce good code, with the goal to replace both the selection `dag` and the fast instruction selector in the future. We look at this approach in the next section.

The new global instruction selection – GlobalISel

Using the selection DAG, we can generate pretty good machine code. The drawback is that it is a very complex piece of software. This means that it is hard to develop, test, and maintain. The FastISel instruction selection works quickly and is less complex, but does not produce good code. Both approaches do not share much code, except for the code generated by TableGen.

Can we have the best of both worlds? One instruction selection algorithm, which is fast, easy to implement, and which produces good code? That is the motivation for adding another instruction selection algorithm, the global instruction selection, to the LLVM framework. The short-term goal is to replace FastISel first, and in the long term the selection DAG, too.

The approach taken by global instruction selection is to build on the existing infrastructure. The whole task is broken down into a sequence of machine function passes. Another major design decision is to not introduce another intermediate representation but instead use the existing `MachineInstr` class. However, new generic opcodes are added.

The current sequence of steps is as follows:

1. The `IRTranslator` pass builds the initial machine instructions using the generic opcodes.

2. The `Legalizer` pass legalizes types and operations in one step. This is different from the selection DAG, which uses two different steps for it. Real CPU architectures are sometimes weird, and it is possible that a certain data type is only supported with one instruction. This case is not handled well by the selection DAG, but it's easy to handle this in the combined step in the global instruction selection.

3. The generated machine instructions still operate on virtual registers. In the `RegBankSelect` pass, a register bank is selected. A register bank represents a type of registers on the CPU, for example, general-purpose registers. This is more coarse-grained than the register definitions in the target description. The important point is that it associates type information with the instruction. The type information is based on the types available in the target, so this is already lower than the generic type in LLVM IR.

4. At this point, the types and operations are known to be legal for the target, and type information is associated with each instruction. The following `InstructionSelect` pass can then easily replace the generic instructions with the machine ones.

After the global instruction selection, the usual backend passes such as instruction scheduling, register allocation, and basic block placement are run.

Global instruction selection is compiled into LLVM, but it is not enabled by default. If you want to use it, you need to give the `-global-isel` option to `llc` or `-mllvm global-isel` to `clang`. You can control what happens if an IR construct cannot be handled by global instruction selection. When you give the `-global-isel-abort=0` option to `llc`, then the selection DAG is used as fallback. With `=1`, the application is terminated. To prevent this, you can give the `-global-isel-abort=0` option to `llc`. And with `=2`, the selection DAG is used as fallback, and a diagnostic message is printed to inform you about the problem.

To add global instruction selection to a target, you only need to override the corresponding functions in the `TargetPassConfig` class of your target. This class is instantiated by the `XXXTargetMachine` class, and the implementation is usually found in the same file. For example, you override the `addIRTranslator()` method to add the `IRTranslator` pass to the machine passes of your target.

The development happens mainly on the AArch64 target, which currently has the best support for global instruction selection. Many other targets, including x86 and Power, have also added support for global instruction selection. One challenge here is that not that much code is generated from the table description, so there is still an amount of manual coding you have to do. Another challenge is that big-endian targets are currently not supported, so pure big-endian targets such as SystemZ cannot use global instruction selection as of today. Both will certainly improve over time.

The Mips target features an implementation of global instruction selection, with the mentioned limitation that it can only be used for little-endian targets. You can enable use of global instruction selection by passing the -global-isel option to the llc tool. Using the sum.ll example file from first section, an invocation looks like this:

```
$ llc -mtriple=mipsel-linux-gnu -global-isel sum.ll
```

Please note that the target mipsel-linux-gnu is the little-endian target. Using the big-endian mips-linux-gnu target results in an error message.

The global instruction selector works much quicker than the selection DAG, and already produces higher code quality than fast instruction selection.

Supporting new machine instructions

The CPU you are targeting may have machine instructions not yet supported by LLVM. For example, manufacturers using the MIPS architecture often add special instructions to the core MIPS instruction set. The specification of the RISC-V instruction set explicitly allows manufacturers to add new instructions. Or you are adding a completely new backend, and then you must add the instructions of the CPU. In the next section, we will add assembler support for a single, new machine instruction to an LLVM backend.

Adding a new instruction to the assembler and code generation

New machine instructions are usually tied to a certain CPU feature. Then the new instruction is only recognized if the user has selected the feature using the --mattr= option to llc.

As an example, we will add a new machine instruction to the MIPS backend. The imaginary, new machine instruction first squares the value of the two input registers $2 and $3 and assigns the sum of both squares to the output register $1:

```
sqsumu $1, $2, $3
```

The name of the instruction is sqsumu, derived from the square and summation operation. The last u in the name indicates that the instruction works on unsigned integers.

The CPU feature we are adding first is called sqsum. This will allow us to call llc with the --mattr=+sqsum option to enable recognition of the new instruction.

Most of the code we will add is in the **TableGen** files which describe the MIPS backend. All the files are located in the `llvm/lib/Target/Mips` folder. The top-level file is `Mips.td`. Look at the file and locate the section in which the various features are defined. Here you add the definition of our new feature:

```
def FeatureSQSum
    : SubtargetFeature<"sqsum", "HasSQSum", "true",
                             "Use square-sum instruction">;
```

The `SubtargetFeature` class takes four template parameters. The first, `sqsum`, is the name of the feature, for use on the command line. The second parameter, `HasSQSum`, is the name of the attribute in the `Subtarget` class representing this feature. The next parameters are the default value and the description of the feature, used for providing help on the command line. TableGen generates the base class for the `MipsSubtarget` class, defined in `MipsSubtarget.h` file. In this file, we add the new attribute in the private part of the class, where all the other attributes are defined:

```
// Has square-sum instruction.
bool HasSQSum = false;
```

In the public part, we also a method to retrieve the value of the attribute. We need this method for the next addition:

```
bool hasSQSum() const { return HasSQSum; }
```

With these additions, we are already able to set the `sqsum` feature on the command line, albeit without effect.

To tie the new instruction to the `sqsum` feature, we need to define a predicate that indicates whether the feature is selected or not. We add this to the `MipsInstrInfo.td` file, either in the section where all the other predicates are defined or simply at the end:

```
def HasSQSum : Predicate<"Subtarget->hasSQSum()">,
                    AssemblerPredicate<(all_of FeatureSQSum)>;
```

The predicate uses the `hasSQSum()` method defined earlier. Additionally, the `AssemblerPredicate` template specifies the condition used when generating the source code for the assembler. We simply refer to the previously defined feature.

We also need to update the scheduling model. The MIPS target uses both the itinerary and the machine-instruction scheduler. For the itinerary model, an `InstrItinClass` record is defined for each instruction in the `MipsSchedule.td` file. Simply add the following line in this file in the section where all the itineraries are defined:

```
def II_SQSUMU : InstrItinClass;
```

We also need to give details about the instruction costs. Usually, you find this information in the documentation for the CPU. For our instruction, we optimistically assume that it just takes one cycle in the ALU. This information is added to the `MipsGenericItineraries` definition in the same file:

```
InstrItinData<II_SQSUMU, [InstrStage<1, [ALU] >] >
```

With this, the update to the itinerary-based scheduling model is complete. The MIPS target also defines a generic scheduling model based on the machine-instruction scheduler model in the `MipsScheduleGeneric.td` file. Because this is a complete model covering all instructions, we also need to add our instruction add. As it is based on multiplication, we simply extend the existing definition for the MULT and MULTu instructions:

```
def : InstrRW<[GenericWriteMul], (instrs MULT, MULTu, SQSUMu)>;
```

The MIPS target also defines a scheduling model for the P5600 CPU in the `MipsScheduleP5600.td` file. Our new instruction is obviously not supported on this target, so we add it to the list of unsupported features:

```
list<Predicate> UnsupportedFeatures = [HasSQSum, HasMips3, …
```

Now we are ready to add the new instruction at the end of the `Mips64InstrInfo.td` file. TableGen definitions are always terse, therefore we dissect them. The definition uses some predefined classes from the MIPS target descriptions. Our new instruction is an arithmetic instruction, and by design, it fits the `ArithLogicR` class. The first parameter, `"sqsumu"`, specifies the assembler mnemonic of the instruction. The next parameter, `GPR64Opnd`, states that the instructions use 64-bit registers as operands and the following `1` parameter indicates that the operands are commutative. Last, an itinerary is given for the instruction. The `ADD_FM` class is given to specify the binary encoding of the instruction. For a real instruction, the parameters must be chosen according to the documentation. Then follows the `ISA_MIPS64` predicate, which indicates for which instruction set the instruction is valid. And last, our `SQSUM` predicate states that the instruction is only valid when our feature is enabled. The complete definition is as follows:

```
def SQSUMu  : ArithLogicR<"sqsumu", GPR64Opnd, 1, II_SQSUMU>,
                  ADD_FM<0x1c, 0x28>, ISA_MIPS64, SQSUM
```

If you only aim to support the new instruction, then this definition is enough. Be sure to finish the definition with `;` in this case. With the addition of a selection DAG pattern, you make the instruction available to the code generator. The instruction uses the two operand registers `$rs` and `$rt` and the destination register `$rd`, all three defined by the `ADD_FM` binary format class. In theory, the pattern to match is then simple: the value of each register is squared using the `mul` multiplication operator, and then the two products are added using the `add` operator and assigned to the destination register `$rd`. The pattern gets a bit more complicated because, with the MIPS instruction set, the result of a multiplication is stored in a special register pair. To be usable, the result must be moved to a general-purpose register. During legalization of operations, the generic `mul` operator is replaced with the MIPS-specific `MipsMult` operation for the multiplication and the `MipsMFLO` operation to move the lower part of the result into a general-purpose register. We must take this into account when writing the pattern, which looks as follows:

```
{
  let Pattern = [(set GPR64Opnd:$rd,
                      (add (MipsMFLO (MipsMult
                          GPR64Opnd:$rs,

                          GPR64Opnd:$rs)),
                          (MipsMFLO (MipsMult
                              GPR64Opnd:$rt,
```

```
                                    GPR64Opnd:$rt)))
                     )];
}
```

As described in the *Instruction selection with the selection DAG* section, if this pattern matches the current DAG node, then our new instruction is selected. Because of the SQSUM predicate, this only happens when the sqsum feature is activated. Let's check it with a test!

Testing the new instruction

If you extend LLVM, then it is good practice to verify it with automated tests. Especially if you want to contribute your extension to the LLVM project, then good tests are required.

After adding a new machine instruction as we did in the last section, we must check two different aspects:

- First, we have to verify that the instruction encoding is correct.

- Second, we must make sure that the code generation works as expected.

The LLVM projects use **LIT**, the **LLVM Integrated Tester**, as the testing tool. Basically, a test case is a file that contains the input, the commands to run, and the checks that should be performed. Adding new tests is as easy as copying a new file into the test directory. To verify the encoding of our new instruction, we use the llvm-mc tool. Besides other tasks, this tool can show the encoding of an instruction. For an ad hoc check, you can run the following command to show the instruction encoding:

```
$ echo "sqsumu \$1,\$2,\$3" | \
   llvm-mc --triple=mips64-linux-gnu -mattr=+sqsum \
           --show-encoding
```

This already shows part of the input and the command to run in an automated test case. To verify the result, you use the FileCheck tool. The output of llvm-mc is piped into this tool. Additionally, FileCheck reads the test case file. The test case file contains lines marked with the CHECK: keyword, after which the expected output follows. FileCheck tries to match these lines against the data piped into it. If no match is found, then an error is displayed. Place the sqsumu.s test case file with the following content into the llvm/test/MC/Mips directory:

```
# RUN: llvm-mc %s -triple=mips64-linux-gnu -mattr=+sqsum \
# RUN:   --show-encoding | FileCheck %s
```

```
# CHECK: sqsumu  $1, $2, $3 # encoding: [0x70,0x43,0x08,0x28]
```

```
    sqsumu $1, $2, $3
```

If you are inside the `llvm/test/Mips/MC` folder, then you can run the test with the following command, which reports success at the end:

```
$ llvm-lit sqsumu.s
-- Testing: 1 tests, 1 workers --
PASS: LLVM :: MC/Mips/sqsumu.s (1 of 1)

Testing Time: 0.11s
  Passed: 1
```

The LIT tool interprets the `RUN:` line, replacing `%s` with the current filename. The `FileCheck` tool reads the file, parses the `CHECK:` lines, and tries to match the input from the pipe. This is a very effective way of testing.

If you are in the `build` directory, you can invoke the LLVM tests with this command:

```
$ ninja check-llvm
```

You can also run the tests contained in one folder, by adding the folder name separated by a dash. To run the tests in the `llvm/test/Mips/MC` folder, you type the following command:

```
$ ninja check-llvm-mips-mc
```

To construct a test case for the code generation, you follow the same strategy. The following `sqsum.ll` file contains LLVM IR code to calculate the hypotenuse square:

```
define i64 @hyposquare(i64 %a, i64 %b) {
  %asq = mul i64 %a, %a
  %bsq = mul i64 %b, %b
  %res = add i64 %asq, %bsq
  ret i64 %res
}
```

To see the generated assembly code, you use the `llc` tool:

```
$ llc -mtriple=mips64-linux-gnu -mattr=+sqsum < sqsum.ll
```

Convince yourself that you see our new sqsum instruction in the output. Please also check that the instruction is not generated if you remove the -mattr=+sqsum option.

Equipped with this knowledge, you can construct the test case. This time, we use two RUN: lines: one to check that our new instruction is generated, and one to check that it is not. We can do both with one test case file because we can tell the FileCheck tool to look for a different label than CHECK:. Put the test case file sqsum.ll with the following content into the llvm/test/CodeGen/Mips folder:

```
; RUN: llc -mtriple=mips64-linux-gnu -mattr=+sqsum < %s |\
; RUN:   FileCheck -check-prefix=SQSUM %s
; RUN: llc -mtriple=mips64-linux-gnu < %s |\
; RUN:   FileCheck --check-prefix=NOSQSUM %s

define i64 @hyposquare(i64 %a, i64 %b) {
; SQSUM-LABEL: hyposquare:
; SQSUM: sqsumu $2, $4, $5
; NOSQSUM-LABEL: hyposquare:
; NOSQSUM: dmult $5, $5
; NOSQSUM: mflo $1
; NOSQSUM: dmult $4, $4
; NOSQSUM: mflo $2
; NOSQSUM: addu $2, $2, $1
  %asq = mul i64 %a, %a
  %bsq = mul i64 %b, %b
  %res = add i64 %asq, %bsq
  ret i64 %res
}
```

As with the other test, you can run the test alone in the folder with the following command:

```
$ llvm-lit squm.ll
```

Alternatively, you can run it from the build directory with the following command:

```
$ ninja check-llvm-mips-codegen
```

With these steps, you enhanced the LLVM assembler with a new instruction, enabled the instruction selection to use this new instruction, and verified that the encoding is correct and the code generation works as expected.

Summary

In this chapter, you learned how the backend of an LLVM target is structured. You used the MIR to examine the state after a pass and you used machine IR to run a single pass. With this knowledge, you can investigate problems in backend passes.

You learned how instruction selection with the help of the selection DAG is implemented in LLVM, and you also were introduced to alternative methods for instruction selection with FastISel and GlobalISel, which helps in deciding which algorithm to choose if your platform offers all of them.

You extended LLVM to support a new machine instruction in the assembler and in the instruction selection, helping you to add support for currently unsupported CPU features. To validate the extension, you developed automated test cases for it.

In the next chapter, we examine another unique feature of LLVM: generating and executing code in one step, also known as **Just-In-Time** (**JIT**) compilation.

10
JIT Compilation

The LLVM core libraries come with the **ExecutionEngine** component, which allows the compilation and execution of IR code in memory. Using this component, we can build **just in time** (**JIT**) compilers, which allow the direct execution of IR code. A JIT compiler works more like an interpreter, in the sense that no object code needs to be stored on secondary storage.

In this chapter, you will learn about applications for JIT compilers, and how the LLVM JIT compiler works in principle. You will explore the LLVM dynamic compiler and interpreter, and you will also learn how to implement a JIT compiler tool on your own. You will also see how to make use of a JIT compiler as part of a static compiler, and the challenges associated with it.

This chapter will cover the following topics:

- Getting an overview of LLVM's JIT implementation and use cases

- Using JIT compilation for direct execution

- Utilizing a JIT compiler for code evaluation

By the end of the chapter, you will know how to develop a JIT compiler, either using a preconfigured class, or a customized version fitting your needs. You will also acquire the knowledge to make use of a JIT compiler inside a traditional static compiler.

Technical requirements

The code files for the chapter can be found at `https://github.com/PacktPublishing/Learn-LLVM-12/tree/master/Chapter10`

You can find the code in action videos at `https://bit.ly/3nllhED`

Getting an overview of LLVM's JIT implementation and use cases

So far, we have only looked at **ahead of time** (**AOT**) compilers. These compilers compile the whole application. Only once the compilation is finished can the application run. If the compilation is performed at the runtime of the application, then the compiler is a JIT compiler. A JIT compiler has interesting use cases:

- **Implementation of a virtual machine**: A programming language can be translated to byte code with an AOT compiler. At runtime, a JIT compiler is used to compile the byte code to machine code. The advantage of this approach is that the byte code is hardware-independent, and thanks to the JIT compiler, there is no performance penalty compared to an AOT compiler. Java and C# use this model today, but the idea is really old: the USCD Pascal compiler from 1977 already used a similar approach.

- **Expression evaluation**: A spreadsheet application can compile often-executed expressions with a JIT compiler. This can speed up the financial simulations, for example. The LLVM debugger LLDB uses the approach to evaluate a source expression at debug time.

- **Database queries**: A database creates an execution plan from a database query. The execution plan describes the operations on tables and columns, which leads to the query answer when executed. A JIT compiler can be used to translate the execution plan into machine code, thereby speeding up the execution of the query.

The static compilation model of LLVM is not as far away from the JIT model as you may think. The LLVM static compiler, `llc`, compiles LLVM IR into machine code and saves the result as an object file on disk. If the object file is not stored on disk but in memory, would the code be executable? Not directly, because references to global functions and global data use relocations instead of absolute addresses.

Conceptually, a relocation describes how to calculate the address, for example, as an offset to a known address. If we resolve the relocations into addresses, like the linker and dynamic loader do, then we can execute the object code. Running the static compiler to compile IR code into an object file in memory, performing a link step on the in-memory object file, and then running the code gives us a JIT compiler. The JIT implementation in the LLVM core libraries is based on this idea.

During the development history of LLVM, there were several JIT implementations, with different feature sets. The latest JIT API is the **on request compilation** (ORC) engine. In case you were wondering about the acronym: it was the lead developer's intention to invent yet another acronym based on Tolkien's universe, after the **ELF (Executable and Linking Format)** and the **DWARF (Debugging Standard)** were already there.

The ORC engine builds on, and extends, the idea of using the static compiler and a dynamic linker on the in-memory object file. The implementation uses a *layered* approach. The two basic levels are the following:

1.   Compile layer

2.   Link layer

On top of the compile layer can sit a layer providing support for *lazy compilation*. A **transformation layer** can be stacked on top or below the lazy compilation layer, allowing the developer to add arbitrary transformation, or simply be notified of certain events. This layered approach has the advantage that the JIT engine is *customizable for diverse requirements*. For example, a high-performance virtual machine may choose to compile everything upfront and make no use of the lazy compilation layer. Other virtual machines will emphasize start up time and responsiveness to the user, and achieve this with the help of the lazy compilation layer.

The older MCJIT engine is still available. The API is derived from an even older, already removed, JIT engine. Over time, the API became a bit bloated, and it lacks the flexibility of the ORC API. The goal is to remove this implementation, as the ORC engine now provides all the functionality of the MCJIT engine. New developments should use the ORC API.

In the next section, we look at 11i, the LLVM interpreter and dynamic compiler, before we dive into implementing a JIT compiler.

Using JIT compilation for direct execution

Running LLVM IR directly is the first idea that comes to mind when thinking about a JIT compiler. This is what the `lli` tool, the LLVM interpreter, and the dynamic compiler do. We will explore the `lli` tool in the next section, and subsequently implement a similar tool on our own.

Exploring the lli tool

Let's try the `lli` tool with a very simple example. Store the following source as a `hello.ll` file. It is the equivalent of a C hello world application. It declares the prototype for the `printf()` function from the C library. The `hellostr` constant contains the message to be printed. Inside the `main()` function, a pointer to the first character of the message is calculated via the `getelementptr` instruction, and this value is passed to the `printf()` function. The application always returns 0. The complete source code is as follows:

```
declare i32 @printf(i8*, ...)


@hellostr = private unnamed_addr constant [13 x i8] c"Hello
                                            world\0A\00"


define i32 @main(i32 %argc, i8** %argv) {
  %res = call i32 (i8*, ...) @printf(
                i8* getelementptr inbounds ([13 x i8],
                    [13 x i8]* @hellostr, i64 0, i64 0))
  ret i32 0
}
```

This LLVM IR file is generic enough that it is valid for all platforms. We can directly execute the IR with the `lli` tool with the help of the following command:

```
$ lli hello.ll
Hello world
```

The interesting point here is how the `printf()` function is found. The IR code is compiled to machine code, and a lookup for the `printf` symbol is triggered. This symbol is not found in the IR, so the current process is searched for it. The `lli` tool dynamically links against the C library, and the symbol is found there.

Of course, the `lli` tool does not link against libraries you created. To enable the use of such functions, the `lli` tool supports the loading of shared libraries and objects. The following C source just prints a friendly message:

```
#include <stdio.h>

void greetings() {
  puts("Hi!");
}
```

Stored in the `greetings.c` file, we use this to explore the loading of objects with the `lli` tool. Compile this source into a shared library. The `-fPIC` option instructs clang to generate position-independent code, which is required for shared libraries. With the `-shared` option given, the compiler creates the `greetings.so` shared library:

```
$ clang -fPIC -shared -o greetings.so greetings.c
```

We also compile the file into a `greetings.o` object file:

```
$ clang -c -o greetings.o greetings.c
```

We now have two files, the `greetings.so` shared library and the `greetings.o` object file, which we will load into the `lli` tool.

We also need an LLVM IR file, which calls the `greetings()` function. For this, create the `main.ll` file, which contains a single call to the function:

```
declare void @greetings(...)

define dso_local i32 @main(i32 %argc, i8** %argv) {
  call void (...) @greetings()
  ret i32 0
}
```

If you try to execute the IR as before, then the `lli` tool is not able to locate the greetings symbol and will simply crash:

```
$ lli main.ll
PLEASE submit a bug report to https://bugs.llvm.org/ and
include the crash backtrace.
```

The greetings () function is defined in an external file, and to fix the crash, we have to tell the lli tool which additional file needs to be loaded. In order to use the shared library, you have to use the -load option, which takes the path to the shared library as an argument:

```
$ lli -load ./greetings.so main.ll
Hi!
```

It is important to specify the path to the shared library, if the directory containing the shared library is not in the search path for the dynamic loader. If omitted, then the library will not be found.

Alternatively, we can instruct the lli tool to load the object file with the -extra-object option:

```
$ lli -extra-object greetings.o main.ll
Hi!
```

Other supported options are -extra-archive, which loads an archive, and -extra-module, which loads another bitcode file. Both options require the path to the file as an argument.

You now know how you can use the lli tool to directly execute LLVM IR. In the next section, we will implement our own JIT tool.

Implementing our own JIT compiler with LLJIT

The lli tool is nothing more than a thin wrapper around LLVM APIs. In the first section, we learned that the ORC engine uses a layered approach. The ExecutionSession class represents a running JIT program. Besides other items, this class holds the used JITDylib instances. A JITDylib instance is a symbol table, which maps symbol names to addresses. For example, this can be the symbols defined in an LLVM IR file, or the symbols of a loaded shared library.

To execute LLVM IR, we do not need to create a JIT stack on our own. The utility LLJIT class provides this functionality. You can also make use of this class when migrating from the older MCJIT implementation. This class essentially provides the same functionality. We begin the implementation with the initialization of the JIT engine in the next subsection.

Initializing the JIT engine for compiling LLVM IR

We first implement the function that sets up the JIT engine, compiles an LLVM IR module, and executes the `main()` function in this module. Later, we use this core functionality to build a small JIT tool. This is the `jitmain()` function:

1. The function needs the LLVM module with the IR to execute. Also needed is the LLVM context class used for this module, because the context class holds important type information. The goal is to call the `main()` function, so we also pass the usual `argc` and `argv` parameters:

```
Error jitmain(std::unique_ptr<Module> M,
              std::unique_ptr<LLVMContext> Ctx, int
              argc,
              char *argv[]) {
```

2. We use the `LLJITBuilder` class to create an `LLJIT` instance. If an error occurs, then we return the error. A possible source for an error is that the platform does not yet support JIT compilation:

```
auto JIT = orc::LLJITBuilder().create();
if (!JIT)
  return JIT.takeError();
```

3. Then we add the module to the main `JITDylib` instance. If configured, then JIT compilation utilizes multiple threads. Therefore, we need to wrap the module and the context in a `ThreadSafeModule` instance. If an error occurs, then we return the error:

```
if (auto Err = (*JIT)->addIRModule(
        orc::ThreadSafeModule(std::move(M),
                              std::move(Ctx))))
  return Err;
```

4. Like the `lli` tool, we also support the symbols from the C library.
    The `DefinitionGenerator` class exposes symbols, and the
    `DynamicLibrarySearchGenerator` subclass exposes the names found in the
    shared library. The class provides two factory methods. The `Load()` method can
    be used to load a shared library, while the `GetForCurrentProcess()` method
    exposes the symbols of the current process. We use the latter function. The symbol
    names can have a prefix, depending on the platform. We retrieve the data layout and
    pass the prefix to the `GetForCurrentprocess()` function. The symbol names
    are then treated in the right way, and we do not need to care about it. As usual, we
    return from the function in case an error occurs:

    ```
    const DataLayout &DL = (*JIT)->getDataLayout();
    auto DLSG = orc::DynamicLibrarySearchGenerator::
        GetForCurrentProcess(DL.getGlobalPrefix());
    if (!DLSG)
      return DLSG.takeError();
    ```

5. We then add the generator to the main `JITDylib` instance. In case a symbol needs
    to be looked up, the symbols from the loaded shared library are also searched:

    ```
    (*JIT)->getMainJITDylib().addGenerator(
        std::move(*DLSG));
    ```

6. Next, we look up the `main` symbol. This symbol must be in the IR module given
    on the command line. The lookup triggers compilation of that IR module. If other
    symbols are referenced inside the IR module, then they are resolved using
    the generator added in the previous step. The result is of the
    `JITEvaluatedSymbol` class:

    ```
    auto MainSym = (*JIT)->lookup("main");
    if (!MainSym)
      return MainSym.takeError();
    ```

7. We ask the returned JIT symbol for the address of the function. We cast this address
    to the prototype of the C `main()` function:

    ```
    auto *Main = (int (*)(
        int, char **))MainSym->getAddress();
    ```

8. Now we can call the `main()` function in the IR module, and pass the `argc` and `argv` parameters, which the function expects. We ignore the return value:

```
(void)Main(argc, argv);
```

9. We report success following execution of the function:

```
  return Error::success();
}
```

This demonstrates how easy it is to use JIT compilation. There is a bunch of other possibilities to expose names, besides exposing the symbols for the current process or from a shared library. The `StaticLibraryDefinitionGenerator` class exposes the symbols found in a static archive, and can be used in the same way as the `DynamicLibrarySearchGenerator` class. The `LLJIT` class also has an `addObjectFile()` method to expose the symbols of an object file. You can also provide your own `DefinitionGenerator` implementation if the existing implementations do not fit your needs. In the next subsection, you extend the implementation into a JIT compiler.

Creating the JIT compiler utility

The `jitmain()` function is easily extended into a small tool, which we do next. The source is saved in a `JIT.cpp` file and is a simple JIT compiler:

1. We must include several header files. The `LLJIT.h` header defines the `LLJIT` class, and the core classes of the ORC API. We include the `IRReader.h` header because it defines a function to read LLVM IR files. The `CommandLine.h` header allows us to parse the command-line options in the LLVM style. Finally, the `InitLLVM.h` header is required for basic initialization of the tool, and the `TargetSelect.h` header for the initialization of the native target:

```
#include "llvm/ExecutionEngine/Orc/LLJIT.h"
#include "llvm/IRReader/IRReader.h"
#include "llvm/Support/CommandLine.h"
#include "llvm/Support/InitLLVM.h"
#include "llvm/Support/TargetSelect.h"
```

2. We add the `llvm` namespace to the current scope:

```
using namespace llvm;
```

3. Our JIT tool expects exactly one input file on the command line, which we declare with the `cl::opt<>` class:

```
static cl::opt<std::string>
     InputFile(cl::Positional, cl::Required,
               cl::desc("<input-file>"));
```

4. To read the IR file, we call the `parseIRFile()` function. The file can be the textual IR representation, or a bitcode file. The function returns a pointer to the created module. Error handling is a bit different because a textual IR file can be parsed, which is not necessarily syntactical correct. The `SMDiagnostic` instance holds the error information in case of a syntax error. The error message is printed, and the application is exited:

```
std::unique_ptr<Module>
loadModule(StringRef Filename, LLVMContext &Ctx,
           const char *ProgName) {
  SMDiagnostic Err;
  std::unique_ptr<Module> Mod =
      parseIRFile(Filename, Err, Ctx);
  if (!Mod.get()) {
    Err.print(ProgName, errs());
    exit(-1);
  }
  return std::move(Mod);
}
```

5. The `jitmain()` function is placed here:

```
Error jitmain(...) { ... }
```

6. Then we add the `main()` function, which initializes the tool and the native target, and parses the command line:

```
int main(int argc, char *argv[]) {
  InitLLVM X(argc, argv);

  InitializeNativeTarget();
  InitializeNativeTargetAsmPrinter();
```

```
InitializeNativeTargetAsmParser();
```

```
cl::ParseCommandLineOptions(argc, argv,
                            "JIT\n");
```

7. Next, the LLVM context class is initialized:

```
auto Ctx = std::make_unique<LLVMContext>();
```

8. Then we load the IR module named on the command line:

```
std::unique_ptr<Module> M =
    loadModule(InputFile, *Ctx, argv[0]);
```

9. Then we can call the `jitmain()` function. To handle errors, we use the
    `ExitOnError` utility class. This class prints an error message and exits the
    application when an error occurred. We also set a banner with the name of the
    application, which is printed before the error message:

```
ExitOnError ExitOnErr(std::string(argv[0]) + ": ");
ExitOnErr(jitmain(std::move(M), std::move(Ctx),
                  argc, argv));
```

10. If the control flow reaches this point, then the IR was successfully executed. We
    return 0 to indicate success:

```
    return 0;
}
```

This is already the complete implementation! We only need to add the build description,
which is the topic of the next subsection.

Adding the CMake build description

In order to compile this source file, we also need to create a `CMakeLists.txt` file with
the build description, saved besides the `JIT.cpp` file:

1. We set the minimal required CMake version to the number required by LLVM and
    give the project the name `jit`:

```
cmake_minimum_required (VERSION 3.13.4)
project ("jit")
```

2. The LLVM package needs to be loaded, and we add the directory of the
    CMake modules provided by LLVM to the search path. Then we include the
    ChooseMSVCCRT module, which makes sure that the same C runtime is used
    as by LLVM:

    ```
    find_package(LLVM REQUIRED CONFIG)
    list(APPEND CMAKE_MODULE_PATH ${LLVM_DIR})
    include(ChooseMSVCCRT)
    ```

3. We also need to add the definitions and the include path from LLVM. The LLVM
    components used are mapped to the library names with a function call:

    ```
    add_definitions(${LLVM_DEFINITIONS})
    include_directories(SYSTEM ${LLVM_INCLUDE_DIRS})
    llvm_map_components_to_libnames(llvm_libs Core OrcJIT
                                              Support
                                              native)
    ```

4. Lastly, we define the name of the executable, the source files to compile, and the
    library to link against:

    ```
    add_executable(JIT JIT.cpp)
    target_link_libraries(JIT ${llvm_libs})
    ```

5. That is everything that is required for the JIT tool. Create and change into
    a build directory, and then run the following command to create and compile
    the application:

    ```
    $ cmake -G Ninja <path to source directory>
    $ ninja
    ```

This compiles the JIT tool. You can check the functionality with the hello.ll file from
the beginning of the chapter:

```
$ JIT hello.ll
Hello world
```

Creating a JIT compiler is surprisingly easy!

The example used LLVM IR as input, but this is not a requirement. The LLJIT class uses the IRCompileLayer class, which is responsible for compiling IR to machine code. You can define your own layer, which accepts the input you need, for example, Java byte code.

Using the predefined LLJIT class is handy, but limits our flexibility. In the next section, we will look at how to implement a JIT compiler using the layers provided by the ORC API.

Building a JIT compiler class from scratch

Using the layered approach of ORC, it is very easy to build a JIT compiler customized for the requirements. There is no one-size-fits-all JIT compiler, and the first section of this chapter gave some examples. Let's have a look at how to set up a JIT compiler.

The ORC API uses layers, which are stacked together. The lowest level is the object linking layer, represented by the llvm::orc::RTDyldObjectLinkingLayer class. It is responsible for linking in-memory objects and turning them into executable code. The memory required for this task is managed by an instance of the MemoryManager interface. There is a default implementation, but we can also use a custom version if we need to.

Above the object linking layer is the compile layer, which is responsible for creating an in-memory object file. The llvm::orc::IRCompileLayer class takes an IR module as input, and compiles it to an object file. The IRCompileLayer class is a subclass of the IRLayer class, which is a generic class for layer implementations accepting LLVM IR.

These two layers already form the core of a JIT compiler. They add an LLVM IR module as input, which is compiled and linked in-memory. To add more functionality, we can add more layers on top of these both. For example, the CompileOnDemandLayer class splits a module, so that only the requested functions are compiled. This can be used to implement lazy compilation. The CompileOnDemandLayer class is also a subclass of the IRLayer class. In a very generic way, the IRTransformLayer class, also a subclass of the IRLayer class, allows us to apply a transformation to the module.

Another important class is the ExecutionSession class. This class represents a running JIT program. Basically, this means that the class manages the JITDylib symbol tables, provides lookup functionality for symbols, and keeps track of the resource managers used.

The generic recipe for a JIT compiler is as follows:

1. Initialize an instance of the `ExecutionSession` class.

2. Initialize the layer, at least consisting of the `RTDyldObjectLinkingLayer` class and the `IRCompileLayer` class.

3. Create the first `JITDylib` symbol table, usually with `main` or a similar name.

The usage is very similar to the `LLJIT` class from the previous section:

4. Add an IR module to the symbol table.

5. Look up a symbol, the triggered compilation of the associated function, and possibly the whole module.

6. Execute the function.

In the next subsection, we will implement a JIT compiler class based on the generic recipe.

Creating a JIT compiler class

To keep the implementation of the JIT compiler class simple, we put everything into the `JIT.h` header file. The initialization of the class is a bit more complex. Due to the handling of possible errors, we need a factory method to create some objects upfront before we can call the constructor. The steps to create the class are as follows:

1. We begin by guarding the header file against multiple inclusion with the `JIT_H` preprocessor definition:

    ```
    #ifndef JIT_H
    #define JIT_H
    ```

2. A bunch of include files is required. Most of them provide a class with the same name as the header file. The `Core.h` header provides a couple of basic classes, including the `ExecutionSession` class. The `ExecutionUtils.h` header provides the `DynamicLibrarySearchGenerator` class to search libraries for symbols, which we already used in the *Implementing our own JIT compiler with LLJIT* section. The `CompileUtils.h` header provides the `ConcurrentIRCompiler` class:

    ```
    #include "llvm/Analysis/AliasAnalysis.h"
    #include "llvm/ExecutionEngine/JITSymbol.h"
    #include "llvm/ExecutionEngine/Orc/CompileUtils.h"
    #include "llvm/ExecutionEngine/Orc/Core.h"
    ```

```
#include "llvm/ExecutionEngine/Orc/ExecutionUtils.h"
#include "llvm/ExecutionEngine/Orc/IRCompileLayer.h"
#include "llvm/ExecutionEngine/Orc/IRTransformLayer.h"
#include
    "llvm/ExecutionEngine/Orc/JITTargetMachineBuilder.h"
#include "llvm/ExecutionEngine/Orc/Mangling.h"
#include
    "llvm/ExecutionEngine/Orc/RTDyldObjectLinkingLayer.h"
#include
    "llvm/ExecutionEngine/Orc/TargetProcessControl.h"
#include "llvm/ExecutionEngine/SectionMemoryManager.h"
#include "llvm/Passes/PassBuilder.h"
#include "llvm/Support/Error.h"
```

3. Our new class is the `JIT` class:

```
class JIT {
```

4. The private data members reflect the ORC layers and a helper class. The
    `ExecutionSession`, `ObjectLinkingLayer`, `CompileLayer`,
    `OptIRLayer`, and `MainJITDylib` instances represent the running
    JIT program, the layers, and the symbol table, as already described. The
    `TargetProcessControl` instance is used for interaction with the JIT target
    process. This can be the same process, another process on the same machine, or a
    remote process on a different machine, possible with a different architecture. The
    `DataLayout` and `MangleAndInterner` classes are required to mangle the
    symbols names in the correct way. The symbol names are internalized, which means
    that all equal names have the same address. To check whether two symbol names
    are equal, it is then sufficient to compare the addresses, which is a very
    fast operation:

```
std::unique_ptr<llvm::orc::TargetProcessControl>
    TPC;
std::unique_ptr<llvm::orc::ExecutionSession> ES;
llvm::DataLayout DL;
llvm::orc::MangleAndInterner Mangle;
std::unique_ptr<llvm::orc::RTDyldObjectLinkingLayer>
    ObjectLinkingLayer;
std::unique_ptr<llvm::orc::IRCompileLayer>
```

```
        CompileLayer;
    std::unique_ptr<llvm::orc::IRTransformLayer>
        OptIRLayer;
    llvm::orc::JITDylib &MainJITDylib;
```

5. The initialization is split into three parts. In C++, a constructor cannot return an error. The simple and recommended solution is to create a static factory method, which can do the error handling prior to constructing the object. The initialization of the layers is more complex, so we introduce factory methods for them, too.

In the create() factory method, we first create a SymbolStringPool instance, which is used to implement string internalization and is shared by several classes. To take control of the current process, we create a SelfTargetProcessControl instance. If we want to target a different process, then we need to change this instance.

Then we construct a JITTargetMachineBuilder instance, for which we need to know the target triple of the JIT process. Next, we query the target machine builder for the data layout. This step can fail if the builder is not able to instantiate the target machine based on the triple provided, for example, because support for this target is not compiled into the LLVM libraries:

```
public:
    static llvm::Expected<std::unique_ptr<JIT>> create() {
        auto SSP =
            std::make_shared<llvm::orc::SymbolStringPool>();
        auto TPC =
            llvm::orc::SelfTargetProcessControl::Create(SSP);
        if (!TPC)
            return TPC.takeError();
        llvm::orc::JITTargetMachineBuilder JTMB(
            (*TPC)->getTargetTriple());
        auto DL = JTMB.getDefaultDataLayoutForTarget();
        if (!DL)
            return DL.takeError();
```

6. At this point, we have handled all the calls that could potentially fail. We are now able to initialize the `ExecutionSession` instance. Finally, the constructor of the `JIT` class is called with all instantiated objects, and the result is returned to the caller:

```
auto ES =
        std::make_unique<llvm::orc::ExecutionSession>(
            std::move(SSP));

    return std::make_unique<JIT>(
        std::move(*TPC), std::move(ES),
        std::move(*DL),
        std::move(JTMB));
}
```

7. The constructor of the `JIT` class moves the passed parameters to the private data members. The layer objects are constructed with a call to a static factory name with the `create` prefix. Each `layer` factory method requires a reference to the `ExecutionSession` instance, connecting the layer to the running JIT session. Except for the object linking layer, which is at the bottom of the layer stack, each layer also requires a reference to the previous layer, illustrating the stacking order:

```
JIT(std::unique_ptr<llvm::orc::TargetProcessControl>
        TPCtrl,
    std::unique_ptr<llvm::orc::ExecutionSession> ExeS,
    llvm::DataLayout DataL,
    llvm::orc::JITTargetMachineBuilder JTMB)
  : TPC(std::move(TPCtrl)), ES(std::move(ExeS)),
    DL(std::move(DataL)), Mangle(*ES, DL),
    ObjectLinkingLayer(std::move(
        createObjectLinkingLayer(*ES, JTMB))),
    CompileLayer(std::move(createCompileLayer(
        *ES, *ObjectLinkingLayer,
        std::move(JTMB)))),
    OptIRLayer(std::move(
        createOptIRLayer(*ES, *CompileLayer))),
    MainJITDylib(ES->createBareJITDylib("<main>")) {
```

8. In the body of the constructor, we add the generator to search the current process for symbols. The `GetForCurrentProcess()` method is special, because the return value is wrapped in an `Expected<>` template, indicating that an `Error` object can also be returned. But we know that no error can occur – the current process will eventually run! Therefore, we unwrap the result with the `cantFail()` function, which terminates the application if an error occurred anyway:

```
MainJITDylib.addGenerator(llvm::cantFail(
    llvm::orc::DynamicLibrarySearchGenerator::
        GetForCurrentProcess(DL.getGlobalPrefix())));
}
```

9. To create the object linking layer, we need to provide a memory manager. We stick here to the default `SectionMemoryManager` class, but we could also provide a different implementation if needed:

```
static std::unique_ptr<
    llvm::orc::RTDyldObjectLinkingLayer>
createObjectLinkingLayer(
    llvm::orc::ExecutionSession &ES,
    llvm::orc::JITTargetMachineBuilder &JTMB) {
  auto GetMemoryManager = []() {
    return std::make_unique<
        llvm::SectionMemoryManager>();
  };
  auto OLLayer = std::make_unique<
      llvm::orc::RTDyldObjectLinkingLayer>(
      ES, GetMemoryManager);
```

10. A slight complication exists for the COFF object file format, which is used on Windows. This file format does not allow functions to be marked as exported. This subsequently leads to failures in checks inside the object linking layer: the flags stored in the symbol are compared with the flags from IR, which leads to a mismatch because of the missing export marker. The solution is to override the flags only for this file format. This finishes construction of the object layer, and the object is returned to the caller:

```
if (JTMB.getTargetTriple().isOSBinFormatCOFF()) {
    OLLayer
```

```
                ->setOverrideObjectFlagsWithResponsibilityFlags(
                    true);
        OLLayer
            ->setAutoClaimResponsibilityForObjectSymbols(
                true);
    }
    return std::move(OLLayer);
}
```

11. To initialize the compiler layer, an `IRCompiler` instance is needed. The
    `IRCompiler` instance is responsible for compiling an IR module into an
    object file. If our JIT compiler does not use threads, then we can use the
    `SimpleCompiler` class, which compiles the IR module using a given
    target machine. The `TargetMachine` class is not thread-safe, likewise the
    `SimpleCompiler` class, too. To support compilation with multiple threads, we
    use the `ConcurrentIRCompiler` class, which creates a new `TargetMachine`
    instance for each module to compile. This approach solves the problem with
    multiple threads:

```
static std::unique_ptr<llvm::orc::IRCompileLayer>
createCompileLayer(
    llvm::orc::ExecutionSession &ES,
    llvm::orc::RTDyldObjectLinkingLayer &OLLayer,
    llvm::orc::JITTargetMachineBuilder JTMB) {
  auto IRCompiler = std::make_unique<
        llvm::orc::ConcurrentIRCompiler>(
        std::move(JTMB));
  auto IRCLayer =
        std::make_unique<llvm::orc::IRCompileLayer>(
            ES, OLLayer, std::move(IRCompiler));
  return std::move(IRCLayer);
}
```

12. Instead of compiling the IR module directly to machine code, we install a layer that optimizes the IR first. This is a deliberate design decision: We turn our JIT compiler into an optimizing JIT compiler, which produces faster code that takes longer to produce, meaning a delay for the user. We do not add lazy compilation, so entire modules are compiled when just a symbol is looked up. This can add up to a significant time before the user sees the code executing.

> **Note**
>
> Please note that introducing lazy compilation is not a proper solution in all circumstances.

Lazy compilation is realized through moving each function into a module of its own, which is compiled when the function name is looked up. This prevents inter-procedural optimizations such as *inlining*, because the inliner pass needs access to the body of the function called to inline them. As a result, the user sees a faster startup with lazy compilation, but the code produced is not as optimal as it can be. These design decisions depend on the intended use. Here, we decide for fast code, accepting slower start up times. The optimization layer is realized as a transformation layer. The `IRTransformLayer` class delegates the transformation to a function, in our case, to the `optimizeModule` function:

```
static std::unique_ptr<llvm::orc::IRTransformLayer>
createOptIRLayer(
    llvm::orc::ExecutionSession &ES,
    llvm::orc::IRCompileLayer &CompileLayer) {
  auto OptIRLayer =
      std::make_unique<llvm::orc::IRTransformLayer>(
          ES, CompileLayer,
          optimizeModule);
  return std::move(OptIRLayer);
}
```

13. The `optimizeModule()` function is an example of a transformation on an IR module. The function gets the module to transform as parameter, and returns the transformed one. Because the JIT can potentially run with multiple threads, the IR module is wrapped in a `ThreadSafeModule` instance:

```
static llvm::Expected<llvm::orc::ThreadSafeModule>
optimizeModule(
```

```
          llvm::orc::ThreadSafeModule TSM,
          const llvm::orc::MaterializationResponsibility
             &R) {
```

14. To optimize the IR, we recall some information from *Chapter 8, Optimizing IR*, in the *Adding an optimization pipeline to your compiler* section. We require a `PassBuilder` instance to create an optimization pipeline. First, we define a couple of analysis managers, and register them afterward at the pass builder. Then we populate a `ModulePassManager` instance with the default optimization pipeline for the O2 level. This is again a design decision: the O2 level produces fast machine code already, but does this faster still than the O3 level. Afterward, we run the pipeline on the module. Finally, the optimized module is returned to the caller:

```
TSM.withModuleDo([](llvm::Module &M) {
  bool DebugPM = false;
  llvm::PassBuilder PB(DebugPM);
  llvm::LoopAnalysisManager LAM(DebugPM);
  llvm::FunctionAnalysisManager FAM(DebugPM);
  llvm::CGSCCAnalysisManager CGAM(DebugPM);
  llvm::ModuleAnalysisManager MAM(DebugPM);
  FAM.registerPass(
      [&] { return PB.buildDefaultAAPipeline(); });
  PB.registerModuleAnalyses(MAM);
  PB.registerCGSCCAnalyses(CGAM);
  PB.registerFunctionAnalyses(FAM);
  PB.registerLoopAnalyses(LAM);
  PB.crossRegisterProxies(LAM, FAM, CGAM, MAM);
  llvm::ModulePassManager MPM =
      PB.buildPerModuleDefaultPipeline(
          llvm::PassBuilder::OptimizationLevel::O2,
          DebugPM);
  MPM.run(M, MAM);
});

return std::move(TSM);
}
```

15. The client of the `JIT` class needs a way to add an IR module, which we provide with the `addIRModule()` function. Remember the layer stack we created: we must add the IR module to the top layer, otherwise we would accidently bypass some layers. This would be a programming error that is not easily spotted: if the `OptIRLayer` member is replaced by a `CompileLayer` member, then our `JIT` class still works, but not as an optimizing JIT because we have bypassed this layer. This is no cause for concern as regards this small implementation, but in a large JIT optimization, we would introduce a function to return the top-level layer:

```
llvm::Error addIRModule(
    llvm::orc::ThreadSafeModule TSM,
    llvm::orc::ResourceTrackerSP RT = nullptr) {
  if (!RT)
    RT = MainJITDylib.getDefaultResourceTracker();
    return OptIRLayer->add(RT, std::move(TSM));
}
```

16. Likewise, a client of our JIT class needs a way to look up a symbol. We delegate this to the `ExecutionSession` instance, passing in a reference to the main symbol table and the mangled and internalized name of the requested symbol:

```
llvm::Expected<llvm::JITEvaluatedSymbol>
lookup(llvm::StringRef Name) {
  return ES->lookup({&MainJITDylib},
                    Mangle(Name.str()));
}
```

Putting the JIT compiler together was quite easy. Initializing the class is a bit tricky, as it involves a factory method and a constructor call for the `JIT` class, and factory methods for each layer. This distribution is caused by limitations in C++, although the code itself is simple.

In the next subsection, we are using our new JIT compiler class to implement a command-line utility.

Using our new JIT compiler class

The interface of our new JIT compiler class resembles the `LLJIT` class used in the *Implementing our own JIT compiler with LLJIT* section. To test our new implementation, we copy the `LIT.cpp` class from the previous section and make the following changes:

1. To be able to use our new class, we include the `JIT.h` header file. This replaces the `llvm/ExecutionEngine/Orc/LLJIT.h` header file, which is no longer required because we are no longer using the LLJIT class.

2. Inside the `jitmain()` function, we replace the call to `orc::LLJITBuilder().create()` with a call to our new `JIT::create()` method.

3. Again, in the `jitmain()` function, we remove the code to add the `DynamicLibrarySearchGenerator` class. Precisely this generator is integrated in the JIT class.

This is already everything that needs to be changed! We can compile and run the changed application as in the previous section, with the same result. Under the hood, the new class uses a fixed optimization level, so with sufficiently large modules, we can note the differences in startup and runtime.

Having a JIT compiler at hand can stimulate new ideas. In the next section, we will look at how we can use the JIT compiler as part of a static compiler to evaluate code at compile time.

Utilizing a JIT compiler for code evaluation

Compiler writers make a great effort to produce optimal code. A simple, yet effective, optimization is to replace an arithmetic operation on two constants by the result value of this operation. To be able to perform the computation, an interpreter for constant expressions is embedded. And to arrive at the same result, the interpreter has to implement the same rules as the generated machine code! Of course, this can be the source of subtle errors.

A different approach would be to compile the constant expression to IR using the same code generations methods, and then have JIT compile and execute the IR. This idea can even be taken a step further. In mathematics, a function always produces the same result for the same input. For functions in computer languages, this is not true. A good example is the `rand()` function, which returns a random value for each call. A function in computer languages, which has the same characteristic as a function in mathematics, is called a **pure function**. During the optimization of expressions, we could JIT-compile and execute pure functions, which only have constant parameters, and replace the call to the function with the result returned from JIT execution. Effectively, we move the execution of the function from runtime to compile time!

Think about cross-compilation

Using a JIT compiler as part of a static compiler is an interesting option. However, if the compiler were to support cross-compilation, then this approach should be well thought-out. The usual candidates causing trouble are floating-point types. The precision of the `long double` type in C often depends on the hardware and the operation system. Some systems use 128-bit floating points, while others only use 64-bit floating points. The 80-bit floating point type is only available on the x86 platform, and usually only used on Windows. Performing the same floating-point operation with different precision can result in huge differences. Evaluation through JIT compilation cannot be used in such cases.

It cannot easily be decided whether a function is pure. The common solution is to apply a heuristic. If a function does not read or write into heap memory, either through pointers or indirectly with the use of aggregate types, and only calls other pure functions, then it is a pure function. The developer can aid the compiler, and mark pure functions, for example, with a special keyword or symbol. In the semantic analysis phase, the compiler can then check for violations.

In the next subsection, we will take a closer look at the implications for language semantics when trying to JIT-execute a function at compile time.

Identifying the language semantics

The difficult part is indeed to decide at the language semantics level which parts of the language are suitable for evaluation at compile time. Excluding access to heap memory is very restrictive. In general terms, it rules out string handling, for example. Using heap memory becomes problematic when the allocated memory survives the lifetime of the JIT-executed function. This is a program state, which can influence other results, and is therefore dangerous. On the other hand, if there are matched calls to `malloc()` and `free()` functions, then the memory is only used for internal calculation. In this case, the use of heap memory would be safe. But precisely this condition is not easy to proof.

At a similar level, an infinite loop inside the JIT-executed function can freeze the compiler. Alan Turing showed in 1936 that no machine can decide whether a function will produce a result or whether it is stuck in an endless loop. Some precautions must be taken to avoid this situation, for example, a runtime limit after which the JIT-executed function is terminated.

And last, the more that functionality is allowed, the more thoughts must be put into security, because the compiler now executes code written by someone else. Just imagine that this code downloads and runs files from the internet or tries to erase the hard disk: with too much state allowed for JIT-executed functions, we also need to think about such scenarios.

The idea is not new. The D programming language has a feature called **compile-time function execution**. The reference compiler **dmd** implements this feature by interpretation of the functions at the AST level. The LLVM-based LDC compiler has an experimental feature to use the LLVM JIT engine for it. You can find out more about the language and the compilers at `https://dlang.org/`.

Ignoring the semantic challenges, the implementation is not that difficult. In the *Building a JIT compiler class from scratch* section, we developed a JIT compiler with the `JIT` class. We feed an IR module in the class, and we can look up and execute a function from this module. Looking at the `tinylang` compiler implementation, we can clearly identify access to constants, because there is a `ConstantAccess` node in the AST. For example, there is code like the following:

```
if (auto *Const = llvm::dyn_cast<ConstantAccess>(Expr)) {
  // Do something with the constant.
}
```

Instead of interpreting the operations in the expression to derive the value of the constant, we can do the following:

1. Create a new IR module.

2. Create an IR function in the module, returning a value of the expected type.

3. Use the existing emitExpr() function to create the IR for the expression and return the calculated value with the last instruction.

4. JIT-execute the function to calculate the value.

Is this worth implementing? LLVM performs constant propagation and function inlining as part of the optimization pipeline. A simple expression such as 4 + 5 is already replaced during IR construction with the result. Small functions such as calculation of the greatest common divisor are inlined. If all parameters are constant values, then the inlined code gets replaced by the result of the calculation through constant propagation.

Based on this observation, an implementation of this approach is only useful if enough language features are available for execution at compile time. If this is the case, then it is fairly easily implemented using the given sketch.

Knowing how to utilize the JIT compiler component of LLVM enables you to use LLVM in whole new ways. Besides implementing a JIT compiler like the Java VM, the JIT compiler can also be embedded in other applications. This allows creative approaches, such as its use inside a static compiler, which you looked at in this section.

Summary

In this chapter, you learned how to develop a JIT compiler. You began with possible applications of JIT compilers, and you explored lli, the LLVM dynamic compiler and interpreter. Using the predefined LLJIT class, you built a tool similar to lli on your own. To be able to take advantage of the layered structure of the ORC API, you implemented an optimizing JIT class. Having acquired all this knowledge, you explored the possibility of using a JIT compiler inside a static compiler, a feature from which some languages can benefit.

In the next chapter, you will examine how to add a backend for a new CPU architecture to LLVM.

11
Debugging Using LLVM Tools

LLVM comes with a set of tools that helps you to identify certain errors in your application. All of these tools make use of the LLVM and **Clang** libraries.

In this chapter, you will learn how to instrument an application with **sanitizers**, how to use the most common sanitizer to identify a wide range of bugs, and how to implement fuzz testing for your application. This will help you to identify bugs that are usually not found with unit testing. You will also learn how to identify performance bottlenecks in your application, running the **static analyzer** to identify problems normally not found by the compiler, and creating your own Clang-based tool with which you can extend Clang with new functionality.

This chapter will cover the following topics:

- Instrumenting an application with sanitizers
- Finding bugs with **libFuzzer**
- Performance profiling with **XRay**
- Checking the source with the **Clang Static Analyzer**
- Creating your own Clang-based tool

By the end of the chapter, you will know how to use various LLVM and Clang tools to identify a large category of errors in an application. You will also acquire the knowledge to extend Clang with new functionality, for example, to enforce a naming convention or to add new source analysis.

Technical requirements

To create the **flame graph** in the *Performance profiling with XRay* section, you need to install the scripts from `https://github.com/brendangregg/FlameGraph`. Some systems, such as **Fedora** and **FreeBSD**, provide a package for these scripts, which you can also use.

To view the **Chrome visualization** in the same section, you need to have the **Chrome** browser installed. You can download the browser from `https://www.google.com/chrome/`, or use the package manager of your system to install the Chrome browser. The code files for the chapter are available at `https://github.com/PacktPublishing/Learn-LLVM-12/tree/master/Chapter11`

You can find the code in action videos at `https://bit.ly/3nllhED`

Instrumenting an application with sanitizers

LLVM comes with a couple of **sanitizers**. These are passes that instrument the **Intermediate Representation** (**IR**) in a way to check for certain misbehaviors of an application. Usually, they require library support, which is part of the `compiler-rt` project. Sanitizers can be enabled in Clang, which makes them very comfortable to use. In the following sections, we will have a look at the available sanitizers, namely, `address`, `memory`, and `thread`. We will first look at the `address` sanitizer.

Detecting memory access problems with the address sanitizer

You use the `address` sanitizer to detect a couple of memory access bugs in an application. This includes common errors such as using dynamically allocated memory after freeing it, or writing to dynamically allocated memory outside the boundaries of the allocated memory.

When enabled, the `address` sanitizer replaces calls to the `malloc()` and `free()` functions with its own version, and instruments all memory access with a checking guard. Of course, this adds a lot of overhead to the application, and you will use the `address` sanitizer only during the testing phase of the application. If you are interested in the implementation details, then you can find the source of the pass in the `llvm/lib/Transforms/Instrumentation/AddressSanitzer.cpp` file and a description of the algorithm used at `https://github.com/google/sanitizers/wiki/AddressSanitizerAlgorithm`.

Let's run a short example to demonstrate the capabilities of the `address` sanitizer. The following example application, `outofbounds.c`, allocates 12 bytes of memory, but initializes 14 bytes:

```
#include <stdlib.h>
#include <string.h>

int main(int argc, char *argv[]) {
  char *p = malloc(12);
  memset(p, 0, 14);
  return (int)*p;
}
```

You can compile and run this application without noticing any problems. This is typical for this kind of error. Even in larger applications, this kind of bug can go unnoticed for a long time. But, if you enable the `address` sanitizer with the `-fsanitize=address` option, then the application stops after detecting the error.

It is also useful to enable debug symbols with the `-g` option, because it helps to identify the location of the error in the source. The following code is an example of how to compile the source file with the `address` sanitizer and debug symbols enabled:

```
$ clang -fsanitize=address -g outofbounds.c -o outofbounds
```

Now, you get a lengthy error report when running the application:

```
$ ./outofbounds
=================================================================
===
==1067==ERROR: AddressSanitizer: heap-buffer-overflow on
address 0x60200000001c at pc 0x00000023a6ef bp 0x7fffffffeb10
sp 0x7fffffffe2d8
WRITE of size 14 at 0x60200000001c thread T0
```

```
    #0 0x23a6ee in __asan_memset /usr/src/contrib/llvm-project/
compiler-rt/lib/asan/asan_interceptors_memintrinsics.cpp:26:3
    #1 0x2b2a03 in main /home/kai/sanitizers/outofbounds.c:6:3
    #2 0x23331f in _start /usr/src/lib/csu/amd64/crt1.c:76:7
```

The report also contains detailed information about the memory content. The important information is the type of error – **heap buffer overflow**, in this case – and the offending source line. To find the source line, you look at the stack trace at location *#1*, which is the last location before the address sanitizer intercepts the execution of the application. It shows *line 6* in the outofbounds.c file, which is the line containing the call to memset() – indeed, the exact place where the buffer overflow happens.

If you replace the line containing memset(p, 0, 14); in the outofbounds.c file with the following code, then you introduce access to memory after the memory is freed. You'll need to store the source in the useafterfree.c file:

```
memset(p, 0, 12);
free(p);
```

Again, if you compile and run it, the use of the pointer after the memory is free is detected:

```
$ clang -fsanitize=address -g useafterfree.c -o useafterfree
$ ./useafterfree
================================================================
===
==1118==ERROR: AddressSanitizer: heap-use-after-free on address
0x602000000010 at pc 0x0000002b2a5c bp 0x7fffffffeb00 sp
0x7fffffffeaf8
READ of size 1 at 0x602000000010 thread T0
    #0 0x2b2a5b in main /home/kai/sanitizers/
useafterfree.c:8:15
    #1 0x23331f in _start /usr/src/lib/csu/amd64/crt1.c:76:7
```

This time, the report points to *line 8*, which contains dereferencing of the p pointer.

On **x86_64 Linux** and **macOS**, you can also enable a leak detector. If you set the ASAN_OPTIONS environment variable to the value detect_leaks=1 before running the application, then you also get a report about memory leaks. On the command line, you do this as follows:

```
$ ASAN_OPTIONS=detect_leaks=1 ./useafterfree
```

The `address` sanitizer is very useful, because it catches a category of bugs that are otherwise difficult to detect. The `memory` sanitizer does a similar task, and we'll look at it in the next section.

Finding uninitialized memory access with the memory sanitizer

Using uninitialized memory is another category of bugs that are hard to find. In **C** and **C++**, the general memory allocation routines do not initialize the memory buffer with a default value. The same is true for automatic variables on the stack.

There are lots of opportunities for errors, and the `memory` sanitizer helps to find the bugs. If you are interested in the implementation details, you can find the source for the `memory` sanitizer pass in the `llvm/lib/Transforms/Instrumentation/MemorySanitizer.cpp` file. The comment at top of the file explains the ideas behind the implementation.

Let's run a small example and save the following source as the `memory.c` file. You should note that the x variable is not initialized, but is used as a `return` value:

```
int main(int argc, char *argv[]) {
   int x;
   return x;
}
```

Without the sanitizer, the application will run just fine. However, you will get an error report if you use the `-fsanitize=memory` option:

```
$ clang -fsanitize=memory -g memory.c -o memory
$ ./memory
==1206==WARNING: MemorySanitizer: use-of-uninitialized-value
    #0 0x10a8f49 in main /home/kai/sanitizers/memory.c:3:3
    #1 0x1053481 in _start /usr/src/lib/csu/amd64/crt1.c:76:7

SUMMARY: MemorySanitizer: use-of-uninitialized-value /home/kai/
sanitizers/memory.c:3:3 in main
Exiting
```

Like the `address` sanitizer, the `memory` sanitizer stops the application at the first found error.

In the next section, we look at how we can use the `thread` sanitizer to detect data races in multi-threaded applications.

Pointing out data races with the thread sanitizer

To leverage the power of modern CPUs, applications now use multiple threads. This is a powerful technique, but it also introduces new sources of errors. A very common problem in multi-threaded applications is that access to global data is not protected, for example, with a **mutex** or **semaphore**. This is called a **data race**. The `thread` sanitizer can detect data races in **Pthread**-based applications and applications using the LLVM **libc++** implementation. You will find the implementation in the `llvm/lib/Transforms/Instrumentation/ThreadSanitize.cpp` file.

To demonstrate the functionality of the `thread` sanitizer, we will create a very simple producer/consumer-style application. The producer thread increments a global variable, while the consumer thread decrements the same variable. The access to the global variable is not protected, so this is clearly a data race. You'll need to save the following source in the `thread.c` file:

```
#include <pthread.h>

int data = 0;

void *producer(void *x) {
  for (int i = 0; i < 10000; ++i) ++data;
  return x;
}

void *consumer(void *x) {
  for (int i = 0; i < 10000; ++i) --data;
  return x;
}

int main() {
  pthread_t t1, t2;
  pthread_create(&t1, NULL, producer, NULL);
  pthread_create(&t2, NULL, consumer, NULL);
```

```
    pthread_join(t1, NULL);
    pthread_join(t2, NULL);
    return data;
}
```

From the preceding code, the `data` variable is shared between two threads. Here, it is of the `int` type to make the example simple. Most often, a data structure such as the `std::vector` class or similar would be used. These two threads run the `producer()` and `consumer()` functions.

The `producer()` function only increments the `data` variable, while the `consumer()` function decrements it. No access protection is implemented, so this constitutes a data race. The `main()` function starts both threads with the `pthread_create()` function, waits for the end of the threads with the `pthread_join()` function, and returns the current value of the `data` variable.

If you compile and run this application, then you will note no error; that is, the return value is always 0. An error, in this case, a return value not equal to 0, will show up if the number of loops performed is increased by a factor of 100. Then, you'll see other values showing up.

You use the `thread` sanitizer to identify the data race. To compile with the `thread` sanitizer being enabled, you'll need to pass the `-fsanitize=thread` option to Clang. Adding debug symbols with the `-g` option gives you line numbers in the report, which helps a lot. Note that you also need to link the `pthread` library:

```
$ clang -fsanitize=thread -g thread.c -o thread -lpthread
$ ./thread

==================
WARNING: ThreadSanitizer: data race (pid=1474)
  Write of size 4 at 0x000000cdf8f8 by thread T2:
    #0 consumer /home/kai/sanitizers/thread.c:11:35
(thread+0x2b0fb2)

  Previous write of size 4 at 0x000000cdf8f8 by thread T1:
    #0 producer /home/kai/sanitizers/thread.c:6:35
(thread+0x2b0f22)

  Location is global 'data' of size 4 at 0x000000cdf8f8
(thread+0x000000cdf8f8)
```

```
   Thread T2 (tid=100437, running) created by main thread at:
      #0 pthread_create /usr/src/contrib/llvm-project/
   compiler-rt/lib/tsan/rtl/tsan_interceptors_posix.cpp:962:3
   (thread+0x271703)
      #1 main /home/kai/sanitizers/thread.c:18:3
   (thread+0x2b1040)


   Thread T1 (tid=100436, finished) created by main thread at:
      #0 pthread_create /usr/src/contrib/llvm-project/
   compiler-rt/lib/tsan/rtl/tsan_interceptors_posix.cpp:962:3
   (thread+0x271703)
      #1 main /home/kai/sanitizers/thread.c:17:3
   (thread+0x2b1021)


SUMMARY: ThreadSanitizer: data race /home/kai/sanitizers/
thread.c:11:35 in consumer
==================
ThreadSanitizer: reported 1 warnings
```

The report points us to *lines 6* and *11* of the source file, where the global variable is accessed. It also shows that two threads, named *T1* and *T2*, accessed the variable, as well as the file and line number of the respective calls to the `pthread_create()` function.

In this section, we learned how to use three sanitizers to identify common problems in applications. The `address` sanitizer helps us to identify common memory access errors, such as out-of-bounds access or using memory after being freed. Using the `memory` sanitizer, we can find accesses to uninitialized memory, and the `thread` sanitizer helps us to identify data races.

In the next section, we try to trigger the sanitizers by running our application on random data, called **fuzz testing**.

Finding bugs with libFuzzer

To test your application, you'll need to write **unit tests**. This is a great way to make sure your software behaves correctly. However, due to the exponential number of possible inputs, you'll probably miss certain weird inputs, and a few bugs as well.

Fuzz testing can help here. The idea is to present your application with randomly generated data, or data based on valid input but with random changes. This is done over and over again, and so your application is tested with a large number of inputs. This is a very powerful testing approach. Literally hundreds of bugs in web browsers and other software have been found with fuzz testing.

LLVM comes with its own fuzz testing library. Originally part of the LLVM core libraries, the **libFuzzer** implementation was finally moved to `compiler-rt`. The library is designed to test small and fast functions.

Let's run a small example. You'll need to provide the `LLVMFuzzerTestOneInput()` function. This function is called by the **fuzzer driver** and provides you with some input. The following function counts consecutive ASCII digits in the input, and then we'll feed the random input to it. You'll need to save the example in the `fuzzer.c` file:

```c
#include <stdint.h>
#include <stdlib.h>

int count(const uint8_t *Data, size_t Size) {
  int cnt = 0;
  if (Size)
    while (Data[cnt] >= '0' && Data[cnt] <= '9') ++cnt;
  return cnt;
}

int LLVMFuzzerTestOneInput(const uint8_t *Data, size_t
                           Size) {
  count(Data, Size);
  return 0;
}
```

From the preceding code, the `count()` function counts the number of digits in the memory pointed to by the `Data` variable. The size of the data is only checked to determine whether there are any bytes available. Inside the `while` loop, the size is not checked.

Used with normal **C strings**, there will be no error because C strings are always terminated by a 0 byte. The `LLVMFuzzerTestOneInput()` function is the so-called **fuzz target**, and it is the function called by libFuzzer. It calls the function we want to test and returns 0, which is currently the only allowed value.

To compile the file with libFuzzer, you add the `-fsanitize=fuzzer` option. The recommendation is to also enable the `address` sanitizer and the generation of debug symbols. Use the following command to compile the file:

```
$ clang -fsanitize=fuzzer,address -g fuzzer.c -o fuzzer
```

When you run the test, a lengthy report is emitted. The report contains more information than a stack trace, so let's have a closer look at it:

1. The first line tells you the seed that was used to initialize the random number generator. You can use the `-seed=` option to repeat this execution:

    ```
    INFO: Seed: 1297394926
    ```

2. By default, libFuzzer limits inputs to at most 4,096 bytes. You can change the default by using the `-max_len=` option:

    ```
    INFO: -max_len is not provided; libFuzzer will not
    generate inputs larger than 4096 bytes
    ```

3. Now, we run the test without providing sample input. The set of all sample inputs is called the corpus, and it is empty for this run:

    ```
    INFO: A corpus is not provided, starting from an empty
    corpus
    ```

4. Some information about the generated test data will follow. It shows you that `28` inputs were tried and `6` inputs, with a combined length of `19` bytes, were found, which together cover `6` coverage points or basic blocks:

    ```
    #28      NEW    cov: 6 ft: 9 corp: 6/19b lim: 4 exec/s: 0
    rss: 29Mb L: 4/4 MS: 4 CopyPart-PersAutoDict-CopyPart-
    ChangeByte- DE: "1\x00"-
    ```

5. After this, a buffer overflow was detected, and it follows the information from the `address` sanitizer. Lastly, the report tells you where the input causing the buffer overflow is saved:

    ```
    artifact_prefix='./'; Test unit written to ./crash-17ba07
    91499db908433b80f37c5fbc89b870084b
    ```

With the saved input, you can execute the test case with just the crashing input again:

```
$ ./fuzzer crash-17ba0791499db908433b80f37c5fbc89b870084b
```

This is obviously a great help to identify the problem. Only, using random data is often not very helpful. If you try to fuzz test the `tinylang` lexer or parser, then pure random data leads to immediate rejection of the input, because no valid token can be found.

In such cases, it is more useful to provide a small set of valid input, called the corpus. Then, the files of the corpus are randomly mutated and used as input. You can think of the input as mostly valid, with just a few bits flipped. This also works great with other input, which must have a certain format. For example, for a library processing **JPEG** and **PNG** files, you will provide some small **JPEG** and **PNG** files as the corpus.

You can save the corpus files in one or more directories and you can create a simple corpus for your fuzz test with the help of the `printf` command:

```
$ mkdir corpus
$ printf "012345\0" >corpus/12345.txt
$ printf "987\0" >corpus/987.txt
```

When running the test, you will provide the directory on the command line:

```
$ ./fuzzer corpus/
```

The corpus is then used as the base for generating random input, as the report tells you:

```
INFO: seed corpus: files: 2 min: 4b max: 7b total: 11b rss:
29Mb
```

If you are testing a function that works on tokens or other magic values, such as a programming language, then you can speed up the process by providing a dictionary with the tokens. For a programming language, the dictionary would contain all the keywords and special symbols used in the language. The dictionary definitions follow a simple key-value style. For example, to define the `if` keyword in the dictionary, you can add the following:

```
kw1="if"
```

However, the key is optional and can be left out. You can then specify the dictionary file on the command line with the `-dict=` option. In the next section, we'll get to know the limitations and alternatives for the libFuzzer implementation.

Limitations and alternatives

The libFuzzer implementation is fast but poses a number of restrictions on the test target. They are as follows:

- The function under test must accept the input as an array in memory. Some library functions require a file path to the data instead, and they cannot be tested with libFuzzer.

- The exit() function should not be called.

- The global state should not be altered.

- Hardware random number generators should not be used.

From the aforementioned restrictions, the first two restrictions are an implication of the implementation of libFuzzer as a library. The latter two restrictions are needed to avoid confusion in the evaluation algorithm. If one of these restrictions is not met, then two identical calls to the fuzz target can give different results.

The best-known alternative tool for fuzz testing is **AFL**, found at https://github.com/google/AFL. AFL needs an instrumented binary (an LLVM plugin for instrumentation is provided) and requires the application to take the input as the file path on the command line. AFL and libFuzzer can share the same corpus and the same dictionary files. Thus, it is possible to test an application with both tools. In cases where libFuzzer is not applicable, AFL may be a good alternative.

There are many more ways of influencing the way libFuzzer works. You can read the reference page at https://llvm.org/docs/LibFuzzer.html for more details.

In the next section, we look at a totally different problem an application can have; we try to identify performance bottlenecks.

Performance profiling with XRay

If your application seems to run slow, then you might want to know where all the time is spent in the code. In this case, instrumenting the code with **XRay** helps you. Basically, at each function entry and exit, a special call into the runtime library is inserted. This allows counting how often a function is called, and also how much time is spent in the function. You find the implementation for the instrumentation pass in the llvm/lib/XRay/ directory. The runtime portion is part of compiler-rt.

In the following example source, real work is simulated by calling the `usleep()` function. The `func1()` function sleeps for 10 μs. The `func2()` function either calls `func1()` or sleeps for 100 μs, depending on whether the n parameter is odd or even. Inside the `main()` function, both functions are called inside a loop. This is already enough to get interesting information. You'll need to save the following source code in the `xraydemo.c` file:

```c
#include <unistd.h>

void func1() { usleep(10); }

void func2(int n) {
  if (n % 2) func1();
  else usleep(100);
}

int main(int argc, char *argv[]) {
  for (int i = 0; i < 100; i++) { func1(); func2(i); }
  return 0;
}
```

To enable the XRay instrumentation during compilation, you will need to specify the `-fxray-instrument` option. Functions with less than 200 instructions are not instrumented. This is an arbitrary threshold defined by the developers, and in our case, the functions would not be instrumented. The threshold can be specified with the `-fxray-instruction-threshold=` option. Alternatively, we can add a function attribute to control whether a function should be instrumented. For example, adding the following prototype would result in always instrumenting the function:

```c
void func1() __attribute__((xray_always_instrument));
```

Likewise, by using the `xray_never_instrument` attribute, you can turn off instrumentation for a function.

We will now use the command-line option and compile the `xraydemo.c` file as follows:

```
$ clang -fxray-instrument -fxray-instruction-threshold=1 -g\
  xraydemo.c -o xraydemo
```

In the resulting binary, instrumentation is turned off by default. If you run the binary, you will note no difference to a not-instrumented binary. The XRAY_OPTIONS environment variable is used to control the recording of runtime data. To enable data collection, you run the application as follows:

```
$ XRAY_OPTIONS= "patch_premain=true xray_mode=xray-basic "\
    ./xraydemo
```

The xray_mode=xray-basic option tells the runtime that we want to use basic mode. In this mode, all runtime data is collected, which can result in huge log files. When the patch_premain=true option is given, then functions that are run before the main() function are instrumented, too.

After running this command, you see a new file in the directory, in which the collected data is stored. You need to use the llvm-xray tool to extract readable information from this file.

The llvm-xray tool supports various subcommands. You use the account subcommand to extract some basic statistics. For example, to get the top 10 most called functions, you add the -top=10 option to limit the output, and the -sort=count option to specify the function call count as the sort criteria. You can influence the sort order with the -sortorder= option. Run the following command to get the statistic:

```
$ llvm-xray account xray-log.xraydemo.xVsWiE -sort=count\
    -sortorder=dsc -instr_map ./xraydemo
Functions with latencies: 3
   funcid        count        sum   function
        1          150   0.166002   demo.c:4:0: func1
        2          100   0.543103   demo.c:9:0: func2
        3            1   0.655643   demo.c:17:0: main
```

You can see that the func1() function is called most often, as well as the accumulated time spent in this function. The example only has three functions, so the –top= option has no visible effect here, but for real applications, it is very useful.

From the collected data, it is possible to reconstruct all the stack frames that occurred during runtime. You use the stack subcommand to view the top 10 stacks. The output shown here is reduced for brevity:

```
$ llvm-xray stack xray-log.xraydemo.xVsWiE -instr_map\
    ./xraydemo
Unique Stacks: 3
```

```
Top 10 Stacks by leaf sum:


Sum: 1325516912
lvl     function           count                  sum
#0      main                   1           1777862705
#1      func2                 50           1325516912



Top 10 Stacks by leaf count:


Count: 100
lvl     function           count                  sum
#0      main                   1           1777862705
#1      func1                100            303596276
```

A **stack frame** is a sequence of how a function is called. The func2() function is called by the main() function, and this is the stack frame with the largest accumulated time. The depth depends on how many functions are called, and the stack frames are usually large.

This subcommand can also be used to create a **flame graph** from the stack frames. With a flame graph, you can easily identify which functions have a large accumulated runtime. The output is the stack frames with count and runtime information. Using the flamegraph.pl script, you convert the data into a **Scalable Vector Graphics** (**SVG**) file, which you can view in your browser.

With the following command, you instruct llvm-xray to output all stack frames with the -all-stacks option. Using the -stack-format=flame option, the output is in the format expected by the flamegraph.pl script. With the -aggregation-type option, you can choose whether stack frames are aggregated by total time or by the number of invocations. The output of llvm-xray is piped into the flamegraph.pl script, and the resulting output is saved in the flame.svg file:

```
$ llvm-xray stack xray-log.xraydemo.xVsWiE -all-stacks\
   -stack-format=flame --aggregation-type=time\
   -instr_map ./xraydemo | flamegraph.pl >flame.svg
```

Open the generated `flame.svg` file in your browser. The graphic looks as follows:

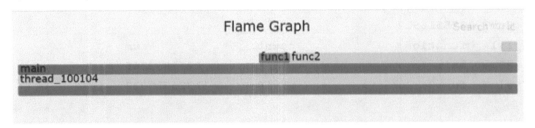

Figure 11.1 – Flame graph produced by llvm-xray

Flame graphs can be confusing at the first look, because the *x* axis does not have the usual meaning of elapsed time. Instead, the functions are simply sorted by name. The colors are chosen to have good contrast and have no other meaning. From the preceding graph, you can easily determine the call hierarchy and the time spent in a function.

Information about a stack frame is displayed only after you move the mouse cursor over the rectangle representing the frame. With a mouse click on the frame, you can zoom into this stack frame. Flame graphs are of great help if you want to identify functions worth optimizing. To find out more about flame graphs, please visit the website of Brendan Gregg, the inventor of flame graphs, http://www.brendangregg.com/flamegraphs.html.

You can use the `convert` subcommand to convert the data into `.yaml` format or into the format used by the **Chrome trace viewer visualization**. The latter is another nice way to create a graphic from the data. To save the data in the `xray.evt` file, you run the following command:

```
$ llvm-xray convert -output-format=trace_event\
    -output=xray.evt -symbolize -sort\
    -instr_map=./xraydemo xray-log.xraydemo.xVsWiE
```

If you do not specify the `-symbolize` option, then no function names are shown in the resulting graph.

Once that is done, open the Chrome browser and type chrome:///tracing. Then, click on the **Load** button to load the `xray.evt` file. You will see the following visualization of the data:

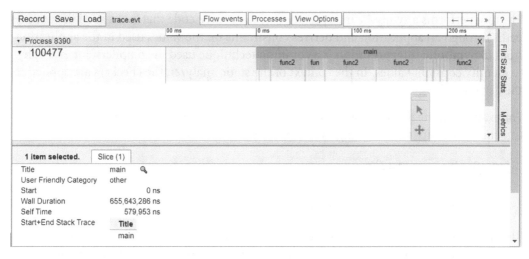

Figure 11.2 – Chrome trace viewer visualization generated by llvm-xray

In this view, the stack frames are sorted by the time the function call occurs. For further interpretation of the visualization, please read the tutorial at `https://www.chromium.org/developers/how-tos/trace-event-profiling-tool`.

> **Tip**
>
> The `llvm-xray` tool has more functionality. You can read about it on the LLVM website at `https://llvm.org/docs/XRay.html` and `https://llvm.org/docs/XRayExample.html`.

In this section, we learned how to instrument an application with XRay, how to collect runtime information, and how to visualize that data. We can use this knowledge to find performance bottlenecks in applications.

Another approach to identifying errors in an application is to analyze the source code, which is done with the static analyzer.

Checking the source with the Clang Static Analyzer

The **Clang Static Analyzer** is a tool that performs additional checking on C, C++, and **Objective C** source code. The checks performed by the static analyzer are more thorough than the checks the compiler performs. They are also more costly in terms of time and required resources. The static analyzer has a set of checkers that check for certain bugs.

The tool performs a symbolic interpretation of the source code that looks at all the code paths through an application and derives constraints on the values used in the application from it. **Symbolic interpretation** is a common technique used in compilers, for example, to identify constant values. In the context of the static analyzer, the checkers are applied to the derived values.

For example, if the divisor of a division is 0, then the static analyzer warns about it. We can check this with the following example stored in the `div.c` file:

```
int divbyzero(int a, int b) { return a / b; }
```

```
int bug() { return divbyzero(5, 0); }
```

The static analyzer will warn about a division by 0 in the example. However, when compiling, the file with the `clang -Wall -c div.c` command will show no warning.

There are two ways to invoke the static analyzer from the command line. The older tool is **scan-build**, which is included in LLVM and can be used for simple scenarios. The newer tool is **CodeChecker**, available at `https://github.com/Ericsson/codechecker/`. For checking a single file, the `scan-build` tool is the easier solution. You simply pass the `compile` command to the tool, and everything else is done automatically:

```
$ scan-build clang -c div.c
scan-build: Using '/usr/local/llvm12/bin/clang-12' for static
analysis
div.c:2:12: warning: Division by zero [core.DivideZero]
  return a / b;
        ~~^~~
1 warning generated.
scan-build: Analysis run complete.
scan-build: 1 bug found.
scan-build: Run 'scan-view /tmp/scan-
build-2021-03-01-023401-8721-1' to examine bug reports.
```

The output on the screen already tells you that a problem was found, that is, the checker with the name `core.DivideZero` was triggered. But that is not all. You will find a complete report in HTML in the mentioned subdirectory of the `/tmp` directory. You can use the `scan-view` command to view the report or open the `index.html` file found in the subdirectory in your browser.

The first page of the report shows you a summary of the found bugs:

sanitizers - scan-build results

User:	kai@freebsd
Working Directory:	/usr/home/kai/sanitizers
Command Line:	clang-12 -c div.c
Clang Version:	clang version 12.0.0
Date:	Sat Apr 3 22:47:20 2021

Bug Summary

Bug Type	Quantity	Display?
All Bugs	1	☑
Logic error		
Division by zero	1	☑

Reports

Bug Group	Bug Type ▾	File	Function/Method	Line	Path Length	
Logic error	Division by zero	div.c	divbyzero	2	3	View Report

Figure 11.3 – Summary page

For each found **error**, the summary page shows the type of the error, the location in the source, and the path length after which the analyzer finds the error. A link to a detailed report for the error is provided.

The following screenshot shows the detailed report for the error:

Bug Summary

File:　/home/kai/sanitizers/div.c
Warning:　line 2, column 12
　　　　Division by zero

Annotated Source Code

Press '?' to see keyboard shortcuts

Show analyzer invocation

☐ Show only relevant lines

```
1  int divbyzero(int a, int b) {
2      return a / b;
```
　　　　　　　　3 ← Division by zero
```
3  }
4
5  int bug() {
6      return divbyzero(5, 0);
```
　　　　　　　1 Passing the value 0 via 2nd parameter 'b' →

　　　　　　2 ← Calling 'divbyzero' →
```
7  }
```

Figure 11.4 – Detailed report

With the detailed report, you are able to verify the error by following the numbered bubbles. In our simple example, it shows in three steps how passing 0 as a parameter value leads to a division by zero error.

Verification through a human is indeed required. If the derived constraints are not precise enough for a certain checker, then false positives are possible, that is, an error is reported for perfectly fine code. Based on the report, you can identify false positives.

You are not limited to the checkers that are provided with the tool. You can also add new checkers. The next section shows how to do this.

Adding a new checker to the Clang Static Analyzer

To add a new checker to the Clang Static Analyzer, you create a new subclass of the `Checker` class. The static analyzer tries all possible paths through the code. The analyzer engine generates events at certain points, for example, before a function call or after a function call. Your class has to provide callbacks for these events if you need to handle them. The `Checker` class and the registrations for the events are provided in the `clang/include/clang/StaticAnalyzer/Core/Checker.h` header file.

Usually, a checker needs to track some symbols. But the checker can't manage the state, because it does not know which code path the analyzer engine currently tries. Therefore, the tracked state must be registered with the engine, and can only be changed using a `ProgramStateRef` instance.

Many libraries provide functions that must be used in pairs. For example, the C standard library provides the `malloc()` and `free()` functions. The memory allocated by the `malloc()` function must be freed exactly one time by the `free()` function. Not calling the `free()` function, or calling it several times, is a programming error. There are many more instances of this coding pattern, and the static analyzer provides checkers for some of them.

The **iconv** library provides functions to convert text from one encoding to another, for example, from Latin-1 encoding to UTF-16 encoding. To perform the conversion, the implementation needs to allocate memory. To transparently manage the internal resources, the `iconv` library provides the `iconv_open()` and `iconv_close()` functions, which must be used in pairs. You implement a checker to check for this.

To detect the errors, the checker needs to track the descriptor returned from the `iconv_open()` function. The analyzer engine returns a `SymbolRef` instance for the return value of the `iconv_open()` function. We associate this symbol with a state to reflect whether `iconv_close()` was called or not. For the state, we create the `IconvState` class, which encapsulates a `bool` value.

The new `IconvChecker` class needs to handle four events:

- `PostCall`, which occurs after a function call. After the `iconv_open()` function is called, we retrieve the symbol for the return value and remember it as being in an open state.

- `PreCall`, which occurs before a function call. Before the `iconv_close()` function is called, we check whether the symbol for the descriptor is in an open state. If not, then the `iconv_close()` function was already called for the descriptor, and we have detected a double call to the function.

- DeadSymbols, which occurs when unused symbols are cleaned up. We check whether an unused symbol for a descriptor is still in an open state. If yes, then we have detected a missing call to iconv_close(), which is a resource leak.

- PointerEscape, which is called when the symbols can no longer be tracked by the analyzer. In this case, we remove the symbol from the state, because we can no longer reason whether the descriptor was closed or not.

The new checker is implemented inside the Clang project. Let's begin with adding the new checker to the collection of all checkers, which is the clang/include/clang/StaticAnalyzer/Checkers/Checkers.td file. Each checker is associated with packages. Our new checker is under development, and therefore it belongs in the alpha package. The iconv API is a POSIX-standardized API, so it also belongs in the unix package. Locate the UnixAlpha section in the Checkers.td file and add the following code to register the new IconvChecker:

```
def IconvChecker : Checker<"Iconv">,
  HelpText<"Check handling of iconv functions">,
  Documentation<NotDocumented>;
```

This adds the new checker to the collection of known **checkers**, sets help text for the command-line option, and states that there is no documentation for this checker.

Next, we implement the checker in the clang/lib/StaticAnalyzer/Checkers/IconvChecker.cpp file:

1. For the implementation, we need to include several header files. The BuiltinCheckerRegistration.h file is required to register the checker. The Checker.h file provides the declaration of the Checker class and the callbacks for the events. The CallEvent.h file declares the class used for call events, and the CheckerContext.h file is required for the declaration of the CheckerContext class, which is the central class providing access to the state of the analyzer:

```
#include "clang/StaticAnalyzer/Checkers/
BuiltinCheckerRegistration.h"
#include "clang/StaticAnalyzer/Core/Checker.h"
#include "clang/StaticAnalyzer/Core/
PathSensitive/CallEvent.h"
#include "clang/StaticAnalyzer/Core/PathSensitive/
CheckerContext.h"
```

2. To avoid typing the namespace names, we use the `clang` and `ento` namespaces:

```
using namespace clang;
using namespace ento;
```

3. We associate a state with each symbol representing an iconv descriptor. The state can be open or closed, and we use a `bool`-type variable, with the `true` value for an open state. The state value is encapsulated in the `IconvState` struct. This struct is used with a `FoldingSet` data structure, which is a hash set that filters duplicate entries. To be usable with this data structure implementation, the `Profile()` method is added here, which sets the unique bits of this struct. We put the struct into an anonymous namespace, to avoid pollution of the global namespace:

```
namespace {
struct IconvState {
  const bool IsOpen;

public:
  IconvState(bool IsOpen) : IsOpen(IsOpen) {}
  bool isOpen() const { return IsOpen; }

  bool operator==(const IconvState &O) const {
    return IsOpen == O.IsOpen;
  }

  void Profile(llvm::FoldingSetNodeID &ID) const {
    ID.AddInteger(IsOpen);
  }
};
}
```

4. The `IconvState` struct represents the state of an iconv descriptor, which is represented by a symbol of the `SymbolRef` class. This is best done with a map, which has the symbol as the key and the state as the value. As explained earlier, the checker cannot hold the state. Instead, the state must be registered with the global program state, which is done with the `REGISTER_MAP_WITH_PROGRAMSTATE` macro. This macro introduces the `IconvStateMap` name, which we use later to access the map:

```
REGISTER_MAP_WITH_PROGRAMSTATE(IconvStateMap, SymbolRef,
                                 IconvState)
```

5. We also implement the `IconvChecker` class in an anonymous namespace. The requested `PostCall`, `PreCall`, `DeadSymbols`, and `PointerEscape` events are template parameters to the `Checker` base class:

```
namespace {
class IconvChecker
    : public Checker<check::PostCall, check::PreCall,
                       check::DeadSymbols,
                       check::PointerEscape> {
```

6. The `IconvChecker` class only has fields of the `CallDescription` type, which are used to identify `iconv_open()`, `iconv()`, and `iconv_close()` function calls in the program:

```
CallDescription IconvOpenFn, IconvFn, IconvCloseFn;
```

7. The `report()` method generates an error report. The important parameters to the method are an array of symbols, the type of the bug, and a bug description. Inside the method, a bug report is created for each symbol, and the symbol is marked as the interesting one for the bug. If a source range is provided as a parameter, then this is also added to the report. Finally, the report is emitted:

```
void
report(ArrayRef<SymbolRef> Syms, const BugType &Bug,
       StringRef Desc, CheckerContext &C,
       ExplodedNode *ErrNode,
       Optional<SourceRange> Range = None) const {
  for (SymbolRef Sym : Syms) {
    auto R = std::make_unique
```

```
                    <PathSensitiveBugReport>(
            Bug, Desc, ErrNode);
        R->markInteresting(Sym);
        if (Range)
          R->addRange(*Range);
        C.emitReport(std::move(R));
    }
  }
```

8. The constructor of the `IconvChecker` class only initializes the `CallDescription` fields using the name of the function:

```
public:
  IconvChecker()
      : IconvOpenFn("iconv_open"), IconvFn("iconv"),
        IconvCloseFn("iconv_close", 1) {}
```

9. The `checkPostCall()` method is called after the analyzer has executed a function call. If the executed function is not a global C function and not named `iconv_open`, then there is nothing to do:

```
void checkPostCall(const CallEvent &Call,
                   CheckerContext &C) const {
    if (!Call.isGlobalCFunction() ||
        !Call.isCalled(IconvOpenFn))
      return;
```

10. Otherwise, we try to get the return value of the function as a symbol. To store the symbol with the open state in the global program state, we need to get a `ProgramStateRef` instance from the `CheckerContext` instance. The state is immutable, so adding the symbol to the state results in a new state. The analyzer engine is informed about the new state with a call to the `addTransition()` method:

```
    if (SymbolRef Handle =
            Call.getReturnValue().getAsSymbol()) {
      ProgramStateRef State = C.getState();
      State = State->set<IconvStateMap>(
          Handle, IconvState(true));
```

```
        C.addTransition(State);
    }
}
```

11. Likewise, the `checkPreCall()` method is called before the analyzer executes a function. Only a global C function with the name `iconv_close` is of interest to us:

```
void checkPreCall(const CallEvent &Call,
                    CheckerContext &C) const {
    if (!Call.isGlobalCFunction() ||
        !Call.isCalled(IconvCloseFn))
        return;
```

12. If the symbol for the first argument of the function, which is the iconv descriptor, is known, then we retrieve the state of the symbol from the program state:

```
    if (SymbolRef Handle =
            Call.getArgSVal(0).getAsSymbol()) {
    ProgramStateRef State = C.getState();
    if (const IconvState *St =
            State->get<IconvStateMap>(Handle)) {
```

13. If the state represents the closed state, then we have detected a double close error, and we generate a bug report for it. The call to `generateErrorNode()` can return a `nullptr` value if an error report was already generated for this path, so we have to check for this situation:

```
    if (!St->isOpen()) {
        if (ExplodedNode *N = C.generateErrorNode()) {
        BugType DoubleCloseBugType(
            this, "Double iconv_close",
            "iconv API Error");
        report({Handle}, DoubleCloseBugType,
            "Closing a previous closed iconv "
            "descriptor",
            C, N, Call.getSourceRange());
        }
        return;
```

```
        }
    }
```

14. Otherwise, we set the state for the symbol to closed:

```
        State = State->set<IconvStateMap>(
            Handle, IconvState(false));
        C.addTransition(State);
    }
}
```

15. The `checkDeadSymbols()` method is called to clean up unused symbols. We loop over all symbols we track and ask the `SymbolReaper` instance whether the current symbol is dead:

```
void checkDeadSymbols(SymbolReaper &SymReaper,
                      CheckerContext &C) const {
    ProgramStateRef State = C.getState();
    SmallVector<SymbolRef, 8> LeakedSyms;
    for (auto SymbolState :
        State->get<IconvStateMap>()) {
      SymbolRef Sym = SymbolState.first;
      IconvState &St = SymbolState.second;

      if (SymReaper.isDead(Sym)) {
```

16. If the symbol is dead, then we need to check the state. If the state is still open, then this is a potential resource leak. There is one exception: `iconv_open()` returns `-1` in the case of an error. If the analyzer is in a code path handling this error, then it is wrong to assume a resource leak, because the function call failed. We try to get the value of the symbol from the `ConstraintManager` instance, and we do not consider the symbol as a resource leak if this value is `-1`. We add a leaked symbol to a `SmallVector` instance, for generating the error report later. Finally, we remove the dead symbol from the program state:

```
        if (St.isOpen()) {
          bool IsLeaked = true;
          if (const llvm::APSInt *Val =
                State->getConstraintManager()
                    .getSymVal(State, Sym))
```

```
            IsLeaked = Val->getExtValue() != -1;
        if (IsLeaked)
        LeakedSyms.push_back(Sym);
    }


        State = State->remove<IconvStateMap>(Sym);
    }
}
```

17. After the loop, we call the `generateNonFatalErrorNode()` method. This method transitions to the new program state, and returns an error node if there is not already an error node for this path. The `LeakedSyms` container holds the (possibly empty) list of leaked symbols, and we call the `report()` method to generate an error report:

```
if (ExplodedNode *N =
        C.generateNonFatalErrorNode(State)) {
    BugType LeakBugType(this, "Resource Leak",
                        "iconv API Error", true);
    report(LeakedSyms, LeakBugType,
        "Opened iconv descriptor not closed", C,
        N);
}
}
```

18. The `checkPointerEscape()` function is called when the analyzer detects a function call for which the parameters cannot be tracked. In such a case, we must assume that we do not know whether the iconv descriptor will be closed inside the function or not. The only exception is a call to the `iconv()` function, which does the conversion and is known to not call the `iconv_close()` function. This finishes the implementation of the `IconvChecker` class:

```
ProgramStateRef
checkPointerEscape(ProgramStateRef State,
                const InvalidatedSymbols &Escaped,
                const CallEvent *Call,
                PointerEscapeKind Kind) const {
    if (Kind == PSK_DirectEscapeOnCall &&
        Call->isCalled(IconvFn))
```

```
        return State;
      for (SymbolRef Sym : Escaped)
        State = State->remove<IconvStateMap>(Sym);
      return State;
    }
  };
  }
```

19. Lastly, the new checker needs to be registered at a `CheckerManager` instance. The `shouldRegisterIconvChecker()` method returns `true` to indicate that `IconvChecker` should be registered by default, and the `registerIconvChecker()` method performs the registration. Both methods are called via the code generated from the `Checkers.td` file:

```
void ento::registerIconvChecker(CheckerManager &Mgr) {
  Mgr.registerChecker<IconvChecker>();
}

bool ento::shouldRegisterIconvChecker(
      const CheckerManager &Mgr) {
  return true;
}
```

This finishes the implementation of the new checker. You just need to add the filename to the list of source filenames in the `clang/lib/StaticAnalyzer/Checkers/CmakeLists.txt` file:

```
add_clang_library(clangStaticAnalyzerCheckers
...
  IconvChecker.cpp
...)
```

To compile the new checker, you change to your build directory and run the `ninja` command:

```
$ ninja
```

You can test the new checker with the following source saved in the `conv.c` file, which has two calls to the `iconv_close()` function:

```
#include <iconv.h>

void doconv() {
  iconv_t id = iconv_open("Latin1", "UTF-16");
  iconv_close(id);
  iconv_close(id);
}
```

You learned how to extend the Clang Static Analyzer with your own checker. You can use this knowledge to either create new general checkers and contribute them to the community, or you can create checkers specifically built for your needs, to raise the quality of your product.

The static analyzer is built leveraging the Clang infrastructure, and the next section introduces you to how can build your own plugin extending Clang.

Creating your own Clang-based tool

The static analyzer is an impressive example of what you can do with the Clang infrastructure. It is also possible to extend Clang with plugins, so you are able to add your own functionality to Clang. The technique is very similar to adding a pass plugin to LLVM.

Let's explore the functionality with a simple plugin. The LLVM coding standard requires function names to begin with a lowercase letter. However, the coding standard has evolved over time, and there are many instances in which a function begins with an uppercase letter. A plugin that warns about a violation of the naming rule can help to fix the issue, so let's give it a try.

Because you want to run a user-defined action over the **abstract syntax tree** (**AST**), you need to define a subclass of the `PluginASTAction` class. If you write your own tool using the Clang libraries, then you define subclasses of the `ASTFrontendAction` class for your actions. The `PluginASTAction` class is a subclass of the `ASTFrontendAction` class, with the additional ability to parse command-line options.

The other class you need is a subclass of the ASTConsumer class. An AST consumer is a class using which you can run an action over an AST, regardless of the origin of the AST. Nothing more is needed for our first plugin. You can create the implementation in the NamingPlugin.cpp file as follows:

1. Begin by including the required header files. Besides the mentioned ASTConsumer class, you also need an instance of the compiler and the plugin registry:

    ```cpp
    #include "clang/AST/ASTConsumer.h"
    #include "clang/Frontend/CompilerInstance.h"
    #include "clang/Frontend/FrontendPluginRegistry.h"
    ```

2. Use the clang namespace and put your implementation into an anonymous namespace to avoid name clashes:

    ```cpp
    using namespace clang;
    namespace {
    ```

3. Next, define your subclass of the ASTConsumer class. Later, you will want to emit warnings if you detect a violation of the naming rule. To do so, you need a reference to a DiagnosticsEngine instance.

4. You'll need to store a CompilerInstance instance in the class, then you can ask for a DiagnosticsEngine instance:

    ```cpp
    class NamingASTConsumer : public ASTConsumer {
      CompilerInstance &CI;

    public:
      NamingASTConsumer(CompilerInstance &CI) : CI(CI) {}
    ```

5. An ASTConsumer instance has several entry methods. The HandleTopLevelDecl() method fits our purpose. The method is called for each declaration at the top level. This includes more than functions, for example, variables. So, you will use the LLVM RTTI dyn_cast<>() function to determine whether the declaration is a function declaration. The HandleTopLevelDecl() method has a declaration group as a parameter, which can contain more than a single declaration. This requires a loop over the declarations. The following code shows us the HandleTopLevelDecl() method:

    ```cpp
    bool HandleTopLevelDecl(DeclGroupRef DG) override {
      for (DeclGroupRef::iterator I = DG.begin(),
    ```

```
                                   E = DG.end();
        I != E; ++I) {
    const Decl *D = *I;
    if (const FunctionDecl *FD =
            dyn_cast<FunctionDecl>(D)) {
```

6. After having found a function declaration, you'll need to retrieve the name of the function. You'll also need to make sure that the name is not empty:

```
    std::string Name =
        FD->getNameInfo().getName().getAsString();
    assert(Name.length() > 0 &&
            "Unexpected empty identifier");
```

If the function name does not start with a lowercase letter, then you'll have found a violation of the naming rule:

```
    char &First = Name.at(0);
    if (!(First >= 'a' && First <= 'z')) {
```

7. To emit a warning, you need a `DiagnosticsEngine` instance. Additionally, you need a message ID. Inside Clang, the message ID is defined as an enumeration. Because your plugin is not part of Clang, you need to create a custom ID, which you then use to emit the warning:

```
    DiagnosticsEngine &Diag =
        CI.getDiagnostics();
    unsigned ID = Diag.getCustomDiagID(
        DiagnosticsEngine::Warning,
        "Function name should start with "
        "lowercase letter");
    Diag.Report(FD->getLocation(), ID);
```

8. Aside from closing all open braces, you need to return `true` from this function to indicate that processing can continue:

```
        }
      }
    }
```

```
        return true;
    }
};
```

9. Next, you need to create the `PluginASTAction` subclass, which implements the interface called by Clang:

```
class PluginNamingAction : public PluginASTAction {
public:
```

The first method you must implement is the `CreateASTConsumer()` method, which returns an instance of your `NamingASTConsumer` class. This method is called by Clang, and the passed `CompilerInstance` instance gives you access to all the important classes of the compiler. The following code demonstrates this:

```
std::unique_ptr<ASTConsumer>
CreateASTConsumer(CompilerInstance &CI,
                  StringRef file) override {
    return std::make_unique<NamingASTConsumer>(CI);
}
```

10. A plugin also has access to command-line options. Your plugin has no command-line parameters, and you will just return `true` to indicate success:

```
bool ParseArgs(const CompilerInstance &CI,
               const std::vector<std::string> &args)
                                            override {
    return true;
}
```

11. The action type of a plugin describes when the action is invoked. The default value is `Cmdline`, which means that the plugin must be named on the command line in order to be invoked. You'll need to override the method and change the value to `AddAfterMainAction`, which automatically runs the action:

```
PluginASTAction::ActionType getActionType() override {
    return AddAfterMainAction;
}
```

12. The implementation of your `PluginNamingAction` class is finished; only the closing braces for the class and the anonymous namespace are missing. Add them to the code as follows:

```
};
}
```

13. Lastly, you need to register the plugin. The first parameter is the name of the plugin, and the second parameter is the help text:

```
static FrontendPluginRegistry::Add<PluginNamingAction>
    X("naming-plugin", "naming plugin");
```

This finishes the implementation of the plugin. To compile the plugin, create a build description in the `CMakeLists.txt` file. The plugin lives outside the Clang source tree, so you need to set up a complete project. You can do so by following these steps:

1. Begin with the definition of the required **CMake** version and the name of the project:

```
cmake_minimum_required(VERSION 3.13.4)
project(naminglugin)
```

2. Next, include the LLVM files. If CMake is not able to find the files automatically, then you have to set the `LLVM_DIR` variable to point to the LLVM directory containing the CMake files:

```
find_package(LLVM REQUIRED CONFIG)
```

3. Append the LLVM directory with the CMake files to the search path, and include some required modules:

```
list(APPEND CMAKE_MODULE_PATH ${LLVM_DIR})
include(ChooseMSVCCRT)
include(AddLLVM)
include(HandleLLVMOptions)
```

4. Then, load the CMake definitions for Clang. If CMake is not able to find the files automatically, then you have to set the `Clang_DIR` variable to point to the Clang directory containing the CMake files:

```
find_package(Clang REQUIRED)
```

5. Next, define where the headers files and the library files are located, and which definitions to use:

```
include_directories("${LLVM_INCLUDE_DIR}"
                    "${CLANG_INCLUDE_DIRS}")
add_definitions("${LLVM_DEFINITIONS}")
link_directories("${LLVM_LIBRARY_DIR}")
```

6. The previous definitions set up the build environment. Insert the following command, defining the name of your plugin, the source file(s) of the plugin, and that it is a Clang plugin:

```
add_llvm_library(NamingPlugin MODULE NamingPlugin.cpp
                 PLUGIN_TOOL clang)
```

On **Windows,** the plugin support is different from the **Unix** platforms, and the required LLVM and Clang libraries must be linked in. The following code ensures this:

```
if(LLVM_ENABLE_PLUGINS AND (WIN32 OR CYGWIN))
  set(LLVM_LINK_COMPONENTS Support)
  clang_target_link_libraries(NamingPlugin PRIVATE
    clangAST clangBasic clangFrontend clangLex)
endif()
```

7. Save both files in the NamingPlugin directory. Create a build-naming-plugin directory at the same level as the NamingPlugin directory, and build the plugin with the following commands:

```
$ mkdir build-naming-plugin
$ cd build-naming-plugin
$ cmake -G Ninja ../NamingPlugin
$ ninja
```

These steps create the NamingPlugin.so shared library in the build directory.

To test the plugin, save the following source as the naming.c file. The Func1 function name violates the naming rule, but not the main name:

```
int Func1() { return 0; }
int main() { return Func1(); }
```

To invoke the plugin, you need to specify the `-fplugin=` option:

```
$ clang -fplugin=./NamingPlugin.so   naming.c
naming.c:1:5: warning: Function name should start with
lowercase letter
int Func1() { return 0; }
    ^
1 warning generated.
```

This kind of invocation requires that you override the `getActionType()` method of the `PluginASTAction` class, and that you return a value different from the `Cmdline` default value.

If you did not do this, for example, because you want to have more control over the invocation of the plugin action, then you can run the plugin from the compiler command line:

```
$ clang -cc1 -load ./NamingPlugin.so -plugin naming-plugin\
  naming.c
```

Congrats, you have built your first Clang plugin!

The disadvantage of this approach is that it has certain limitations. The `ASTConsumer` class has different entry methods, but they are all coarse-grained. This can be solved by using a `RecursiveASTVisitor` class. This class traverses all AST nodes, and you can override the `VisitXXX()` methods you are interested in. You can rewrite the plugin to use the visitor with the following steps:

1. You need an additional `include` for the definition of the `RecursiveASTVisitor` class. Insert it as follows:

    ```
    #include "clang/AST/RecursiveASTVisitor.h"
    ```

2. Then, define the visitor as the first class in the anonymous namespace. You will only store a reference to the AST context, which will give you access to all the important methods for AST manipulation, including the `DiagnosticsEngine` instance required for emitting the warning:

    ```
    class NamingVisitor
        : public RecursiveASTVisitor<NamingVisitor> {
    private:
    ```

```
    ASTContext &ASTCtx;

public:
    explicit NamingVisitor(CompilerInstance &CI)
        : ASTCtx(CI.getASTContext()) {}
```

3. During traversal, the `VisitFunctionDecl()` method is called whenever a function declaration is discovered. Copy the body of the inner loop inside the `HandleTopLevelDecl()` function here:

```
    virtual bool VisitFunctionDecl(FunctionDecl *FD) {
        std::string Name =
            FD->getNameInfo().getName().getAsString();
        assert(Name.length() > 0 &&
            "Unexpected empty identifier");
        char &First = Name.at(0);
        if (!(First >= 'a' && First <= 'z')) {
            DiagnosticsEngine &Diag =
                ASTCtx.getDiagnostics();
            unsigned ID = Diag.getCustomDiagID(
                DiagnosticsEngine::Warning,
                "Function name should start with "
                "lowercase letter");
            Diag.Report(FD->getLocation(), ID);
        }
        return true;
    }
};
```

4. This finishes the visitor implementation. In your `NamingASTConsumer` class, you will now only store a visitor instance:

```
    std::unique_ptr<NamingVisitor> Visitor;

public:
    NamingASTConsumer(CompilerInstance &CI)
        : Visitor(std::make_unique<NamingVisitor>(CI)) {}
```

5. You will remove the `HandleTopLevelDecl()` method, because the functionality is now in the visitor class, so you'll need to override the `HandleTranslationUnit()` method instead. This class is called once for each translation unit, and you will start the AST traversal here:

```
void
HandleTranslationUnit(ASTContext &ASTCtx) override {
  Visitor->TraverseDecl(
    ASTCtx.getTranslationUnitDecl());
}
```

This new implementation has exactly the same functionality. The advantage is that it is easier to extend. For example, if you want to examine variable declarations, then you implement the `VisitVarDecl()` method. Or if you want to work with a statement, then you implement the `VisitStmt()` method. Basically, you have a visitor method for each entity of the C, C++, and Objective C languages.

Having access to the AST allows you to build plugins that perform complex tasks. Enforcing naming conventions, as described in this section, is a useful addition to Clang. Another useful addition you could implement as a plugin is the calculation of a software metric such as **cyclomatic complexity**. You can also add or replace AST nodes, allowing you, for example, to add runtime instrumentation. Adding plugins allows you to extend Clang in the way you need it.

Summary

In this chapter, you learned how to apply various sanitizers. You detected pointer errors with the `address` sanitizer, uninitialized memory access with the `memory` sanitizer, and detected data races with the `thread` sanitizer. Application errors are often triggered by malformed input, and you implemented fuzz testing to test your application with random data.

You instrumented your application with XRay to identify the performance bottlenecks, and you also learned about the various ways to visualize data. In this chapter, you also used the Clang Static Analyzer to find possible errors through interpretation of the source, and you learned how to build your own Clang plugin.

These skills will help you to raise the quality of the applications you build. It is certainly good to find runtime errors before your application users complain about them. Applying the knowledge gained in this chapter, you can not only find a wide range of common errors but also extend Clang with new functionality.

In the next chapter, you will learn how to add a new backend to LLVM.

12
Create Your Own Backend

LLVM has a very flexible architecture. You can also add a new target backend to it. The core of a backend is the target description, from which most of the code is generated. However, it is not yet possible to generate a complete backend, and implementing the calling convention requires manually written code. In this chapter, we will learn how to add support for a historical CPU.

In this chapter, we will cover the following:

- Setting the stage for a new backend introduces you to the M88k CPU architecture and shows you where to find the information you need.

- Adding the new architecture to the Triple class teaches you how to make LLVM aware of a new CPU architecture.

- In Extending the ELF file format definition in LLVM, you will add support for the M88k-specific relocations to the libraries and tools that handle ELD object files.

- In Creating the target description, you will develop all the parts of the target description in the TableGen language.

- In Implementing the DAG instruction selection classes, you will create the passes and supporting classes required for instruction selection.

- Generating assembler instructions teaches you how to implement the assembler printer, which is responsible for textual assembler generation.

- In Emitting machine code, you learn about which additional classes you must provide to enable the **machine code (MC)** layer to write code to object files.

- In Adding support for disassembling, you will learn how to implement support for a disassembler.

- In Piecing it all together, you will integrate the source for the new backend into the build system.

By the end of this chapter, you will know how to develop a new and complete backend. You will know about the different parts a backend is made of, giving you a deeper understanding of the LLVM architecture.

Technical requirements

The code files for the chapter are available at `https://github.com/PacktPublishing/Learn-LLVM-12/tree/master/Chapter12`

You can find the code in action videos at `https://bit.ly/3nllhED`

Setting the stage for a new backend

Whether it's needed commercially to support a new CPU or it's only for a hobby project to add support for some old architecture, adding a new backend to LLVM is a major task. The following sections outline what you need to develop a new backend. We will add a backend for the Motorola M88k architecture, which is a RISC architecture from the 1980s.

Taken together, the M88k architecture is long out of production, but we found enough information and tools to make it an interesting goal to add an LLVM backend for it. We will begin with a very basic task and extend the `Triple` class.

Adding the new architecture to the Triple class

An instance of the `Triple` class represents the target platform LLVM is producing code for. To support a new architecture, the first task is to extend the `Triple` class. In the `llvm/include/llvm/ADT/Triple.h` file, you add a member to the `ArchType` enumeration and a new predicate:

```
class Triple {
public:
  enum ArchType {
  // Many more members
    m88k,            // M88000 (big endian): m88k
  };

  /// Tests whether the target is M88k.
  bool isM88k() const {
    return getArch() == Triple::m88k;
  }
```

```
// Many more methods
};
```

Inside the `llvm/lib/Support/Triple.cpp` file, there are numerous methods that use the `ArchType` enumeration. You need to extend all of them; for example, in the `getArchTypeName()` method, you need to add a new case statement:

```
  switch (Kind) {
// Many more cases
  case m88k:            return "m88k";
  }
```

In most cases, the compiler will warn you if you forget to handle the new `m88k` enumeration member in one of the functions. Next, we will expand the **Executable and Linkable Format (ELF)** definition.

Extending the ELF file format definition in LLVM

The ELF file format is one of the binary object file formats that LLVM has support for to read and write. ELF itself is defined for many CPU architectures, and there is also a definition for the M88k architecture. All we need to do is to add the definition of the relocations and some flags. The relocations are given in *Chapter 4, Object Files*, of the *System V ABI M88k Processor* supplement book:

1. We need to type the following into the `llvm/include/llvm/BinaryFormat/ELFRelocs/M88k.def` file:

```
  #ifndef ELF_RELOC
  #error "ELF_RELOC must be defined"
  #endif
  ELF_RELOC(R_88K_NONE, 0)
  ELF_RELOC(R_88K_COPY, 1)
  // Many more...
```

2. We also add some flags to the `llvm/include/llvm/BinaryFormat/ELF.h` file and include the relocation definitions:

```
  // M88k Specific e_flags
  enum : unsigned {
```

```
    EF_88K_NABI = 0x80000000,   // Not ABI compliant
    EF_88K_M88110 = 0x00000004  // File uses 88110-
                                // specific
                                // features
};


// M88k relocations.
enum {
#include "ELFRelocs/M88k.def"
};
```

The code can be added anywhere in the file, but it is best to keep a sorted order and insert it before the code for the MIPS architecture.

3. We also need to expand some other methods. In the `llvm/include/llvm/Object/ELFObjectFile.h` file are some methods that translate between enumeration members and strings. For example, we must add a new case statement to the `getFileFormatName()` method:

```
    switch (EF.getHeader()->e_ident[ELF::EI_CLASS]) {
// Many more cases
    case ELF::EM_88K:
        return "elf32-m88k";
    }
```

4. Similarly, we extend the `getArch()` method.

5. Last, we use the relocation definitions in the `llvm/lib/Object/ELF.cpp` file, in the `getELFRelocationTypeName()` method:

```
    switch (Machine) {
// Many more cases
    case ELF::EM_88K:
      switch (Type) {
#include "llvm/BinaryFormat/ELFRelocs/M88k.def"
      default:
        break;
      }
      break;
    }
```

6. To complete the support, you can also add the relocations in the `llvm/lib/ObjectYAML/ELFYAML.cpp` file, in the method that maps the `ELFYAML::ELF_REL` enumeration.

7. At this point, we have completed the support of the m88k architecture in the ELF file format. You can use the `llvm-readobj` tool to inspect an ELF object file, for example, created by a cross-compiler on OpenBSD. Likewise, you can create an ELF object file for the m88k architecture with the `yaml2obj` tool.

> **Is adding support for an object file format mandatory?**
>
> Integrating support for an architecture into the ELF file format implementation requires only a couple of lines. If the architecture for which you create an LLVM backend uses the ELF format, then you should take this route. On the other hand, adding support for a completely new binary file format is itself a complicated task. In this case, a possible approach is to only output assembler files and use an external assembler to create object files.

With these additions, the implementation of the ELF file formats now supports the M88k architecture. In the next section, we create the target description for the M88k architecture, which describes the instructions, registers, calling convention, and other details of the architecture.

Creating the target description

The **target description** is the heart of a backend implementation. In an ideal world, we could generate the whole backend from the target description. This goal has not yet been reached, and therefore, we need to extend the generated code later. Let's dissect the target description, beginning with the top-level file.

Implementing the top-level file of the target description

We put the files of our new backend into the `llvm/lib/Target/M88k` directory. The target description is in the `M88k.td` file:

1. In this file, we first need to include basic target description classes predefined by LLVM and then the files we are going to create in the next sections:

```
include "llvm/Target/Target.td"


include "M88kRegisterInfo.td"
```

```
include "M88kCallingConv.td"
include "M88kSchedule.td"
include "M88kInstrFormats.td"
include "M88kInstrInfo.td"
```

2. Next, we also define the supported processor. Among other things, this translates into the parameter for the –mcpu= option:

```
def : ProcessorModel<"mc88110", M88kSchedModel, []>;
```

3. With all these definitions done, we now can piece our target together. We define these subclasses, in case we need to modify some of the default values. The M88kInstrInfo class holds all the information about the instructions:

```
def M88kInstrInfo : InstrInfo;
```

4. We define a parser for the .s assembly files, and we additionally state that register names are always be prefixed with %:

```
def M88kAsmParser : AsmParser;
def M88kAsmParserVariant : AsmParserVariant {
  let RegisterPrefix = "%";
}
```

5. Next, we define a class for the assembly writer, which is responsible for writing .s assembly files:

```
def M88kAsmWriter : AsmWriter;
```

6. And lastly, all these records are put together to define the target:

```
def M88k : Target {
  let InstructionSet = M88kInstrInfo;
  let AssemblyParsers    = [M88kAsmParser];
  let AssemblyParserVariants = [M88kAsmParserVariant];
  let AssemblyWriters = [M88kAsmWriter];
  let AllowRegisterRenaming = 1;
}
```

Now that the top-level file is implemented, we create the included files, starting with the register definition in the next section.

Adding the register definition

A CPU architecture usually defines a set of registers. The characteristics of these registers can vary greatly. Some architectures allow access to subregisters. For example, the x86 architecture has special register names to access only a part of a register value. Other architectures do not implement this. Besides general-purpose, floating-point, and vector registers, an architecture may also define special registers, for example, for status codes or for the configuration of floating-point operations. You need to define all this information for LLVM.

The M88k architecture defines general-purpose registers, floating-point registers, and control registers. To keep the example small, we will only define the general-purpose registers. We begin with defining a super-class for the registers. The encoding for registers uses only 5 bits, so we limit the field holding the encoding. We also define that all the generated C++ code should reside in the M88k namespace:

```
class M88kReg<bits<5> Enc, string n> : Register<n> {
  let HWEncoding{15-5} = 0;
  let HWEncoding{4-0} = Enc;
  let Namespace = "M88k";
}
```

The M88kReg class is used for all register types. We define a special class for general-purpose registers:

```
class GRi<bits<5> Enc, string n> : M88kReg<Enc, n>;
```

Now we can define all 32 general-purpose registers:

```
foreach I = 0-31 in {
  def R#I : GRi<I, "r"#I>;
}
```

The single registers need to be grouped in register classes. The sequence order of the registers also defines the allocation order in the register allocator. Here, we simply add all registers:

```
def GPR : RegisterClass<"M88k", [i32], 32,
                        (add (sequence "R%u", 0, 31))>;
```

And last, we need to define an operand based on the register class. The operand is used in selecting DAG nodes to match a register, and it can also be extended to denote method names for printing and matching the register in assembly code:

```
def GPROpnd : RegisterOperand<GPR>;
```

This finishes our definition of the registers. In the next section, we use these definitions to define the calling convention.

Defining the calling convention

A **calling convention** defines how parameters are passed to functions. Usually, the first parameters are passed in registers, and the rest of the parameters are passed on the stack. There must also be rules on how aggregates are passed and how values are returned from a function. From the definition given here, analyzer classes are generated, which are used later during the lowering of calls.

You can read about the calling convention used on the M88k architecture in *Chapter 3, Low-Level System Information*, of the *System V ABI M88k Processor* supplement book. Let's translate this into the TableGen syntax:

1. We define a record for the calling convention:

   ```
   def CC_M88k : CallingConv< [
   ```

2. The M88k architecture only has 32-bit registers, therefore values of smaller data types need to be promoted to 32 bit:

   ```
   CCIfType< [i1, i8, i16], CCPromoteToType<i32>>,
   ```

3. The calling convention states that for aggregate return values, a pointer to the memory is passed in the r12 register:

   ```
   CCIfSRet<CCIfType< [i32], CCAssignToReg< [R12] >>>,
   ```

4. The registers r2 to r9 are used to pass parameters:

   ```
   CCIfType< [i32,i64,f32,f64],
             CCAssignToReg< [R2, R3, R4, R5, R6, R7, R8,
                R9] >>,
   ```

5. Every additional parameter is passed on the stack, in 4 bytes-aligned slots:

```
    CCAssignToStack<4, 4>
  ]>;
```

6. An additional record defines how results are passed to the calling function. 32-bit values are passed in the r2 register, and 64-bit values use the r2 and r3 registers:

```
def RetCC_M88k : CallingConv<[
  CCIfType<[i32,f32], CCAssignToReg<[R2]>>,
  CCIfType<[i64,f64], CCAssignToReg<[R2, R3]>>
  ]>;
```

7. And last, a calling convention also states which registers have to be preserved by the called function:

```
def CSR_M88k :
          CalleeSavedRegs<(add (sequence "R%d", 14,
          25), R30)>;
```

If needed, you can also define multiple calling conventions. In the next section, we will have a brief look at the scheduling model.

Creating the scheduling model

The scheduling model is used by the code generation to order the instructions in an optimal way. Defining a scheduling model improves the performance of the generated code, but it is not necessary for code generation. Therefore, we only define a placeholder for the model. We add the information that the CPU can issue at most two instructions at once, and that it is an in-order CPU:

```
def M88kSchedModel : SchedMachineModel {
  let IssueWidth = 2;
  let MicroOpBufferSize = 0;
  let CompleteModel = 0;
  let NoModel = 1;
}
```

You can find recipes on how to create a complete scheduling model in the talk *Writing Great Schedulers* on YouTube at https://www.youtube.com/watch?v=brpomKUynEA.

Next, we will define the instruction formats and the instructions.

Defining the instruction formats and the instruction information

We have already looked at the instruction formats and the instruction information in *Chapter 9, Instruction Selection*, in the *Supporting new machine instructions* section. To define the instructions for the M88k architecture, we follow the same approach. First, we define a base class for the instruction records. The most important field of this class is the Inst field, which holds the encoding for the instruction. Most of the other field definitions just assign a value to a field defined in the Instruction superclass:

```
class InstM88k<dag outs, dag ins, string asmstr,
        list<dag> pattern, InstrItinClass itin =
          NoItinerary>
  : Instruction {
  field bits<32> Inst;
  field bits<32> SoftFail = 0;
  let Namespace = "M88k";
  let Size = 4;
  dag OutOperandList = outs;
  dag InOperandList = ins;
  let AsmString   = asmstr;
  let Pattern = pattern;
  let DecoderNamespace = "M88k";
  let Itinerary = itin;
}
```

This base class is used for all instruction formats, so it is also used for the F_JMP format. You take the encoding for the user manual of the processor. The class has two parameters, which must be part of the encoding. The func parameter defines bits 11 to 15 of the encoding, which defines the instruction as a jump with or without saving the return address. The next parameter is a bit that defines whether the next instruction is executed unconditionally or not. This is similar to the delay slot of the MIPS architecture.

The class also defines the rs2 field, which holds the encoding of the register holding the target address. The other parameters are the DAG input and output operand, the textual assembler string, a DAG pattern used to select this instruction, and an itinerary class for the scheduler model:

```
class F_JMP<bits<5> func, bits<1> next,
             dag outs, dag ins, string asmstr,
             list<dag> pattern,
             InstrItinClass itin = NoItinerary>
  : InstM88k<outs, ins, asmstr, pattern, itin> {
  bits<5> rs2;
  let Inst{31-26} = 0b111101;
  let Inst{25-16} = 0b0000000000;
  let Inst{15-11} = func;
  let Inst{10}    = next;
  let Inst{9-5}   = 0b00000;
  let Inst{4-0}   = rs2;
}
```

And with this, we can finally define the instruction. A jump instruction is the last instruction in a basic block, so we need to set the isTerminator flag. Because control flow can't fall through this instruction, we also have to set the isBarrier flag. We take the values for the func and next parameters from the user manual of the processor.

The input DAG operand is a general-purpose register and refers to the operand from the preceding register's information. The encoding is stored in the rs2 field, from the preceding class definition. The output operand is empty. The assembler string gives the textual syntax of the instruction and also refers to the register operand. The DAG pattern uses the predefine brind operator. This instruction is selected if the DAG contains an indirect branch node with the target address hold in a register:

```
let isTerminator = 1, isBarrier = 1 in
  def JMP : F_JMP<0b11000, 0, (outs), (ins GPROpnd:$rs2),
                  "jmp $rs2", [(brind GPROpnd:$rs2)]>;
```

We need to define records for all instructions in this way.

In this file, we also implement other necessary patterns for instruction selection. A typical application is a constant synthesis. The M88k architecture has 32 bit-wide registers, but the instructions with immediate values as operands support only 16 bit-wide constants. As a consequence, operations such as a bitwise and between a register and a 32-bit constant have to be split into two instructions that use 16-bit constants.

Luckily, a flag in the and instruction defines whether an operation applies to the lower or the upper half of the register. With operators LO16 and HI16 used to extract the lower or upper half of a constant, we can formulate a DAG pattern for an and operation between a register and a 32 bit-wide constant:

```
def : Pat<(and GPR:$rs1, uimm32:$imm),
          (ANDri (ANDriu GPR:$rs1, (HI16 i32:$imm)),
                                   (LO16 i32:$imm))>;
```

The ANDri operator is the and instruction that applies the constant to the lower half of the register, and the ANDriu operator uses the upper half of the register. Of course, before we can use these names in the pattern, we must define the instruction like we defined the jmp instruction. This pattern solves the problem using a 32-bit constant with an and operation, generating two machine instructions for it during instruction selection.

Not all operations can be represented by the predefined DAG nodes. For example, the M88k architecture defined bit field operations, which can be seen as generalizations of the normal and/or operations. For such operations, it is possible to introduce new node types, for example, for the set instruction:

```
def m88k_set : SDNode<"M88kISD::SET", SDTIntBinOp>;
```

This defines a new record of the SDNode class. The first argument is the C++ enumeration member that denotes the new operation. The second parameter is the so-called type profile and defines the type and number of parameters and the result type. The predefined SDTIntBinOp class defines two integer parameters and an integer result type, which is suitable for this operation. You can look up the predefined classes in the llvm/include/llvm/Target/TargetSelectionDAG.td file. If there is no suitable predefined type profile, then you can define a new one.

For calling functions, LLVM requires certain definitions that cannot be predefined because they are not completely target-independent. For example, for returns, we need to specify a `retflag` record:

```
def retflag : SDNode<"M88kISD::RET_FLAG", SDTNone,
                     [SDNPHasChain, SDNPOptInGlue, SDNPVariadic]>;
```

Comparing this to `m88k_set` the record, this also defines some flags for the DAG node: the chain and glue sequences are used, and the operator can take a variable number of arguments.

> **Implement the instructions iteratively**
>
> A modern CPU can easily have thousands of instructions. It makes sense to not implement all instructions at once. Instead, you should first concentrate on basic instructions such as logical operations and call and return instructions. This is enough to get a very basic backend working. To this base, you then add more and more instruction definitions and patterns.

This finishes our implementation of the target description. From the target description, a lot of code is automatically generated with the `llvm-tblgen` tool. To complete the instruction selection and other parts of the backend, we still need to develop a C++ source using the generated code. In the next section, we implement the DAG instruction selection.

Implementing the DAG instruction selection classes

A large portion of the DAG instruction selector is generated by the `llvm-tblgen` tool. We still need to create classes using the generated code and put everything together. Let's begin with a part of the initialization process.

Initializing the target machine

Each backend has to provide at least one `TargetMachine` class, usually a subclass of the `LLVMTargetMachine` class. The `M88kTargetMachine` class holds a lot of the details required for code generation, and it also acts as a factory for other backend classes, most notably for the `Subtarget` class and the `TargetPassConfig` class. The `Subtarget` class holds the configuration for the code generation, such as which features are enabled. The `TargetPassConfig` class configures the machine passes of the backend. The declaration for our `M88kTargetMachine` class is in the `M88ktargetMachine.h` file and looks like this:

```
class M88kTargetMachine : public LLVMTargetMachine {
public:
  M88kTargetMachine(/* parameters */);
  ~M88kTargetMachine() override;
  const M88kSubtarget *getSubtargetImpl(const Function &)
                                          const override;
  const M88kSubtarget *getSubtargetImpl() const = delete;
  TargetPassConfig *createPassConfig(PassManagerBase &PM)
                                          override;
};
```

Please note that there can be a different subtarget for each function.

The implementation in the `M88kTargetMachine.cpp` file is straightforward. Most interesting is the setup of the machine passes for this backend. This creates the connection to the selection DAG (and, if desired, to global instruction selection). The passes created in the class are later added to the pass pipeline to produce object files or assemblers from the IR:

```
namespace {
class M88kPassConfig : public TargetPassConfig {
public:
  M88kPassConfig(M88kTargetMachine &TM, PassManagerBase
    &PM)
      : TargetPassConfig(TM, PM) {}
```

```
   M88kTargetMachine &getM88kTargetMachine() const {
     return getTM<M88kTargetMachine>();
   }


   bool addInstSelector() override {
     addPass(createM88kISelDag(getM88kTargetMachine(),
                               getOptLevel()));
     return false;
   }
};
} // namespace


TargetPassConfig *M88kTargetMachine::createPassConfig(
    PassManagerBase &PM) {
   return new M88kPassConfig(*this, PM);
}
```

The SubTarget implementation return from the M88kTargetMachine class gives access to other important classes. The M88kInstrInfo class returns information about instructions, including registers. The M88kTargetLowering class provides a lowering of call-related instructions and also allows adding custom DAG rules. Most of the class is generated by the llvm-tblgen tool, and we need to include the generated header.

The definition in the M88kSubTarget.h file is as follows:

```
#define GET_SUBTARGETINFO_HEADER
#include "M88kGenSubtargetInfo.inc"

namespace llvm {
class M88kSubtarget : public M88kGenSubtargetInfo {
  Triple TargetTriple;
  virtual void anchor();

  M88kInstrInfo InstrInfo;
  M88kTargetLowering TLInfo;
  M88kFrameLowering FrameLowering;

public:
```

```
M88kSubtarget(const Triple &TT, const std::string &CPU,
              const std::string &FS,
              const TargetMachine &TM);

void ParseSubtargetFeatures(StringRef CPU, StringRef FS);

const TargetFrameLowering *getFrameLowering() const
  override
{ return &FrameLowering; }
const M88kInstrInfo *getInstrInfo() const override
{ return &InstrInfo; }
const M88kRegisterInfo *getRegisterInfo() const override
{ return &InstrInfo.getRegisterInfo(); }
const M88kTargetLowering *getTargetLowering() const
  override
{ return &TLInfo; }
};
} // end namespace llvm
```

Next, we implement the selection DAG.

Adding the selection DAG implementation

The selection DAG is implemented in the `M88kDAGtoDAGISel` class in the file of the same name. Here, we benefit from having created the target machine description: most of the functionality is generated from this description. In a very first implementation, we only need to override the `Select()` function and forward it to the generated `SelectCode` function. More functions can be overridden for certain cases, for example, if we need to extend the preprocessing of the DAG or if we need to add special inline assembler constraints.

Because this class is a machine function pass, we also provide a name for the pass. The main bulk of the implementation comes from the generated file, which we include in the middle of the class:

```
class M88kDAGToDAGISel : public SelectionDAGISel {
  const M88kSubtarget *Subtarget;
public:
  M88kDAGToDAGISel(M88kTargetMachine &TM,
```

```
                         CodeGenOpt::Level OptLevel)
        : SelectionDAGISel(TM, OptLevel) {}


  StringRef getPassName() const override {
    return "M88k DAG->DAG Pattern Instruction Selection";
  }


#include "M88kGenDAGISel.inc"


  void Select(SDNode *Node) override {
    SelectCode(Node);
  }
};
```

We also add the factory function to create the pass in this file:

```
FunctionPass *llvm::createM88kISelDag(M88kTargetMachine &TM,
                                      CodeGenOpt::Level
                                        OptLevel) {
  return new M88kDAGToDAGISel(TM, OptLevel);
}
```

Now we can implement the target-specific operations, which cannot be expressed in the target description.

Supporting target-specific operations

Let's turn to the `M88kTargetLowering` class, defined in the `M88kISelLowering.h` file. This class configures the instruction DAG selection process and enhances the lowering with target-specific operations.

In the target description, we defined new DAG nodes. The enumeration used with the new types is also defined in this file, continuing the numbering with the last predefined number:

```
namespace M88kISD {
enum NodeType : unsigned {
  FIRST_NUMBER = ISD::BUILTIN_OP_END,
  RET_FLAG,
```

```
  SET,
};
} // end namespace M88kISD
```

The class needs to provide the required lowering methods for the function calls.
To keep it simple, we look only at returning values. The class can also define the
LowerOperation() hook method for operations that need custom handling.
We can also enable custom DAG combining methods, for which we define the
PerformDAGCombine() method:

```
class M88kTargetLowering : public TargetLowering {
  const M88kSubtarget &Subtarget;

public:
  explicit M88kTargetLowering(const TargetMachine &TM,
                              const M88kSubtarget &STI);

  SDValue LowerOperation(SDValue Op, SelectionDAG &DAG) const
                                                        override;

  SDValue PerformDAGCombine(SDNode *N, DAGCombinerInfo &DCI)
                                                  const override;

  SDValue LowerReturn(SDValue Chain, CallingConv::ID CallConv,
          bool IsVarArg,
          const SmallVectorImpl<ISD::OutputArg> &Outs,
          const SmallVectorImpl<SDValue> &OutVals,
          const SDLoc &DL,
          SelectionDAG &DAG) const override;
};
```

The implementation of the class is in the `M88kISelLowering.cpp` file. First, we look at how to lower a return value:

1. The generated functions for the calling convention are needed, so we include the generated file:

```
#include "M88kGenCallingConv.inc"
```

2. The `LowerReturn()` method takes a lot of arguments, which are all defined by the `TargetLowering` superclass. The most important ones are the `Outs` vector, which holds the description of the return argument, and the `OutVals` vector, which holds the DAG nodes for the return values:

```
SDValue M88kTargetLowering::LowerReturn(SDValue Chain,
                CallingConv::ID CallConv,
                bool IsVarArg,
                const SmallVectorImpl<ISD::OutputArg>
                  &Outs,
                const SmallVectorImpl<SDValue> &OutVals,
                const SDLoc &DL, SelectionDAG &DAG) const {
```

3. We analyze the return argument with the help of the `CCState` class, passing a reference to the generated `RetCC_M88k` function. As result, we have classified all the return arguments:

```
MachineFunction &MF = DAG.getMachineFunction();
SmallVector<CCValAssign, 16> RetLocs;
CCState RetCCInfo(CallConv, IsVarArg, MF, RetLocs,
                                *DAG.getContext());
RetCCInfo.AnalyzeReturn(Outs, RetCC_M88k);
```

4. In case of a `void` function, there is nothing to do and we return. Please note that the type of the returned node is `RET_FLAG`. We defined this in the target description as the new `ret_flag` node:

```
if (RetLocs.empty())
  return DAG.getNode(M88kISD::RET_FLAG, DL,
                          MVT::Other, Chain);
```

5. Otherwise, we need to loop over the return arguments. For each return argument, we have an instance of the CCValAssign class, which tells us how we have to treat the argument:

```
SDValue Glue;
SmallVector<SDValue, 4> RetOps;
RetOps.push_back(Chain);
for (unsigned I = 0, E = RetLocs.size(); I != E;
     ++I) {
  CCValAssign &VA = RetLocs[I];
  SDValue RetValue = OutVals[I];
```

6. The values may need to be promoted. We add a DAG node with the required extension operation, if necessary:

```
switch (VA.getLocInfo()) {
case CCValAssign::SExt:
  RetValue = DAG.getNode(ISD::SIGN_EXTEND, DL,
                         VA.getLocVT(), RetValue);
  break;
case CCValAssign::ZExt:
  RetValue = DAG.getNode(ISD::ZERO_EXTEND, DL,
                         VA.getLocVT(), RetValue);
  break;
case CCValAssign::AExt:
  RetValue = DAG.getNode(ISD::ANY_EXTEND, DL,
                         VA.getLocVT(), RetValue);
  break;
case CCValAssign::Full:
  break;
default:
  llvm_unreachable("Unhandled VA.getLocInfo()");
}
```

7. When the value has the right type, we copy the value into a register for returning it and chain and glue the copies together. This finishes the loop:

```
Register Reg = VA.getLocReg();
Chain = DAG.getCopyToReg(Chain, DL, Reg, RetValue,
```

```
                                        Glue);
    Glue = Chain.getValue(1);
    RetOps.push_back(DAG.getRegister(Reg,
                                  VA.getLocVT()));
  }
```

8. Last, we need to update the chain and the glue:

```
    RetOps[0] = Chain;
    if (Glue.getNode())
      RetOps.push_back(Glue);
```

9. We will then return the `ret_flag` node, connecting the result of the lowering:

```
    return DAG.getNode(M88kISD::RET_FLAG, DL,
      MVT::Other,
                      RetOps);
  }
```

To be able to call functions, we must implement the `LowerFormalArguments()` and `LowerCall()` methods. Both methods follow a similar approach and hence are not shown here.

Configuring the target lowering

The methods to lower function calls and arguments must always be implemented, as they are always target-dependent. Other operations may or may not have support in the target architecture. To make the lowering process aware of it, we set up the configuration in the constructor of the `M88kTargetLowering` class:

1. The constructor takes `TargetMachine` and `M88kSubtarget` instances as parameters and initializes the corresponding fields with them:

```
M88kTargetLowering::M88kTargetLowering(
    const TargetMachine &TM, const M88kSubtarget &STI)
  : TargetLowering(TM), Subtarget(STI) {
```

2. We add all the register classes first. We have only general-purpose registers defined, therefore it is just a simple call:

```
    addRegisterClass(MVT::i32, &M88k::GPRRegClass);
```

3. After all the register classes are added, we compute the derived properties for the registers. For example, since the registers are 32 bits wide, this function marks the 64-bit data type as requiring two registers:

```
computeRegisterProperties(Subtarget.getRegisterInfo());
```

4. We also need to tell which register is used for the stack pointer. On the M88k architecture, the r31 register is used:

```
setStackPointerRegisterToSaveRestore(M88k::R31);
```

5. We also need to define how boolean values are represented. Basically, we say here that the values 0 and 1 are used. Other possible options are to look only at bit 0 of the value, ignoring all other bits, and setting all bits of the value either to 0 or 1:

```
setBooleanContents(ZeroOrOneBooleanContent);
```

6. For every operation that needs special handling, we must call the setOperationAction() method. The method takes the operation, the value type, and the action to take as input. If the operation is valid, then we use the Legal action value. If the type should be promoted, then we use the Promote action value, and if the operation should result in a library call, then we use the LibCall action value.

   If we give the Expand action value, then the instruction selection first tries to expand this operation into other operations. If this is not possible, then a library call is used. And last, we can implement our own action if using the Custom action value. In this case, the LowerOperation() method is called for a node with this operation. As an example, we set the CTTZ count trailing zeros operation to the Expand action. This operation will be replaced by a sequence of primitive bit operations:

```
setOperationAction(ISD::CTTZ, MVT::i32, Expand);
```

7. The M88k architecture has a bit field operation, for which it is not easy to define a pattern in the target description. Here, we tell the instruction selection that we want to perform additional matching on or DAG nodes:

```
setTargetDAGCombine(ISD::OR);
}
```

Depending on the target architecture, setting the configuration in the constructor can be much longer. We only defined the bare minimum, ignoring, for example, floating-point operations.

We have marked the or operation to perform custom combining on it. As a result, the instruction selector calls the `PerformDAGCombine()` method before calling the generated instruction selection. This function is called in the various phases of the instruction selection, but usually, we perform our matching only after the operations are legalized. The common implementation is to look at the operation and branch to a function handling the matching:

```
SDValue M88kTargetLowering::PerformDAGCombine(SDNode *N,
                                   DAGCombinerInfo &DCI) const {
  if (DCI.isBeforeLegalizeOps())
    return SDValue();
  switch (N->getOpcode()) {
  default:
    break;
  case ISD::OR:
    return performORCombine(N, DCI);
  }
  return SDValue();
}
```

In the `performORCombine()` method, we try to check whether we can generate a set instruction for the or operation. The set instruction sets a number of consecutive bits to 1, starting at a specified bit offset. This is a special case of the or operation, with the second operand being a constant matching this format. Because the or instruction of the M88k architecture works only on 16-bit constants, this matching is beneficial, because otherwise, we would have to synthesize the constant, resulting in two or instructions. This method uses the `isShiftedMask()` helper function to determine whether the constant values have the required form.

If the second operand is a constant of the required form, then this function returns a node representing the set instruction. Otherwise, the return value `SDValue()` indicates that no matching pattern was found and that the generated DAG pattern matcher should be called:

```
SDValue performORCombine(SDNode *N,
    TargetLowering::DAGCombinerInfo &DCI) {
  SelectionDAG &DAG = DCI.DAG;
```

```
    uint64_t Width, Offset;
    ConstantSDNode *Mask =
                    dyn_cast<ConstantSDNode>(N->getOperand(
                    1));
    if (!Mask ||
        !isShiftedMask(Mask->getZExtValue(), Width, Offset))
      return SDValue();

    EVT ValTy = N->getValueType(0);
    SDLoc DL(N);
    return DAG.getNode(M88kISD::SET, DL, ValTy,
            N->getOperand(0),
            DAG.getConstant(Width << 5 | Offset, DL,
                MVT::i32));
}
```

To finish the implementation of the whole lowering process, we need to implement the
M88kFrameLowering class. This class is responsible for handling the stack frame. This
includes generating the prologue and epilogue code, handling register spills, and more.
For the very first implementation, you can just provide empty functions. Obviously, for
complete functionality, this class must be implemented.

This finishes our implementation of the instruction selection. Next, we look at how the
final instructions are emitted.

Generating assembler instructions

The instruction selection implemented in the previous sections lowers the IR instructions
into MachineInstr instances. This is already a much lower representation of
instruction, but it is not yet the machine code itself. The last pass in the backend
pipeline is to emit the instructions, either as assembly text or into an object file. The
M88kAsmPrinter machine pass is responsible for this task.

Basically, this pass lowers a MachineInstr instance to an MCInst instance, which
is then emitted to a streamer. The MCInst class represents the real machine code
instruction. This additional lowering is required because the MachineInstr class still
does not have all the required details.

For the first approach, we can limit our implementation to overriding the `emitInstruction()` method. You need to override more methods for supporting several operand types, mainly to emit the correct relocations. This class is also responsible for handling inline assemblers, which you also need to implement if needed.

Because the `M88kAsmPrinter` class is again a machine function pass, we also override the `getPassName()` method. The declaration of the class is as follows:

```
class M88kAsmPrinter : public AsmPrinter {
public:
  explicit M88kAsmPrinter(TargetMachine &TM,
                          std::unique_ptr<MCStreamer>
                          Streamer)
      : AsmPrinter(TM, std::move(Streamer)) {}

  StringRef getPassName() const override
  { return "M88k Assembly Printer"; }

  void emitInstruction(const MachineInstr *MI) override;
};
```

Basically, we must handle two different cases in the `emitInstruction()` method. The `MachineInstr` instance can still have operands, which are not real machine instructions. For example, this is the case for the return `ret_flag` node, having the `RET` opcode value. On the M88k architecture, there is no `return` instruction. Instead, a jump to the address store in the `r1` register is made. Therefore, we need to construct the branch instruction when we detect the `RET` opcode. In the default case, the lowering only needs the information from the `MachineInstr` instance, and we delegate this task to the `M88kMCInstLower` class:

```
void M88kAsmPrinter::emitInstruction(const MachineInstr *MI) {
  MCInst LoweredMI;
  switch (MI->getOpcode()) {
  case M88k::RET:
    LoweredMI = MCInstBuilder(M88k::JMP).addReg(M88k::R1);
    break;

  default:
    M88kMCInstLower Lower(MF->getContext(), *this);
```

```
    Lower.lower(MI, LoweredMI);
    break;
  }
  EmitToStreamer(*OutStreamer, LoweredMI);
}
```

The `M88kMCInstLower` class has no predefined superclass. Its main purpose is to handle the various operand types. As we currently only have a very limited set of supported operand types, we can reduce this class to having only a single method. The `lower()` method sets the opcode and the operand of the `MCInst` instance. Only register and immediate operands are handled; other operand types are ignored. For the full implementation, we also need to handle memory addresses:

```
void M88kMCInstLower::lower(const MachineInstr *MI, MCInst
&OutMI) const {
  OutMI.setOpcode(MI->getOpcode());
  for (unsigned I = 0, E = MI->getNumOperands(); I != E; ++I)
  {
    const MachineOperand &MO = MI->getOperand(I);
    switch (MO.getType()) {
    case MachineOperand::MO_Register:
      if (MO.isImplicit())
        break;
      OutMI.addOperand(MCOperand::createReg(MO.getReg()));
      break;

    case MachineOperand::MO_Immediate:
      OutMI.addOperand(MCOperand::createImm(MO.getImm()));
      break;

    default:
      break;
    }
  }
}
```

The assembler printer needs a factory method, which is called during initialization, for example, from the `InitializeAllAsmPrinters()` method:

```
extern "C" LLVM_EXTERNAL_VISIBILITY void
LLVMInitializeM88kAsmPrinter() {
  RegisterAsmPrinter<M88kAsmPrinter> X(getTheM88kTarget());
}
```

Finally, having lowered the instructions to real machine code instructions, we are still not done. We need to implement various small pieces for the MC layer, which we look at in the next section.

Emitting machine code

The MC layer is responsible for emitting machine code in textual or binary form. Most of the functionality is either implemented in the various MC classes and only needs to be configured, or the implementation is generated from the target description.

The initialization of the MC layer takes place in the `MCTargetDesc/M88kMCTargetDesc.cpp` file. The following classes are registered with the `TargetRegistry` singleton:

- `M88kMCAsmInfo`: This class provides basic information, such as the size of a code pointer, the direction of stack growth, the comment symbol, or the name of assembler directives.

- `M88MCInstrInfo`: This class holds information about instructions, for example, the name of an instruction.

- `M88kRegInfo`: This class provides information about registers, for example, the name of a register, or which register is the stack pointer.

- `M88kSubtargetInfo`: This class holds the data of the scheduling model and the methods to parse and set CPU features.

- `M88kMCAsmBackend`: This class provides helper methods to get the target-dependent relocation data for fixups. It also contains factory methods for the object writer classes.

- `M88kMCInstPrinter`: This class contains helper methods to textually print instructions and operands. If an operand defines a custom print method in the target description, then it must be implemented in this class.

- `M88kMCCodeEmitter`: This class writes the encoding of an instruction to a stream.

Depending on the scope of a backend implementation, we do not need to register and implement all of these classes. You can omit to register the `MCInstPrinter` subclass if you do not support textual assembler output. If you do not add support writing of object files, you can omit the `MCAsmBackend` and `MCCodeEmitter` subclasses.

We begin the file by including the generated parts and providing factory methods for it:

```
#define GET_INSTRINFO_MC_DESC
#include "M88kGenInstrInfo.inc"
#define GET_SUBTARGETINFO_MC_DESC
#include "M88kGenSubtargetInfo.inc"
#define GET_REGINFO_MC_DESC
#include "M88kGenRegisterInfo.inc"

static MCInstrInfo *createM88kMCInstrInfo() {
  MCInstrInfo *X = new MCInstrInfo();
  InitM88kMCInstrInfo(X);
  return X;
}


static MCRegisterInfo *createM88kMCRegisterInfo(
                                      const Triple &TT) {
  MCRegisterInfo *X = new MCRegisterInfo();
  InitM88kMCRegisterInfo(X, M88k::R1);
  return X;
}


static MCSubtargetInfo *createM88kMCSubtargetInfo(
            const Triple &TT, StringRef CPU, StringRef
            FS) {
  return createM88kMCSubtargetInfoImpl(TT, CPU, FS);
}
```

We also provide some factory methods for classes implemented in other files:

```
static MCAsmInfo *createM88kMCAsmInfo(
                const MCRegisterInfo &MRI, const Triple &TT,
                const MCTargetOptions &Options) {
```

```
    return new M88kMCAsmInfo(TT);
}


static MCInstPrinter *createM88kMCInstPrinter(
                const Triple &T, unsigned SyntaxVariant,
                const MCAsmInfo &MAI, const MCInstrInfo &MII,
                const MCRegisterInfo &MRI) {
    return new M88kInstPrinter(MAI, MII, MRI);
}
```

To initialize the MC layer, we only need to register all the factory methods with the
TargetRegistry singleton:

```
extern "C" LLVM_EXTERNAL_VISIBILITY
void LLVMInitializeM88kTargetMC() {
  TargetRegistry::RegisterMCAsmInfo(getTheM88kTarget(),
                                        createM88kMCAsmInfo);
  TargetRegistry::RegisterMCCodeEmitter(getTheM88kTarget(),

                                        createM88kMCCodeEmitter);
  TargetRegistry::RegisterMCInstrInfo(getTheM88kTarget(),
                                        createM88kMCInstrInfo);
  TargetRegistry::RegisterMCRegInfo(getTheM88kTarget(),
                                        createM88kMCRegisterInfo);
  TargetRegistry::RegisterMCSubtargetInfo(getTheM88kTarget(),
                                        createM88kMCSubtargetInfo);
  TargetRegistry::RegisterMCAsmBackend(getTheM88kTarget(),
                                        createM88kMCAsmBackend);
  TargetRegistry::RegisterMCInstPrinter(getTheM88kTarget(),
                                        createM88kMCInstPrinter);
}
```

Additionally, in the MCTargetDesc/M88kTargetDesc.h header file, we also need to
include the header portion of the generated source, to make it available to others, too:

```
#define GET_REGINFO_ENUM
#include "M88kGenRegisterInfo.inc"
#define GET_INSTRINFO_ENUM
```

```
#include "M88kGenInstrInfo.inc"
#define GET_SUBTARGETINFO_ENUM
#include "M88kGenSubtargetInfo.inc"
```

We put the source files for the registered classes all in the MCTargetDesc directory. For the first implementation, it is sufficient to provide just stubs for these classes. For example, as long as support for memory addresses is not added to the target description, no fixups will be generated. The M88kMCAsmInfo class can be very quickly implemented, as we only need to set some properties in the constructor:

```
M88kMCAsmInfo::M88kMCAsmInfo(const Triple &TT) {
  CodePointerSize = 4;
  IsLittleEndian = false;
  MinInstAlignment = 4;
  CommentString = "#";
}
```

Having implemented the support classes for the MC layer, we are now able to emit the machine code into files.

In the next section, we implement the class required for disassembling, which is the reverse action: turning an object file back into assembler text.

Adding support for disassembling

The definition of the instructions in the target description allows the construction of decoder tables, which are used to disassemble an object file into a textual assembler. The decoder tables and a decoder function are generated by the llvm-tblgen tool. Besides the generated code, we only need to provide the code to register and initialize the M88kDisassembler class and some helper functions to decode registers and operands. We place the implementation in the Disassembler/M88kDisassembler.cpp file.

The getInstruction() method of the M88kDisassembler class does the decoding work. It takes an array of bytes as input and decodes the next instruction into an instance of the MCInst class. The class declaration is as follows:

```
using DecodeStatus = MCDisassembler::DecodeStatus;

namespace {

class M88kDisassembler : public MCDisassembler {
```

```
public:
  M88kDisassembler(const MCSubtargetInfo &STI, MCContext &Ctx)
      : MCDisassembler(STI, Ctx) {}
  ~M88kDisassembler() override = default;

  DecodeStatus getInstruction(MCInst &instr, uint64_t &Size,
                              ArrayRef<uint8_t> Bytes,
                              uint64_t Address,
                              raw_ostream &CStream) const
                                                        override;
};
}
```

The generated classes refer unqualified to the DecodeStatus enumeration, so we have to make this name visible.

To initialize the disassembler, we define a factory function that simply instantiates a new object:

```
static MCDisassembler *
createM88kDisassembler(const Target &T,
                       const MCSubtargetInfo &STI,
                       MCContext &Ctx) {
  return new M88kDisassembler(STI, Ctx);
}
```

In the LLVMInitializeM88kDisassembler() function, we register the factory function at the target registry:

```
extern "C" LLVM_EXTERNAL_VISIBILITY void
LLVMInitializeM88kDisassembler() {
  TargetRegistry::RegisterMCDisassembler(
      getTheM88kTarget(), createM88kDisassembler);
}
```

This function is called from the InitializeAllDisassemblers() function or the InitializeNativeTargetDisassembler() function, when the LLVM core libraries are initialized.

The generated decoder function expects helper functions to decode registers and operands. The reason for this is that the encoding of those elements often involves special cases not expressed in the target description. For example, the distance between two instructions is always even, so the lowest bit can be ignored because it is always zero.

To decode the registers, the DecodeGPRRegisterClass() function has to be defined. The 32 registers are encoded with a number between 0 and 31, and we can use the static GPRDecoderTable table to map between the encoding and the generated enumeration for the registers:

```
static const uint16_t GPRDecoderTable[] = {
    M88k::R0,   M88k::R1,   M88k::R2,   M88k::R3,
    M88k::R4,   M88k::R5,   M88k::R6,   M88k::R7,
    M88k::R8,   M88k::R9,   M88k::R10,  M88k::R11,
    M88k::R12,  M88k::R13,  M88k::R14,  M88k::R15,

    M88k::R16,  M88k::R17,  M88k::R18,  M88k::R19,
    M88k::R20,  M88k::R21,  M88k::R22,  M88k::R23,
    M88k::R24,  M88k::R25,  M88k::R26,  M88k::R27,
    M88k::R28,  M88k::R29,  M88k::R30,  M88k::R31,
};

static DecodeStatus
DecodeGPRRegisterClass(MCInst &Inst, uint64_t RegNo,
                       uint64_t Address,
                       const void *Decoder) {
  if (RegNo > 31)
    return MCDisassembler::Fail;

  unsigned Register = GPRDecoderTable[RegNo];
  Inst.addOperand(MCOperand::createReg(Register));
  return MCDisassembler::Success;
}
```

All other required decoder functions follow the same pattern as the
DecodeGPRRegisterClass() function:

1. Check that the value to decode fits the required size restriction. If not, then return
    the MCDisassembler::Fail value.

2. Decode the value and add it to the MCInst instance.

3. Return MCDisassembler::Success to indicate success.

Then, we can include the generated decoder tables and function:

```
#include "M88kGenDisassemblerTables.inc"
```

Finally, we are able to define the getInstruction() method. This method has two
result values, the decoded instruction and the size of the instruction. If the byte array is
too small, the size must be set to 0. This is important because the size parameter is used by
the caller to advance the pointer to the next memory location, even if the decoding failed.

In the case of the M88k architecture, the method is simple, because all instructions are 4
bytes long. So, after extracting 4 bytes from the array, the generated decoder function can
be called:

```
DecodeStatus M88kDisassembler::getInstruction(
    MCInst &MI, uint64_t &Size, ArrayRef<uint8_t> Bytes,
    uint64_t Address, raw_ostream &CS) const {
  if (Bytes.size() < 4) {
    Size = 0;
    return MCDisassembler::Fail;
  }
  Size = 4;

  uint32_t Inst = 0;
  for (uint32_t I = 0; I < Size; ++I)
    Inst = (Inst << 8) | Bytes[I];

  return decodeInstruction(DecoderTableM88k32, MI, Inst,
                           Address, this, STI);
}
```

This finishes the implementation of the disassembler.

After we have implemented all the classes, we only need to set up the build system to pick up the new target backend, which we will add in the next section.

Piecing it all together

Our new target, located in the `llvm/lib/Target/M88k` directory, needs to be integrated into the build system. To make development easy, we add it as an experimental target in the `llvm/CMakeLists.txt` file. We replace the existing empty string with the name of our target:

```
set(LLVM_EXPERIMENTAL_TARGETS_TO_BUILD "M88k"  … )
```

We also need to provide a `llvm/lib/Target/M88k/CMakeLists.txt` file to build our target. Besides listing the C++ files for the target, it also defines the generation of the source from the target description.

Generating all the types of sources from the target description

Different runs of the `llvm-tblgen` tool generate different portions of C++ code. However, I recommend adding the generation of all parts to the `CMakeLists.txt` file. The reason for this is that it provides better checking. For example, if you make an error with the instruction encoding, then this is only caught during the generation of the code for the disassembler. So, even if you do not plan to support the disassembler, it is still worth generating the source for it.

The file looks as follows:

1. First, we define a new LLVM component named `M88k`:

    ```
    add_llvm_component_group(M88k)
    ```

2. Next, we name the target description file, add statements to generate the various source pieces with TableGen, and define a public target for it:

    ```
    set(LLVM_TARGET_DEFINITIONS M88k.tdtablegen(LLVM
    M88kGenAsmMatcher.inc -gen-asm-matcher)
    tablegen(LLVM M88kGenAsmWriter.inc -gen-asm-writer)
    tablegen(LLVM M88kGenCallingConv.inc -gen-callingconv)
    tablegen(LLVM M88kGenDAGISel.inc -gen-dag-isel)
    tablegen(LLVM M88kGenDisassemblerTables.inc
                                      -gen-disassembler)
    ```

```
tablegen(LLVM M88kGenInstrInfo.inc -gen-instr-info)
tablegen(LLVM M88kGenMCCodeEmitter.inc -gen-emitter)
tablegen(LLVM M88kGenRegisterInfo.inc -gen-register-info)
tablegen(LLVM M88kGenSubtargetInfo.inc -gen-subtarget)

add_public_tablegen_target(M88kCommonTableGen)
```

3. We must list all the source files the new component is made of:

```
add_llvm_target(M88kCodeGen
  M88kAsmPrinter.cpp M88kFrameLowering.cpp
  M88kISelDAGToDAG.cpp M88kISelLowering.cpp
  M88kRegisterInfo.cpp M88kSubtarget.cpp
  M88kTargetMachine.cpp )
```

4. Last, we include the directories with the MC and disassembler classes in the build:

```
add_subdirectory(MCTargetDesc)
add_subdirectory(Disassembler)
```

Now we are ready to compile the LLVM with the new backend target. On the build directory, we can simply run this:

```
$ ninja
```

This detects the changed CmakeLists.txt file, runs the configuration step again, and compiles the new backend. To check that all went well, you can run this:

```
$ bin/llc --version
```

The output should contain the following line in the Registered Target section:

```
m88k       - M88k
```

Hurray! We finished the backend implementation. Let's try it out. The following f1 function in LLVM IR performs a bitwise AND operation between the two parameters of the function and returns the result. Save it in the example.ll file:

```
target triple = "m88k-openbsd"
define i32 @f1(i32 %a, i32 %b) {
  %res = and i32 %a, %b
  ret i32 %res
}
```

Run the llc tool as follows to see the generated assembler text on the console:

```
$ llc < example.ll
        .text
        .file    "<stdin>"
        .globl    f1                               # -- Begin
function f1
        .align    3
        .type    f1,@function
f1:                                     # @f1
        .cfi_startproc
# %bb.0:
        and %r2, %r2, %r3
        jmp %r1
.Lfunc_end0:
        .size    f1, .Lfunc_end0-f1
        .cfi_endproc
                                        # -- End function
        .section         ".note.GNU-stack","",@progbits
```

The output is in valid GNU syntax. For the f1 function, and and jmp instructions are generated. The parameters are passed in the %r2 and %r3 registers, which are used in the and instruction. The result is stored in the %r2 register, which is also the register to return 32-bit values. The return from the function is realized with a branch to the address hold in the %r1 register, which also matches the ABI. It all looks very good!

With the topics you learned about in this chapter, you can now implement your own LLVM backend. For many relatively simple CPUs such as **digital signal processors (DSPs)**, you do not need to implement more than we did here. Of course, the implementation for the M88k CPU architecture does not yet support all features of the architecture, for example, floating-point registers. However, you now know all the important concepts applied in LLVM backend development, and with this, you will be able to add any missing parts!

Summary

In this chapter, you learned how to develop a new backend target for LLVM. You first collected the required documentation and made LLVM aware of the new architecture by enhancing the `Triple` class. The documentation also includes the relocation definition for the ELF file format, and you added support for that to LLVM.

You learned about the different parts the target description contains, and using the C++ source generated from it, you learned how to implement an instruction selection. For outputting the generated code, you developed an assembler printer and learned which support classes are needed to write to an object file. You also learned how to add support for disassembling, which is used to turn an object file back into assembler text. Lastly, you extended the build system to include the new target in the build.

You are now equipped with everything you need to use LLVM in creative ways in your own projects. The LLVM ecosystem is very active, and new features are added all the time, so be sure to follow all developments!

Being a compiler developer myself, it was a pleasure for me to write about LLVM and discover some new features along the way. Have fun with LLVM!

Other Books You May Enjoy

If you enjoyed this book, you may be interested in these other books by Packt:

LLVM Techniques, Tips, and Best Practices Clang and Middle-End Libraries

Min-Yih Hsu

ISBN: 978-1-83882-495-2

- Find out how LLVM's build system works and how to reduce the building resource
- Get to grips with running custom testing with LLVM's LIT framework
- Build different types of plugins and extensions for Clang
- Customize Clang's toolchain and compiler flags
- Write LLVM passes for the new PassManager
- Discover how to inspect and modify LLVM IR
- Understand how to use LLVM's profile-guided optimizations (PGO) framework
- Create custom compiler sanitizers

Modern C++ Programming Cookbook - Second Edition

Marius Bancila

ISBN: 78-1-80020-898-8

- Understand the new C++20 language and library features and the problems they solve
- Become skilled at using the standard support for threading and concurrency for daily tasks
- Leverage the standard library and work with containers, algorithms, and iterators
- Solve text searching and replacement problems using regular expressions
- Work with different types of strings and learn the various aspects of compilation
- Take advantage of the file system library to work with files and directories
- Implement various useful patterns and idioms
- Explore the widely used testing frameworks for C++

Packt is searching for authors like you

If you're interested in becoming an author for Packt, please visit authors. packtpub.com and apply today. We have worked with thousands of developers and tech professionals, just like you, to help them share their insight with the global tech community. You can make a general application, apply for a specific hot topic that we are recruiting an author for, or submit your own idea.

Leave a review - let other readers know what you think

Please share your thoughts on this book with others by leaving a review on the site that you bought it from. If you purchased the book from Amazon, please leave us an honest review on this book's Amazon page. This is vital so that other potential readers can see and use your unbiased opinion to make purchasing decisions, we can understand what our customers think about our products, and our authors can see your feedback on the title that they have worked with Packt to create. It will only take a few minutes of your time, but is valuable to other potential customers, our authors, and Packt. Thank you!

Index